The Enterprise University
Power, Governance and Rei

Throughout the industrialised world universities have undergone remarkable changes since the mid-1980s. In Australia interest in reform has been intense and the scope of change profound. *The Enterprise University: Power, Governance and Reinvention in Australia* is a book grounded upon detailed case studies, interviews and site visits used to develop profiles of 17 Australian universities, half of the higher education sector. Marginson and Considine describe a new form of university governance, characterised by management instruments and executive power, bypassing of the traditional disciplines, and strategies of imitation that define the identity of the Australian university and try to position it in a global context.

Critical of traditional definitions of collegiality and professional control, *The Enterprise University* finds there are new opportunities to use university reinvention as a deeper structural process, in which respect for disciplinary strength and diversity is the price paid for a shared culture of performance, and institutions or groups of institutions have the incentive to forge different paths. Rather than imitating an imagined world of North American private universities, *The Enterprise University* highlights national and regional distinctiveness in the battle for global relevance.

Simon Marginson is Director of the Monash University Centre for Research in International Education. His books include *Education and Public Policy in Australia* (1993) and *Markets in Education* (1997).

Mark Considine works in the Department of Political Science at the University of Melbourne. Among his books are *Public Policy: A Critical Approach* (1994), and with Ann Capling and Michael Crozier *Australian Politics in the Global Era* (1998).

The Enterprise University

Power, Governance and Reinvention in Australia

Simon Marginson
Monash University

Mark Considine
University of Melbourne

CAMBRIDGE UNIVERSITY PRESS
Cambridge, New York, Melbourne, Madrid, Cape Town,
Singapore, São Paulo, Delhi, Tokyo, Mexico City

Cambridge University Press
The Edinburgh Building, Cambridge CB2 8RU, UK

Published in the United States of America by Cambridge University Press, New York

www.cambridge.org
Information on this title: www.cambridge.org/9780521794480

First published 2000
Re-issued 2011

A catalogue record for this publication is available from the British Library

ISBN 978-0-521-79118-2 Hardback
ISBN 978-0-521-79448-0 Paperback

Cambridge University Press has no responsibility for the persistence or
accuracy of URLs for external or third-party internet websites referred to in
this publication, and does not guarantee that any content on such websites is,
or will remain, accurate or appropriate.

Contents

Tables and figures

Tables

Figure

Preface

The Enterprise University: Power, Governance and Reinvention in Australia
was written on the basis of data generated during a three-year Australian
Research Council Large Grant project. Without the ARC's willingness
to support explanatory and critical studies of social phenomena, and
allocate financial support for such studies on academic grounds, the
study and book would not have been possible.

The authors prepared the whole text collaboratively. The first version
of chapter 5 was drafted by Rachel Boston. We are very grateful to
Rachel, both for her outstanding research assistance in the organisation
of the case studies and her input to the analysis and synthesis. She also
contributed much to the spirit which animated the project. Bob Bessant
was part of the original research team and contributed to the early design
and case study stages. We thank him for his insights, and criticisms of
some of the early working papers that preceded this book. The Centre for
the Study of Higher Education at the University of Melbourne was a
supportive and efficient home for the project for the duration of the
funding. We also gained much from the voluntary contributions of many
university officers and academics who assisted us. In all but one university (where our request to conduct a study was refused, for reasons
unclear) we received generous co-operation. During the case studies we
were often pleased to find an unexpected openness and frankness in
people's reflections on organisational questions.

In the preparation of the book we benefited from the comments of two
anonymous readers that generated considerable revision and development. At the penultimate stage the whole manuscript was read by Gary
Rhoades, Grant Harman, Stuart Macintyre, Ruth Neumann and
Genevieve Timmons and their thoughtful comments had a significant
impact on the final text. Bryan Turner, then Dean of Arts at Deakin and
Homer Le Grand, then Dean of Arts at Melbourne, read early versions of
chapter 4 and offered helpful insights into the circuitry of executive
power. It was a pleasure to work with Cambridge University Press in the
production of the book and we thank especially Phillipa McGuinness and
Peter Debus. When market value sometimes seems to be the be-all and

end-all of publishing, Cambridge demonstrates an exemplary commitment both to scholarly work as an end in itself, and to its effective
communication. Thank you also to Carla Taines (editor) and Jo Waite
(cover design). Many other colleagues and friends contributed indirectly
to the ideas here: some are acknowledged in the footnotes. The authors
bear responsibility for the words herein.

Our families provide settings in which book preparation contends with
much else for time, but one in which centred and satisfying intellectual
work is immeasurably enhanced. Our partners Melba and Genevieve
have our gratitude for this and also our sympathy for the times when
authors do not make good company.

Abbreviations and shortened forms

A	answer
ACT	Australian Capital Territory
ACU	Australian Catholic University
Adelaide	University of Adelaide
AGPS	Australian Government Publishing Service
ANU	Australian National University
ARC	Australian Research Council
AVCC	Australian Vice-Chancellors' Committee
Ballarat	University of Ballarat
BHP	Broken Hill Proprietary Limited
Bond	Bond University
CAE	college of advanced education
Central Queensland	Central Queensland University
CEO	chief executive officer
Charles Sturt	Charles Sturt University
Coll.	College
CQU	Central Queensland University
CRC	Cooperative Research Centre
CSIRO	Commonwealth Scientific and Industrial Research Organisation
CTEC	Commonwealth Tertiary Education Commission
Curtin	Curtin University of Technology
Deakin	Deakin University
DEET	Department of Employment, Education and Training
DEETYA	Department of Employment, Education, Training and Youth Affairs
DETYA	Department of Education, Training and Youth Affairs
DVC	deputy vice-chancellor
ECU	Edith Cowan University
Edith Cowan	Edith Cowan University

EIP	Evaluations and Investigations Program
Flinders	Flinders University of South Australia
Griffith	Griffith University
GT	Gumtree
HE	Higher Education
HECS	Higher Education Contribution Scheme
HED	Higher Education Division
IAE	Institute of Advanced Education
IMF	International Monetary Fund
Inst.	Institute
IT	information technology
IT	Institute of Technology
James Cook	James Cook University of North Queensland
La Trobe	La Trobe University
Macquarie	Macquarie University
Melbourne	University of Melbourne
Monash	Monash University
Murdoch	Murdoch University
New England	University of New England
New South Wales	University of New South Wales
Newcastle	University of Newcastle
Notre Dame	Notre Dame University, Australia
NHMRC	National Health and Medical Research Council
NSW	New South Wales
NT	Northern Territory
NTEU	National Tertiary Education Union
NTU	Northern Territory University
NU	New University
OECD	Organization for Economic Cooperation and Development
PhD	Doctor of Philosophy
PVC	pro vice-chancellor
Q	question
Qld	Queensland
Queensland	University of Queensland
QUT	Queensland University of Technology
RB	Redbrick
RMIT	Royal Melbourne Institute of Technology University
SA	South Australia
South Australia	University of South Australia
Southern Cross	Southern Cross University
Southern Queensland	University of Southern Queensland

SS	Sandstone
Sunshine Coast	University of the Sunshine Coast
Swinburne	Swinburne University of Technology
SWOT	strengths, weaknesses, opportunities and threats
Sydney	University of Sydney
TAFE	Technical and Further Education
Tasmania	University of Tasmania
Tech.	Technology
UC	University of Canberra
UK	United Kingdom
UNE	University of New England
Uni	university
UNSW	University of New South Wales
US	United States
USA	United States of America
USA	University of South Australia
USQ	University of Southern Queensland
UT	Unitech
UTS	University of Technology, Sydney
UWA	University of Western Australia
UWS	University of Western Sydney
VC	vice-chancellor
VUT	Victoria University of Technology
WA	Western Australia
Western Australia	University of Western Australia
Western Sydney	University of Western Sydney
Wollongong	University of Wollongong

1   Introduction

Paradise lost?

By any reckoning universities are unusual institutions. At home as the refuge for both iconoclasts and ideologues, they mix cathedral ritual and astrophysics without apparent embarrassment. In political terms they have usually been recessive, standing at arm's length from commerce and never doing all that well in the race to pucker-up to power. Traditional to a fault, they fail however to live comfortably in the past. Craven curiosity leads to the shattering of icons and a low view of conventions. The idea of the university, together with its realisation as a place of work, is about as far removed from standard, modern ideas about power, control and management as it is possible to travel. Or is it?

To a significant extent universities have been self-organising institutions. They have chosen for themselves a mixed history of medieval authority and modern science which has been invested in traditions of scholarly exchange and a shared intellectual responsibility for things past. To emphasise their independence from temporal imperatives they have retained the monastic and cathedral symbolism of rectors, deans and readers. They have sought to count rank and ritual as equal to cash reward. Faculties are still places where an Edwardian ethic of counting medals next to pay-rises reigns intact. Entwined into this formal pageantry, like Ariadne's thread, has been an individualism which asserts itself as a total right to academic freedom, expressed with equal plausibility as a responsibility to both defend and criticise the dominant cultures of the day. Without evident discomfort this same energy has driven genetic engineers and physicists to extend the borders of the known universe and, as they say, go where no enterprise has gone before, dragging commerce and politics with one hand and holding the book of common prayer in the other.

This unique set of paradoxes and occasional contradictions confounds every sensible explanation of how modern organisations ought to work. There is no single, unified chain of command. Basic questions about the purpose of the work, the nature of tasks and the use of technology are decided differently by each local initiative. Most contributors accept central directives only rather reluctantly and will side with students, colleagues in other institutions, or with abstract principle rather than with their own managers, most of whom are regarded as 'meeting-hounds', pen-pushers and obstacles to true science.

To compare the university to the modern corporation, the classical bureaucracy or the imagined community is, in the minds of many academics, to compare music to money, or literature to town hall legislation. In the end they are thought to be alike in all unimportant respects. That universities function at all in organisational terms may therefore be viewed as the ultimate proof that what would never work in theory is often found in practice.

This evident discordance between the way the university has chosen to order and organise itself and the systems of power by which other important institutions govern themselves has been a source of tension over a long period. A historian of the university could write about late medieval pressures to turn universities into agents of a unified monarchy, or their awkward compact with the emergent nation states of the eighteenth century. Just as interesting is the history of university involvement in industrialisation, with the establishment of the professions, and the prosecution of modern warfare. In each case university governance learned something from the secular science we now call management. In each case it chose to synthesise elements of the old and new, to reinvent its own internal culture, and to self-organise a unique form of university authority.

The purpose of this book is not to write the history of those earlier encounters between universities and other forms of governance, but instead to investigate the latest and contemporary encounter, using Australian universities as the empirical framework. In approaching the task we tried hard to avoid the innocent conceit which thinks any challenge to the university must be a threat to all things great and good. Nor were we surprised to find that an entrepreneurial spirit is now sweeping the cloisters. We live in the age of business and it is plain to everyone that the money-changers have long since mortgaged the temple. What *was* often surprising to us, during the course of the case studies underpinning this book, was the speed and extent of the changes now taking place.

The changes in the universities are manifest more obviously in management structures and institutional systems than in academic units, and more in research than in undergraduate teaching. But it is clear that the managerial dimension is quite rapidly working its way through the whole institutional setting. Sometimes we were astonished at the eagerness of these once stuffy and conservative institutions to reinvent themselves, not just in marketing terms, but in terms of their day-to-day lives, their very identities. Since those case studies were conducted, the evidence suggests that these processes of reinvention have become more daring and more fraught, and the institutional transformations if anything more dramatic.

The Enterprise University

The objective of *The Enterprise University* – like that of the research project on which it is based – is to 'capture' and interpret the main features of the new kind of higher education institution now emerging, opening that institution to scrutiny and debate. The book sets out to do this first of all by focusing on governance and institutional cultures, through the lens of executive leadership, decision-making systems, and research management. It then extends its findings to issues of competition between institutions, managerial strategies, forms of institutional identity and reinvention, and diversity or convergence within and between individual universities. (The study was confined to large doctoral universities because in Australia these institutions comprise virtually the whole of the higher education sector.)[1]

The findings of the book are grounded in 17 case studies of universities in Australia, in that rather unruly body of statistics and interpretative literature which make up the field of higher education studies, and in the on-going international discussion about the university as an institution. The results of the study have also been interpreted with an eye to the global literature on changes in public policy. The emphasis is not so much on what the data reveal about individual institutions – we do not provide 'league table' comparisons, or catalogue individual strengths and weaknesses – but on the more general patterns.

The book finds that a revolution is well under way. Forms of university governance and academic work that survived previous restructures are now under more direct assault. In many places, claims to privilege and special status outside the market have been rejected. In others, the battle over the intellectual purpose of the university is being fought on increasingly unequal terms. Certainly the post-second world war concord which saw universities accept their place as servants of an expanding definition of the public interest has begun to fracture. Those senior executives controlling the future of universities have both more power and less room to manoeuvre than before, while those dependent upon them for leadership have fewer alternative means to define their futures than previously was the case. More independent of government, it seems that universities are iron-bound by a new necessity in which outside pressures and certain distinctive inner cultures coincide.

Strong, increasingly independent forms of executive control give expression to the contemporary university's idea of itself as an 'academic

enterprise'.We have chosen the title *The Enterprise University* to symbolise
the emergent institutional type. We suspect that the emergence of the
Enterprise University constitutes a new phase in the history of the university. In the Enterprise University, forms of organisation and methods
of work are undergoing crucial changes.

- University purpose is now defined by forms of strong executive
  control.
- University missions and governing bodies start to take on a distinctly
  corporate character (drawn not so much from business itself as from
  an 'ideal form' corporation modelled in public sector reform), marketing mediates much of the relationship with the world outside, and
  performance targets are superimposed on scholarly honorifics.
- Established academic institutions including senates and councils,
  academic boards, departments and collegial rules have been supplemented (and sometimes supplanted) by vice-chancellors' advisory
  committees and private 'shadow' university structures.
- The basic frame of academic work is also subject to this 'dual
  structure', with departments and disciplines contesting space with
  institutes, Cooperative Research Centres (CRCs) and a variety of
  ephemeral 'soft money'-funded entities.
- Driving these changes is a redefined internal economy in which under-
  funding drives a 'pseudo-market' in fee incomes, soft budget allocations for special purposes and contested earnings for new enrolments
  and research grants.
- Some elements of this 'market', particularly the education of international students, are driven by a frankly commercial and entrepreneurial spirit, now a key (though by no means always dominant)
  element of the enterprise culture.
- Definitions of quality and lines of accountability are drawn less from
  traditional public sector and political cultures, and more from the
  private sector and the culture of economic consumption, whether
  expressed through university-student relations, university-industry
  relations or university-government relations.
- The paradox of this new openness to outside funding and competition
  is a process of 'isomorphistic closure' through which universities with
  diverse histories choose from an increasingly restricted menu of
  commercial options and strategies.

To describe these phenomena we prefer the term 'Enterprise University' to alternatives such as 'academic capitalism', 'entrepreneurial
university' or 'corporate university'.Those other terms all suggest a one-
dimensional institution solely dominated by profit-seeking, an organisational culture totally reduced to the business form.While parts of the

new university are pure corporation, universities as a whole are more complex than that. 'Enterprise' captures both economic and academic dimensions, and the manner in which research and scholarship survive but are now subjected to new systems of competition and demonstrable performance. 'Enterprise' is as much about generating institutional prestige as about income. In the Enterprise University, the economic and academic dimensions are both subordinated to something else. Money is a key objective, but it is also the means to a more fundamental mission: to advance the prestige and competitiveness of the university as an end in itself. At the same time, academic identities, in their variations, are subordinated to the mission, marketing and strategic development of the institution and its leaders.

We do not argue that all these changes threaten an end to the academy, nor do we see the character of the new university as completely resolved or final. There can be little dispute about the need for universities to play an active and constructive role in the economic and social renewal of their communities. That this involves closer ties with business and greater attention to the needs of consumers should not be in doubt. On the other hand, it is by no means self-evident to us that the ideal of a broad-based public good is obsolete, or that each university should function as a stand-alone corporation, with regard not for community welfare or social betterment, but only for its own interests.

What is in doubt, at least in the evidence here, is the extent to which universities must mirror markets in order to serve markets, must become corporations in order to treat with firms, or should organise themselves in the manner of an industry in order to play a useful role in assisting industries to innovate, plan and manage their fortunes.

In other words, we see a serious deficiency in the norms and models of good governance which have emerged to assist universities in their struggle to stay relevant to new conditions. At a time when they might have helped pioneer creative organisational structures and indigenous 'learning cultures' capable of greater flexibility, they too often appear to have surrendered to highly derivative and dependent notions of themselves.

Over and again we found those in positions of greatest influence fixed on simplistic outside norms of governance. This was more than mere striving for excellence or a search for new ideas. Being useful to business is being widely interpreted as being like business. Having a good reputation in the international field is subsumed under the rubric of being a 'Harvard of the West', or a 'Stanford of the South'. In other words, the desire to excel is being too often defined primarily as a struggle to compete and as a rush to imitate.

This might be of less consequence in a university system with solid and robust internal resources. In such a world the urgings of an administrator class with a sharp eye for new methodologies would be balanced within a matrix of strong professions, independent students and articulate civil interests. But in organisations already depleted by over-enrolment, under-investment and declining career opportunities, the imitate-or-perish imperative meets weak resistance.

This then is our central discovery and core argument: universities now seem less sure of themselves. They are constantly being reinvented, yet are less capable of genuine self-production than before. The decline in robust, indigenous cultures and inventive forms of self-governance suggests a brash but brittle lurch into the world of enterprise. This has less to do with private ownership, fees and exports than might be supposed. Private participation is hardly new to education. One could imagine its greater expansion taking place without a direct threat to norms of equity and excellence. But the decline of stronger sources of intellectual coherence inside the universities and their replacement by derivative forms of top-down private organisation suggest that the new private relationships might be based more on pandering and procuring rather than partnership and genuine pluralism.

In becoming the Enterprise University, the university seems at risk of losing sight of its own distinctive features and achievements. In fact it might be losing control over the very means by which its own identity is formed. In very few cases did we find an executive strategy of enterprise and renewal that was matched by internal structures capable of mobilising what Clark calls the 'academic heartland' of ordinary staff and students.[2]

While this might plausibly be regarded as a likely consequence of the early stage of development towards new goals, the evidence to the contrary is striking. Universities are path-dependent: they continue from the place they start. In the great majority of instances, the changes they make are forced upon them, and they show little capacity to forge unique adaptations. Finding this capacity is the most urgent necessity that now confronts them.

Nor is the insight limited only to Australian universities. The content of this book is largely Australian: nevertheless, as chapter 3 explores in more detail, many of its findings are salient in other nations. To establish the full global and comparative dimensions would require another book. Here we merely note that although some unique local features often survive, similar reforms are taking place almost everywhere. There is gathering evidence which tells us that university systems (always prone to powerful examplars and global imitation) are moving closer to each other.[3] For reasons discussed in chapters 2 and 3, the Australian case is distinguished not because higher education here is different from the rest, but because in Australia the common global trends showed themselves rather early, and have been carried further and more consistently than in many places. As such, the Australian case might provide other nations with a forecast – and a warning – of where the common pattern is taking them.

Governance and identity

The third part of this chapter explains our approach to the study and analysis of *The Enterprise University*, and outlines the contents of the book. But first we need to touch on one crucial aspect: why we have chosen to focus on university governance and institutional identity.

The Enterprise University does not aim to cover every aspect of the contemporary university, which would constitute a very large book indeed. Rather, we have started from a focus on governance, and worked outward from there. In this study governance is treated as a core aspect of the university, one that helps to shape many others.

Here 'governance' is broadly defined to encompass internal re-lationships, external relationships, and the intersection between them. Institutions such as universities are doubly structured, by internal configurations of power, and by their intersection with outside interests. Governance occupies the pivotal position between the inner world (or worlds) of the university, and its larger environment. Not everything in higher education can be explained by governance, or is contained in its practices, but when we are talking about *institutions* of higher education, then governance is always present.

Governance is concerned with the determination of value inside universities, their systems of decision-making and resource allocation, their mission and purposes, the patterns of authority and hierarchy, and the relationship of universities as institutions to the different academic worlds within and the worlds of government, business and community without. It embraces 'leadership', 'management' and 'strategy'. Govern-ance affects specialised administrative activities such as fund-raising, financial planning or industrial relations (though this is not a book on how to carry out such functions). Governance does not contain in itself the sum of teaching and research, but it affects them. It provides the conditions which enable teaching and research to take place.

Governance is central to the large question of where the university as an institution is heading. A study of academic cultures can tell us something about those disciplines, their networking practices and their social effects; a study of governance encompasses much of this, and it also explains the institutional setting in which disciplinary practices are played out. Aspects of governance, notably leadership and management, are often seen as *the* key to improving the universities, or sorting out their problems. Perhaps too much so: one argument of *The Enterprise University* is that more attention should be paid to the creative power of the academic disciplines in shaping the future of the university. Nevertheless, it is hard to avoid the practical impact of governance. It has become all too easy to imagine the university without one or another of the academic disciplines; it is impossible to imagine the academic disciplines without their institutional setting, and its governance.

Governance sits between government, the primary agent in funding and in fashioning the policy settings, and academic work and community service. It also mediates the expanding relationships with business and industry, and between teaching and research. The 'internal' and 'external' dimensions are articulated in more than one way. For example, leaders use the selective deployment of external pressures to drive internal changes, and they also operate as agents of the schools and faculties outside the university. In recent years there has been a concentration of decision-making at the point of institutional management and leadership. Certain decisions once made by national or state government, about resource deployment for example, have been transferred to the universities themselves. Other decisions once made by academic units are now determined from above by professional managers or technicians. Many see this concentration of nodal power as overdue, as essential to the effective running of universities in the manner of government departments or business firms. Others see it as the primary cause of what they perceive as a crisis of university purposes and values. Either way, governance is critical.

As an institution the university is undergoing major changes. In some sites it is in difficulty. Certain of its traditions have been fundamentally destabilised. One reason is the growing impact of the global dimension: universities are among the most 'globalised' of institutions. Another is the changing character of government, for example the partial withdrawal of government from its earlier role as the site for drawing together social capital. A third is the entry of knowledge-related functions and technologies into every area of working life (the advent of the 'knowledge economy'). Universities have become universally important. A much larger group of users is now making claims on them. They are also contested by a growing number of other institutions where knowledge is produced and disseminated. Clearly, if the university is to work its way through all of this, while satisfying its different 'publics' without and within, governance will be at the heart of it.

Governance is where the academic disciplines are joined to other social institutions, where universities become externally referenced and collectively conscious. Governance is where the *identity* of each university as a distinctive social and cultural institution is shaped, within a 'global knowledge economy'.[4] Here the potential of governance is ambiguous. On one hand, it can be the medium for the one-way subordination of universities to other social agents or designs. On the other, it offers the one distinctive means whereby individual universities can remake themselves along innovative lines; and universities as a group can offer the wider community an example of self-invention.

Trends in governance

In a nutshell, *The Enterprise University* identifies five principal trends in governance.

First, there is a new kind of executive power, characterised by a will to manage and, in some respects, a freedom to act greater than was once the case. The executive leaders of the Enterprise University are generic rather than localised managers. They manage according to seemingly universal principles of 'good practice' and they enjoy an operational separation from the internal context (that which is managed). They mediate the university's external relations and fashion its strategies. Executive leaders interpret the 'outside' factors of government, business, and local and global competition as they see them. They are their own switching station, between the external pressures and the internal changes they want to achieve.

Second, there are structural innovations: the remaking or replacement of collegial or democratic forms of governance with structures that operationalise executive power and create selective mechanisms for participation, consultation and internal market research. There is a characteristic shift from the formal to the semi-formal: the new structures enable freedom of action and information flow, without many previous constraints of legislative forms and representative governance. Senior executive groups – sometimes including faculty deans as members of the executive, sometimes holding the faculties at arm's length so as to increase the scope for central executive power – have come to dictate the formal agenda, and enjoy more financial discretion than others in the Enterprise University. The role of university corporations, outside the reach of governing bodies and collegial debate, is also growing, often in sensitive and lucrative areas (fee-based international education, research, technologies) subject to commercial-in-confidence proceedings.

Third, we find an enhanced flexibility of personnel and resources, of means of communication, and of the very location of power and authority. In the Enterprise University managers can never get enough flexibility, as the ritualistic demands for industrial deregulation show. Universities are no longer governed by legislation: they are more commonly ruled by formulae, incentives, targets and plans. These mechanisms

are more amenable to executive-led re-engineering than are the deliberations of a council or an academic board, and less accessible to
counter-strategies of resistance. They also fit with management-
controlled tools such as soft money budgets, commercial companies,
temporary institutes for research or teaching, fund-raising and marketing
campaigns, all drawn together in a complex web of accountability tied
only to the senior executive office. However, enhanced flexibility has a
downside, evident in the trend to short-term goal-feeding and decision
cycles, opportunism and posturing.

Fourth, there is a discernible decline in the role of the academic
disciplines in governance. The disciplines, and the collegial cultures and
networks which sustain them, are often seen as a nuisance by executive
managers and outside policy-makers. Partly inaccessible to control from
above, they can be obstacles to the remaking of institutional structures,
the recasting of courses in line with new requirements, and the freer
movement of resources. (Here there appears to be a strong resemblance
between university management's critique of disciplines, and economic
organisation theory's more general lament about the CEOs' inability to
control junior functionaries in large corporations.) This 'problem' has
prompted a quite widespread movement away from academic departments, which are discipline-based, and in favour of cross-disciplinary
schools and research centres in which identities and resources are
amenable to a high degree of selection and restructuring from above. The
other method of tackling the disciplines has been to implement funding
and performance systems driving academic work via a common cross-
disciplinary model, flattening out the distinctions between different kinds
of knowledges, while enabling the university centre to reach directly into
the work program and resource base. The framing of faculty leaders as
executive deans, and sometimes as 'superdeans' controlling several disciplines, can also weaken disciplinary identity in academic organisation,
cutting the old ties of obligation between leaders and the collegial
networks below.

Fifth, as in many other public and private organisations, there are
new methods of devolution. Devolution is a key mechanism of the new
executive power, a part of centralised control and not its antithesis.
Superdeans, faculty leader-managers and heads of departments and
schools are granted budgetary autonomy within the framework of institutional plans, performance measures and targets, and often a partial
responsibility for generating base-line resources. Targets are powerful
constraints which hem in the devolved manager, restraining her/his
capacity to innovate or resist. That manager's objectives, means of
action and the measures of performance are increasingly controlled from
above (though the degree of system coherence and integration can vary

markedly between institutions). This allows university leaders to throw off the constraints of pastoral responsibility and channel the burden of expectation, and blame for failure, down to their subordinates. In keeping with the 'great leader' notion which seems integral to corporate culture, the gift of devolution is given to individuals rather than to academic or operational collectivities. When responsibility is devolved to a faculty or department, that now often means faculty dean or departmental head, with increased line management responsibility.

Older forms of devolution are no longer favoured. Without exception the university leaders in our study saw collegial forms of decision-making as an obstacle to managerial rationalities. Some also put a case against disciplinary organisation, though others were more circumspect. Often, the strong departments in established universities are more robust than academic boards (which are losing power over the identity of the university almost everywhere) but in both respects academic tradition is losing ground, and is being replaced – or, in older universities, part-replaced, in complex synergies – with more malleable forms.

Along with what was an often conservative and authoritarian collegial tradition, there was a more recently created democratic tradition in universities, expressed through reforms that created increased staff and student representation on councils and committees, and the widespread introduction of elected departmental heads. Typically, these reforms followed the 'student power' era of the late 1960s and early 1970s. The democratic tradition in governance provided greater space for young academics, students, general staff and women in all categories. Undoubtedly it played a role in modernising the universities. Nevertheless, along with the collegial tradition, in the present period this democratic tradition is also being pushed aside, and most of its gains are being reversed. Often, the more engaged, marketing-savvy and transparent character of the new corporate forms, and the more aggressive assertion of the merit principle in corporate university organisation, serve to disguise this shift from collegiality and democracy to executive power.

Changes in common

One of the striking features of the organisational changes now taking place in Australian universities is that these are changes *in common*. They were happening in every university we visited, albeit with varying timing and extent. There is marked variation in the original character of those universities, as chapter 7 will discuss. Yet a common organisational template is apparent. The new and more mobile forms of executive power, the growth of deputy vice-chancellor (DVC) and pro vice-chancellor (PVC) positions and executive deans, the vice-chancellors' executive groups at the operational hub of the universities, the role of budget systems and 'drivers'[5], the declining role of academic boards and changing character of councils, the running of research as a system of measured performance, the language of strategic positioning and planning: all are relatively new, and all are apparent almost everywhere. We find ourselves witnesses to a government-inspired, management-driven convergence in which some original differences between universities are diminishing or have disappeared. There are gains in this, and also significant losses.

In the processes of change and convergence, educational and scholarly goals are being challenged and diminished – and sometimes altogether displaced – by the new set of institutional and financial goals. Not only have older participative structures lost authority in governance, the collaborative ('collegial') networks in teaching and research are being hedged by budget systems and crowded out by more centralised modes of decision-making and performance control, albeit centralised modes that are administered through devolved structures. At the same time universities in Australia – like those in many other countries – are affected by the trend to 'market bureaucracy' in public organisations, characterised by forms of quasi-economic competition, and pseudo price signals in the allocation of resources.[6] Funding policy is a principal instrument of institutional convergence.

The study

Methods

The empirical core of *The Enterprise University* has been derived largely from a three-year research study of 17 Australian higher education institutions, covering about half of the Australian system. The case study data were synthesised into major themes so as to make the best use of the research and to create a more readable book. Most of the writing took place between late 1997 and early 1999 and benefited from statistics and academic literature available after the case work. The final revisions occurred early in 2000.

Higher education institutions are studied using theories and methods drawn from several disciplines, including political science and policy studies, sociology, history, psychology and economics. Research on higher education often draws on more than one such discipline. Some of this work is philosophically informed and rigorous, some of it mathematical in form, some of it constructed as metaphor and myth.[7] A large part of the literature on the university has little or no empirical character, and is concerned to argue a case for or against one or another body of reforms.

We share with the field of higher education studies its multi-disciplinary character: we have been informed by political science, sociology, political economy, history and other social theory, as well as the range of writing specifically on higher education. However, we found ourselves unmoved by the hectoring tone of much of the reformist literature, and sceptical about prescriptions not grounded in detailed knowledge of what universities actually do. Equally, we were unimpressed by those broad-brush condemnations of the university that are derived solely from utopian principles, free from any encounter with institutional realities. Rather than deciding in advance exactly what was wrong, and how to put things right, we preferred to treat the Enterprise University as a puzzle to be investigated. Our bias in this study is to the empirical, and to opening new questions rather than trailing old coats. If new answers are to be found, we hoped this might be the way to find them.

Thus we set out to examine the real experiences of Australian universities, at a crucial turning point in the evolution of the academic mission: its encounter with the global, the corporate, and late-modernising systems of organisation. In doing so, and given our prior assumption about the centrality of governance, we aimed to get as close as possible to the institutional fabric of the universities in our study, especially their leadership and management. Our individual analytical frameworks are spelt out in detail elsewhere.[8] In interpreting specific university behaviours we found insights from a number of different authors to be useful. These included Pfeffer and Salancik's work on resource dependence, DiMaggio and Powell on institutional isomorphism (imitating behaviours), and Hirsch's discussion of markets in positional goods like education.[9]

As joint authors of *The Enterprise University* we brought somewhat different perspectives to bear on the project: part of the work was to bring these together. One of us is a political scientist whose recent work has drawn on contemporary theories of social organisation, including the properties of self-organisation. The other works in education policy studies using political economy from the Cambridge school and theories of power/knowledge and globalisation. Each had written about 'managerialism' and critiqued the wave of economically driven reforms in the universities and the public sector.[10] In our previous work we argued that new forms of governance had emerged in the late 1980s. University management was influenced by organisational economics and images of corporate organisation thought to be found in the private sector; some of the same influences were at work in the wider public sectors of Australia and New Zealand in the 1980s and 1990s. We saw in this a challenge to previous notions of the public interest, and in certain respects a reduced capacity in universities to carry out teaching, research and community service.

Despite these earlier conclusions, we saw the three-year research project as an opportunity to look at the problem afresh. The approach paid dividends, in the sense that by the end of the project we had shifted ground on some issues. The reality turned out to be more nuanced and contradictory than we had expected. For example, we often found ourselves rather less sympathetic to traditional collegial university governance than hitherto. While it is vitally important that universities devise ways of drawing on the talents and purposes of a wider group, the older forms of collegial power-sharing now seem to us simply inadequate to meet the challenges within and without. These failings of collegiality also help explain the easy dominance of the new executive strategies.

There is no doubt that some changes in contemporary university organisation constitute advances. In the virtues of transparency and openness, in the clarity about resource deployment, and in the greater external responsiveness are elements that we would want to take into any future discussion of the university as an institution. Yet what we found also confirmed some of our deeper concerns. The modernisation of management and the extension of economic responsiveness seem inextricably linked to the faltering of academic identity, to reliance on money as the meta-measure of value, and a corrosive cynicism about individual motives and social purposes. In our judgement, it is now essential that the universities disentangle these contrary elements, the pluses and minuses.

A more discerning reform strategy is needed. This is the next step beyond executive enhancement and marketing, a step which situates the self-interest of the university not as one that terminates in itself, but one that is re-grounded in its larger social purposes: a step which treats the academy as a joint project of the community in which it acts and of the many diverse staff and student groups whose talents it seeks to extend.

The cases

Our principal research method was that of intensive institutional case study and largely consisting of extended individual interviews, supplemented by documentary reading and historical data. We wanted to hear directly from those involved in the governance of universities what it was that they saw themselves doing. We were mindful of David Harvey's point that: 'Those who define the material practices, forms and meanings of money, time, or space fix certain basic rules of the social game'.[11]

We judged that the hopes, fears, fantasies and ideals of vice-chancellors, deans, registrars and readers, however mysterious and contentious, would have much to tell us. Typically we asked them, 'What is it you are trying to build?', 'What are you hoping to achieve?', 'What are the tools you prefer to use to get there?'.

Some will object that this is a rather naive view and that 'real power' is less about human footsteps than about the sand on which they fall. We saw some value in bringing these 'environmental' aspects of the issue to the fore. A subsidary part of the research program was the collection and analysis of system-wide data, much of it drawn from the excellent Department of Education, Training and Youth Affairs statistical series and DETYA's commissioned research studies; chapters 2, 3 and 7 of *The Enterprise University* have drawn heavily from these contextual materials. But in the end one project can only do so much. Our primary research strategy was to focus on formal and informal decision-making inside the university. This gave us a set of research questions to ask our informants, including the nature of formal distinctions established by rank and statute, the role of key committees and planning processes, and source of values, new strategies and goals.

While this is not a study closely focused on financial administration and the saliency of financial decisions in universities – such a study would be useful and would complement *The Enterprise University* – in developing the research questions we sought to apply the insights of resource dependency theory to the budget, finance and corporate governance aspects.[12] In addition to inquiries about statutory structures we also tried wherever possible to follow Pfeffer's advice concerning the cultural differences in the assessment of power: 'The best diagnostic tool is the pattern of interaction among individuals involved in the decision. Who gets consulted, at what point, and with what result provides information about where power resides.'[13]

In our selection of case studies we had two driving interests. First and foremost, we wished to cover enough of the field to enable us to make plausible generalisations about the character of 'the new university' if such an organisation could be found. This required coverage of half or more of Australia's universities. Second, we suspected that the impact of change might be quite different in old and new, large and small, rich and poor institutions. We therefore sought to structure the sample of cases to include these key forms of expected diversity. Chapter 7 deals directly with this intra-system diversity.

The universities included in the project enrolled well over half of Australia's higher education students. These included five of the six 'Sandstone' universities founded in Australia before the first world war (Queensland, Sydney, Tasmania, Adelaide, Western Australia), two of the three large 'Redbrick' institutions begun in the 1940s–1950s (NSW and Monash), pre-1987 'Gumtree' universities founded between the early 1960s and the mid-1970s (James Cook, Griffith, Newcastle, Deakin and

Flinders), two of the former large institutes of technology that we designate as 'Universities of Technology' or 'Unitechs' (Queensland and the University of Technology in Sydney), and three other post-1986 universities, which we designate as 'New Universities' (Central Queensland, Southern Cross and Edith Cowan).[14] The strongest universities, the Sandstones and Redbricks, were overrepresented at six out of nine, while the New Universities were somewhat underrepresented.[15]

Case studies were conducted with the co-operation of the universities. Interviewees typically included the vice-chancellor or in his/her absence a DVC, the deputy vice-chancellor or pro vice-chancellor (PVC) research, further DVCs and/or PVCs at need, the senior officer responsible for strategic planning, at least one faculty dean and/or a superdean covering a number of faculties, one or more departmental heads, academics not holding managerial roles. Our method for obtaining interviews was to ask our designated contact person at each institution to arrange meetings with key office bearers, and to nominate any others they felt were 'important to the University's current authority structure or mission'. We spoke to some other members of the university with an insight into power and authority structures, or versed in the academic study of university systems, not selected by our contact person. This included some chairs of academic boards and long-serving members of councils or senates. We also consulted union and collegial networks where possible to seek their recommendations regarding key people to interview.

All but a handful of the interviews or parts of interviews were conducted on the basis that we could record, transcribe and quote from them on a 'not for direct attribution' basis. It was the vice-chancellors who tended to be the most confident and certain in their comments and they ranged freely across the full gamut of internal and external issues. More junior officers often seemed concerned about how their superiors would respond to what they said. Even DVCs and PVCs carefully confined themselves to their brief, somewhat in the manner of portfolio ministers. The group least well represented in this study were ordinary working academics. Occasionally they appear as committee members or office bearers on academic boards but it is indicative that a method deliberately chosen to find those with influence did not uncover strong collegial representation. Still less did it point us to unions, students or community representatives on councils or advisory boards. We accept that a different method might produce a different result concerning these interests. In this study we placed the major priority on interviewing office holders and other readily identified 'key players'. While it was probably inevitable that this method would bias the study towards office-bearers rather than 'informal power brokers', it was far from certain that it would fail to bring to light the roles of staff serving on key committees, boards or councils. The bias, in other words, was towards institutions but not necessarily towards individuals within those institutions, with the exception of vice-chancellors.

Limitations

During the three years of the project, there were substantial changes at most of the institutions under study. Inevitably, we found ourselves trying to freeze-frame a moving picture. Senior manager-leader positions were especially dynamic. One of the vice-chancellors we interviewed appeared twice, in different institutions; a second was interviewed at one university and was about to arrive at another when we were passing through, and a third was interviewed about his previous appointment in the first weeks of starting a new one. Three of the DVCs researched have since become vice-chancellors. University operations are equally subject to change. The universities under scrutiny have changed between the time of the case study and the compilation of this book, and by the time of publication these universities will have shifted again. The result is that the study's conclusions hold up better and last longer at the general level than in relation to particular institutions – and those conclusions need to be continually tested against new evidence.

A second limitation of the study is its reliance on the institution, rather than the academic unit (faculty, school, department, centre) or academic discipline (engineering, accounting, history, etc.) as the unit of analysis. This starting point highlights institutional aspects and obscures teaching and research; and it draws attention to distinctions between institutions, while obscuring the distinctions between fields. It also lessens the attention given to organisational variations within institutions. We chose the institution level because it *is* important, as both a site of administrative practices and a focus of debate about universities. A growing number of crucial decisions are made there. Nevertheless, studies using other units of analysis would also tell us something and would complement *The Enterprise University*, particularly in relation to issues of scholarly diversity.

A third limitation springs from the focus on managers rather than academics. Much is happening in the domain of academic work. *The Enterprise University* does not claim to be a sociological study of academic work practices. Such studies, several of which are referred to in the book, constitute another useful complement to our approach.

The book

The first two-thirds of *The Enterprise University* focus on the common pattern of changes in governance. Chapters 2 and 3 discuss the external

environment (national and global) and the government–institution relationship; chapters 4 to 6 are about internal governance. Chapter 7
broadens the discussion to institutional difference and national system
dynamics. Chapter 8 draws out the broader implications of the changes
in governance for institutional character, and weighs the overall strengths
and weaknesses of the Enterprise University.

Chapter 2 examines the recent history of Australian government policy
in the university sector, and the shift from 'policy' to 'governance' evident
in recent reforms. Notwithstanding the fiscal imperative of 'small government' and the trend to self-managing universities, government continues
to be the major force in shaping the Enterprise University. The first part
of chapter 3 sets out the global political, economic and cultural context
of the Enterprise University, touching on recent studies of the university
as an institution, including Readings' *The university in ruins* (1996)
and Slaughter and Leslie's *Academic capitalism* (1997). The second part
of the chapter provides contextual data on resource trends in Australia,
on the growth in the executive layer, and on tensions between the
'academic' and the 'administrative' as evidenced in recent research.

Chapters 4 to 6 set down the main empirical findings on governance,
covering executive leadership (chapter 4), operational structures (chapter
5) and the management of research (chapter 6). These chapters draw
extensively on material from project interviews.

Chapter 7 takes the study beyond the Enterprise University imagined
as a single institutional type to acknowledge competition, variation and
commonality: it explores the *national system dynamics* of this new type of
university. It examines the Enterprise University in Australia using five
different categories of university. In this manner it joins the analyses of
changes in governance and identity as outlined for all universities in
chapters 2–6, to cross-system considerations. It finds that while some
universities are prospering more than others, in the playing out of system
relationships all Australian universities are bound by certain limitations.
Tendencies to institution-driven imitation are corroding the capacity for
academic invention, and are limiting institutional innovation to a narrow
band of 'reinvention' strategies consistent with the Enterprise University.

This brings us to the heart of the question of university identity. The
problem is not so much that individual universities choose the 'wrong
model', as that the competitive dynamic, sustained by government
system-setting and the Darwinian devices of induced funding scarcity
and ever increasing pressures on managers, has locked them all into
common modes of behaviour that their senior executives have all too
willingly embraced. Governance of the Enterprise University is sustained
both by internal leadership and decision-making structures and cultures
and in national policy and systems of funding and accountability. It is

institutional *and* systemic. Here institutional leaders play the crucial role because of their unique capacity to mediate inner and outer worlds. Yet by placing all of their eggs in the basket of a burdened and often beleaguered leadership, both governments and the universities themselves have truncated universities' capacity for organisational creativity.

The pattern of inter-institutional mimicry, growing marketing dependence and genuflection to content-free generic corporate models would be a problem if it occurred in a supermarket chain or a car manufacturer. In universities, and in a national university system, it indicates an emerging crisis of great concern. Though the long-term survival of the universities as institutions is not at risk, their capacity for self-creation is certainly in grave doubt.

The implications are explored more fully in the concluding chapter 8. It advocates changed forms of governance, including a national policy that discourages conformism and supports innovation, seeks a broader range of internal inputs into institutional development, and fosters a relationship between academic goals and corporate goals based upon continuing independence.

2 Roots of the Enterprise University (1): From policy to governance

Devolution and conformity

There was a time when Australian governments regarded universities as separate, sovereign institutions seeking and sharing a common public purpose in higher education. This time has passed. The paradox of the present period is that the more governments encourage the deregulation and privatisation of higher education, the less autonomous do the institutions of higher education become. Instead the logic of head-to-head competition between universities, market-signals and private incentives generates a new common project – to imitate the private universities of North America in a search for global relevance. It is a project found in higher education systems in many parts of the world

In place of the earlier time of stable purposes has come a period of change, uncertainty and diverse projects of both a public and private nature. Government has not withdrawn from the field but we now observe the emergence of a form of academic enterprise in which public actors seek new forms of influence over both what is done and how it is done. And there appears to be a new paradox in government determination to find a more simple and direct method of 'steering from a distance'. The use of quasi-markets and competitive pressures results in new forms of closure and control over those who are charged with implementation. This is both the achievement and primary confusion in the new higher education industry. It is at once a more devolved system of rule and also one which is ever more exacting in its demand for a standard output.

We describe this shift as one from a public interest in the creation of 'policy' to one driven by a new awareness of the functions of 'governance'. We accept that this is something of an exaggeration. The two are always somewhat entwined. There is policy inside all forms of governance and often some structure of power is implied in any policy initiative. But the essence of the argument seems to hold up. While policy has been a story written in the form of intentions and their implementation, governance has become a narrative of micro-managements, structural-economic reform, budgeting and diverse commercial gestures. The new

governance is shy of defining its policy intentions too specifically, preferring the language of choice and diversity as a means to lower the public
vision closer to the ground. It is also rather agnostic about its implementation requirements, giving each institution the chance to find its
chosen path to a common reinvention.

For the universities this narrative was first visible as the arrows shot by
a series of inspectors charged with the review of higher education
(Murray, Martin, Hoare, West). It was also found in the way institutions
sought to alter the terms of their dependence upon one another. What we
are calling academic enterprise appears, in other words, to be the part-
formed progeny of both public policy and private interest. Accordingly
it bears the mark and purpose of a newly emerging understanding of
the role of the public sphere in a period of economic restructure.
Those titanic struggles for a new future which are so casually described
as 'economic rationalism', 'managerialism' or 'new public management'
are in fact a complex achievement of public purpose and economic
energy. We do not claim that everything that needs to be said about the
present can be read from this past but we see some important elements
of 'path dependence' in the way universities currently seek to position
themselves. This is less about any fixed trajectory and more about the way
they mobilise aspects of their understanding of the past as a tool for
contemporary work.

Imitation rituals

The simplest but by no means the most important clue to this process is
found in many of our interviews where, as noted, senior managers sought
to respond to Canberra by using the same strategies as a means to extend
influence over the internal governance of their own university. This
'outside-in' play of influences both enhances executive power at the top
and also opens the universities to ever more specific demands from
outside. This kind of 'imitation ritual' proves to have a series of powerful and interesting manifestations. Its homogenising effects help explain
how comparatively precise demands (such as numerical performance
measures for academic output in research) cascade into sophisticated
forms of organisational restructure.

The chain of influence is difficult to trace to a single source. The
executives in credit rating agencies, OECD publicists and corporate
think-tanks suggest themselves. But what we can say for certain is that
this outlook entered public policy in the cabinet room and from here
flowed directly into a wider understanding of the nature of governance.
Cabinet leaders in the 1980s lamented an Australia that was 'slipping
behind'.[1] They began to accept the idea that more active and tougher

management (politicians with their sleeves rolled up) would both bring
down the deficit and raise up the poor. A new instrumentalism began to
pervade policy debates and its weapon of choice was the performance
target.

Senior management inside the university soon began to resent Canberra's string-pulling but found themselves powerless to resist these
pressures. Canberra showed it could break from its prolix past and made
its dependants do 'more with less'. Within two years the universities were
found doing to their own faculties and schools what Canberra had just
done to them. Budget siphoning, productivity cuts and strategic planning
taxes soon pulled local authority into line with executive intentions.
Cynics find in this reflexive turn of mind on the part of university
leaderships a form of inauthenticity, perhaps even malevolence. We have
certainly met a few senior executives whose strategies might support such
a conclusion. But the more general account shows managerial imitation
as the most potent form of organisational learning available to universities. Imitation gave them a means both to meet external objectives and
a way to fashion tools for reforming their own institutions. In this sense
nothing proved to be more welcome than a tyrant at the door.

Interestingly these imitation rituals also held true between institutions.
The University of Melbourne sought to mimic Harvard or Stanford. The
University of Ballarat modelled the University of Iowa or some other
upwardly mobile regional icon. Global and regional distinctions then
began to turn on a smaller number of measures and were located in
the histories of fewer and fewer institutions. Imitation rites therefore
emptied out the space they then sought to fill with a common cure.

In this chapter we seek to chart some important parts of the course
which has taken the Australian university from its modern re-birth in the
post-war period to its reinvention at the end of the century. This is not a
history. Others have provided this already, including two of our own
researchers writing in other places. Instead we will simply review what
took place from the standpoint of its significance for the governance of
the university and the emergence of the Enterprise University as a unifying ideal for reformers and critics alike.

It is useful to anticipate some of the main directions of change before
we set off to explain them. The period we are interested in is bracketed
by two important reports, the first by Martin in 1964 and the second
by West in 1998.[2] Martin expresses the view of his day in arguing for
an expanded tertiary sector, a strong focus upon industry (rather than
business)[3] and a recognition that national investment in education is a
source of national prosperity. At the other end of this period we see West
advocating a privatised model of higher education and expressing the
views of his contemporaries who approach education 'as if' it were
a business enterprise. Between these two bookends we find a process

of institutional change culminating in the Dawkins reforms which gave effect to some of the new deregulatory ideals concerning higher education, while also attempting to maintain a strong form of governmental policy steering.

Prehistory of the present

The Martin Report (1964)

To understand how larger movements in the idea of the 'good life' of citizens was played out in the higher education system we need to revisit some of the intentions and institutions put in place after the second world war.

The Martin Report in 1964 provides a summary and a symbol of this earlier vision. Like Murray[4] seven years before him, Martin and his collaborators saw the universities as a tool to work public policy objectives through academic purposes. He made explicit the desire to link educational objectives to the national economic interest. This project would help motivate and direct the 20-year expansion which saw Australia double its efforts and which resulted in a complete transformation of higher education from a semi-private domain of upper-class culture and state-based training for the elite professions into a system of mass credentialling designed to capture the spirit of optimism of the long boom.

If these objectives were rendered in economic terms, and certainly that was how Martin framed his report, they also implied a powerful social program. Like much of this Keynesian period the program was driven by an overwhelming confidence in the role of the national government as an agent of popular participation. Higher education would now be seen as a means to lift the involvement of participants towards the goal of self-development. Nor was this viewed as a compromise between public and private ends. Instead, Martin argued that the private gains to be achieved by students were 'only a fraction' of what society itself would achieve as more and more people became educated.[5] This was not the 'civilising' project which had once brought reformers into the debate about primary and secondary schooling. Rather it showed how far the Keynesian logic of consensus had stretched into all fields of public policy. The gains were economic, technical and very much about national position in the postwar economy. This was also the first clear statement of the commitment to treat skill and professional development as a national resource to be developed and exploited like any other.

The Whitlam years (1972–75)

Among many interesting characteristics of this approach was the preparedness to allow institutions a free hand in the development of these resources. Martin and his generation cared little for administrative matters and, aside from gestures towards modern management practice, did very little to force universities to change their internal systems of government. This carried through until the Whitlam years (the period of the reforming Labor government of 1972–75). Peter Karmel's 1973 report, *Schools in Australia*, was concerned with inequality within the primary and secondary education systems and only touched upon the universities in passing.[6] Nevertheless the thinking behind this report and the sentiments it provoked inside the Whitlam government help explain a number of important shifts in the early 1970s. In showing that educational inequality was a direct threat to the opportunities of many Australian children, Karmel attacked the foundation stone of private education.

Government, he argued, had a responsibility to see that each child could fully extend their talents and he put this claim squarely in the realm of citizenship rights.[7] It was a short step from this position to one which also argued that access to university education should be free. This became one of the major achievements of the Whitlam government and together with the Tertiary Education Allowance Scheme (TEAS) which provided all students with a stipend, this change in funding drew the Commonwealth government ever further into the higher education policy debate. As with the previous reforms, however, most attention was focused upon finance rather than upon outcomes and the means to achieve them. While the federal Department of Education was growing in size and importance as a result of the greater level of funding flowing to universities, institutes of technology and colleges of advanced education, the bulk of this growth was among administrators charged with assessing claims and issuing cheques. Policy development was still ranked low.

The growth of tertiary enrolments was accompanied by an expansion in the range of degree courses made available to students. Certainly the accreditation process required institutions to consider the impact of federally funded student load, but while this was expanding there were few means to target particular disciplines or projects. Instead the different types of institution pursued their own strategy. The universities, for the most part, stuck to a traditional fare and simply absorbed more students. The institutes of technology engaged in some innovation in the applied sciences in fields such as environmental science and human behaviour. But it was the former teachers' colleges and some of the colleges of advanced education (CAEs), which engaged in the most exotic innovations in the arts and humanities fields. By the end of the 1980s Australia had three distinct higher education sectors, each granting degrees and each laying claim to having a research tradition, even if that was somewhat more an ideal than a reality in the case of the institutes and colleges. Nevertheless, federal policy-making and funding had stimulated these ideals and it was for the governments of the 1980s to sort out how they were to be achieved.

The new public management

There is little doubt that some form of systemic change was likely to occur in the higher education sector in the 1980s. The expansions and diversity of the previous decade was already reaching its limits as the Fraser Liberal–National Party government (1975–83) battled youth unemployment and budget deficits in the late 1970s. Like other major spending areas at state and federal level, education was bound to feel the effect of any shift in thinking among policy elites. The shift in the late 1970s began to alter the methods governments used to pursue their objectives. This questioning started in the mid-1970s when the Whitlam government appointed the Coombs Commission which reported in 1976, and asked, ever so politely, for more 'accountable management'. Coombs also inquired whether governments always asked for the kind of information which would guarantee that policy had been implemented.

This rather gentle critique took several years to produce fruit but its point was not lost on insiders who were disappointed with the Whitlam government and who subsequently went to work with the state Labor governments of the 1980s. The disappointment had two elements. The first sprang from a fundamental flaw in the Keynesian model which had underpinned much of the post-war period. According to this view, governments could bring about desired changes in the behaviours of firms and individuals by manipulating the large levers of demand and supply, and in particular by stimulating the economy with expenditure on public works. This led to a complacency among policy-makers in regard to the real behaviours of firms and individuals. If this or that manufacturer failed to use the opportunities provided in order to pro-duce more efficiently, then little could be done. If a spending program did not achieve all of its immediate objectives, then at least the overall contribution to the stimulation of demand was enough to justify it. By the late 1970s very few among the policy elites in Australia or elsewhere in the OECD were content to accept this line.

A second, and related disappointment was with the role played by public servants during the Whitlam period. A general, vague but palpable resentment emerged throughout the late 1970s among those who had served in this government or who had been close to it. Whitlam himself had been a traditionalist when it came to politician–bureaucrat relation-ships. He gave the orders and then left all the rest to the public service.

His government's expansion of the role of the minister's private office to include policy matters seemed to break with this tradition but in practice these staff were confined to policy development and did little to improve public service accountability.

Coombs was interested in management issues and his report stimulated those who came after to think more seriously about the shape, purpose and dynamics of the public service. His argument was not much more developed than this. He favoured innovation. He liked experiments. He wished the public service to better resemble the cross-section of Australian society. Later governments at federal and state level had difficulty in reconciling these enthusiasms with the hard reality of budget pressures and the rising cost of public sector debt. But one certain legacy from the Coombs period was a stronger interest in accountability.

Inquiries in South Australia and New South Wales working for new Labor governments began to show interest in corporate planning and program budgeting techniques. The newly elected Cain government in Victoria committed itself to performance contracts for senior executives and required public authorities to pay a 'dividend' on their investments.[8] From these small beginnings came a new model of public management. It aimed at a rare combination of qualities. On one hand, it imagined the state as a corporation run by a *cabinet-as-board-of-directors*. This allowed ministers to exact far greater information from their public servants and to fix more exactly the terms on which public servants were to measure their performance. Reform-minded governments could quickly see this as a means to stop the implementation failure that had dogged the Whitlam government. Of course not only was this a way to be sure that the government program was fully adopted, it also promised a means to help finance initiatives during a time of fiscal stress. Savings from improved performance figured largely in the explanations given by governments of the 1980s for the means to fund new activities.

The second aspect of new public management was more problematic and led to critics characterising it as mere 'managerialism' (see for example Bryson in 1986[9]). While its political aim might have been to strengthen the hand of ministers and other policy-makers within government, the most immediate practical outcome of these reforms was to greatly enhance the role of senior bureaucrats and especially those charged with the reform of the public service. They quickly set about hiring consultants and subjecting departments to expensive and lengthy reviews, the consequence of which was much reshuffling of programs, some pruning of expenditure but not much worthwhile change.

The best of these reforms saw significant improvements in accountability and more efficient use of resources but the worst of them tended to institutionalise the view that lots of internal upheaval was a good method for disturbing vested interests and granting managers an opportunity to demonstrate toughness, zeal and of course, their individual worthiness for further advancement.

The Hawke government (from 1983)

The Hawke Labor government elected in 1983 was comparatively slow to embrace the assumed virtues of the new public management. Its main concern was to establish a neo-Keynesian accord with unions and business and much of its early enthusiasm was devoted to this end. However by 1985 the economic omens were less favourable to policies of stimulation and public expenditure. Pressure mounted for restraint and reorganisation. From 1985 onwards the government devoted much greater energy to finding a means to 'do more with less'. This inevitably led to cuts in expenditure programs and to the embrace of a more management-centred view of the public sector. Greater integration and control at the top of the public service was sought though contracts for departmental secretaries and performance pay for them and their immediate subordinates. Policy integration was sought through the creation of 'super ministries' which saw a senior cabinet minister assume control over two or more junior portfolios.

In order to achieve both efficiency and better performance, the new methodology was forced to eschew the twin evils of excessive control and careless autonomy. This it sought to do by tying departments to precise performance plans, linked to government policy. These plans, in turn, were to be the means for releasing funds. Much effort was spent examining the finances of departments and other public organisations in order to set these payments close to the level of subsistence, thus reducing their capacity to use 'hollow logs' and other stockpiles as a means to shirk the government (or senior management) policy discipline. Central agencies such as Treasury, Prime Minister and Cabinet, and Finance developed acute skills in this form of calculation and they enjoyed strong political support from the government's Expenditure Review Committee, a key cabinet committee during the Hawke period.

Dawkins and after

The Dawkins revolution

The imaginative reach of neo-liberal policies towards the universities was first powerfully demonstrated by Hawke's minister for Education and Training, John Dawkins. The introduction of new public management into the universities lagged behind its adoption by the administrative arms of the state, but once it became entrenched it was not to be dislodged.

The turning point was in the reform policies of 1987–89. There was an immense difference between government–university relations before and after 1987. Compared to that difference, the future transition from Labor government (1983–96) to Coalition government (1996 onwards) would be less significant, although some important differences between the two kinds of government would become evident.

Under both Labor government and Coalition government, the broad priorities of the new public management were to be substantially the same. In order to absorb greater and greater numbers of those school-leavers unable to find jobs in open employment, the university system was required to take more domestic entrants. Although this was couched in terms of a greater social commitment to the 'clever country' and improved 'human capital' for the workforce, time investment in apprenticeship training by government and industry fell at the same, suggesting a more pragmatic explanation for the enrolment explosion. To cope with the budgetary fall-out from this greater rate of enrolment, the new public management imposed on students a co-payment for the services they received and encouraged institutions to recruit full-fee overseas students. These changes to financing were associated with a new kind of policy-driven reform that worked its way inside the universities and onto the once sacred terrain of academic freedom. System-level changes created a more competitive relationship between individual institutions, installed efficiency imperatives in day-to-day conduct, and encouraged the emergence of entrepreneurial managements focused on the economic 'bottom-line'.

Here the stance of Australian governments was similar to that of many other nations,[10] except that in Australia market reform was introduced relatively quickly, and public fiscal support for the universities was to fall relatively rapidly, by comparative standards (see chapter 3).

For Dawkins and the Labor government the model was not so much the market as the corporation, not so much the theory of competitive allocation through prices and choices, but the theory of the large, multi-form (M-form) corporation regulating itself through targets, management plans and performance controls. We will return to the Dawkins vision later in this chapter to position our own study as a measure of some of its chief initiatives, but for now the point to focus upon is the one to do with the emergence of new economic criteria for assessing the 'public interest' in higher education.

In one very important sense the two guiding motifs of the Labor and Coalition governments owe a common debt to economic theories of organisation. Both sides of politics sought a new governing rationality for intellectual *production* in the arguments and perceived achievements of the business sector. Labor's productivist concept of value led it towards an idea of reform which saw the economic criteria of accountability as more 'hard nosed' and material than other social criteria. Both sought to honour the triumph of the private sector in the period which followed the crisis of social democracy and the loss of faith in government after the fiscal crisis of the mid- to late 1970s. These issues have been well debated elsewhere, including in other work we have done on public sector reform, education and globalisation.[11]

The story, as it is now well understood by all sides of the debate, begins with differences of view over the role played by the public sector in either fostering the building of a mature society, or in the weakening of society through inefficient allocation and rent-seeking. This struggle between alternate visions of renewal sprang from the same seed but took root in different terrain. Between the two developed a remarkably sharp and bitter cleavage in the imaginations of public leaders, including politicians and bureaucrats, senior executives and the employees of public bodies. At stake were the core values and ideals of citizenship that would under-pin a new world system based on global competition and economic vulnerability. In this system there would be a new cultural formation in which the idea of individual responsibility and risk would rise above the received but discredited concepts of the nation as an industrial compromise between labour and capital.

Of the two political imaginations, Labor's vision was both the more complex and the more unstable – in Keating's celebrated phrase they wanted 'econocrats and bleeding hearts' all in together.[12] The embrace of the market was to be framed by concerns for the most disadvantaged. Hard-working East Asian economies provided an imagined (and some-times fantasised) account of sudden prosperity born of sustained, state-driven growth.

In higher education this view took shape as a unique mix of policy assertiveness and massive investment in growth. Labor created 16 new universities through upgrading and merger in four years, forced high school retention rates up in most states and convinced a new generation of adolescents that university was the logical choice for a post-school commitment. Certainly this helped Labor manage a youth unemploy-ment problem which threatened their social democratic credentials. But equally significant was the openness with which the government ap-proached the universities themselves. New entrants were simply allowed to flow into existing courses and institutions with little attention to career options or ways to mark out a new pathway for less academically formed students. A host of 'generic brand' programs in business studies and professional writing began to populate in suburban and regional campuses. 'Full education' emerged as a substitute for 'full employment' and a temporary alternative to life on the dole.

The new universities

Among the coterie of young ministers enthralled with the new management faith, none was more tenacious than John Dawkins. As Finance minister in 1983–84 he had led the charge on public service reform, and even though government attention at the time lay elsewhere, his efforts drew acclaim in the senior cabinet.

Dawkins' first major ministerial opportunity came in mid-1987 when he was put in charge of the new 'super ministry' of Employment, Education and Training. The creation of this ministry sent a clear signal to universities – henceforth the higher education sector – that programs were to be administered in a department with a clear economic orientation. Dawkins also immediately made it clear that his was to be a microeconomic approach to reform, meaning he would seek ways to improve productivity in education and training.

The Green Paper, *Higher education: a policy discussion paper* (1987), released shortly after his ascent to power, was as bold and threatening a document as the universities had ever faced. It proposed to elevate the institutes of technology and colleges of advanced education to the level of universities (despite the fact that this was actually a state prerogative). It proposed mergers among these institutions in order to achieve economies of scale and specialisation. It lampooned university management practices as inefficient and in particular made fun of the academy's collegial practices such as electing deans.

Closely linked to these structural changes, the report championed the idea that higher education be viewed as an industry. Prior reviews had advocated closer links with industry but had stopped short of collapsing the categories of academia and private enterprise. Dawkins and his corporate management enthusiasts had no such hesitation. In particular they favoured the greater use of user payments and other pseudo-market mechanisms inside higher education. Here the first foray had been attempted by the previous minister, Susan Ryan when, in 1985, she provided guidelines to encourage fee-charging for international students. But with the Green Paper this approach moved from the margins to the centre.

Dawkins and his supporters also saw great opportunity for this 'education industry' to export its product into Asia, thus helping improve the current account deficit which was so much on the mind of the government at this time.

Among these threats and challenges there was one big item of good news: graduates were to increase from 80 000 to 125 000 per year over 15 years. This would soften resistance to the other changes and provide the government with an invaluable bargaining chip in negotiations with institutions. The rising tide of enrolments would lift all boats.

Behind the scenes Dawkins sought support and ideas from a number of senior figures in the higher education sector. Known as the 'purple circle', the group included Mal Logan from Monash, Don Watts from Curtin University of Technology and later the private Bond University, the economist Helen Hughes, Don Aitkin from the ANU and soon Dawkins' chair of the newly formed Australian Research Council, Bob Smith from University of WA, Jack Barker from Ballarat CAE and Brian Smith from RMIT. Dawkins' senior adviser Paul Hickey was also active. This group debated the virtues of deregulation and the impediments to getting greater efficiency from the current system. Notable absentees from Dawkins' list included Peter Karmel, the doyen of education policy-makers and former chair of the Commonwealth Tertiary Education Commission (CTEC), the government's own regulator, Paul Bourke of the Australian National University's Institute of Advanced Studies, and the most publicly prominent vice-chancellor, the University of Melbourne's David Penington. All, particularly Penington, were to become critics of the new policies.

Shotgun marriages

Not everyone was convinced, however. The CTEC saw fees and competition between institutions as a doubtful initiative that was unlikely to 'encourage efficiency in the use of scarce resources'.[13] And to the Liberal-leaning Sandstone universities the Dawkins approach was interventionist, impertinent and likely to lower the tone of the whole system. David Penington from the University of Melbourne took up the fight on his own behalf and on behalf of those other elite institutions who found the Green Paper entirely too enthusiastic about changing missions, research programs and internal structures.

The seven months of heated discussion of the Green Paper made little impact and in July 1988 Dawkins released *Higher education: a policy statement*. It so closely resembled the Green Paper that critics were soon asking 'How do you turn a Green Paper into a White Paper? Just photocopy it!' Nor were critics inside government given space to manoeuvre. The minister abolished CTEC, removing its effective chair Hugh Hudson, and then divided its functions among groups far less able to rally criticism regarding government policy.

This then was the background to the institutional changes that led to the creation of the current group of universities. More than this, it was also the genesis of a new logic of sector-wide governance which was to deeply inscribe itself upon the psyche of each contemporary bureaucrat and university leader drawn by its siren call.

The Enterprise University

Table 2.1 Institutions in the unified national system[a] of higher education in Australia, 1987 compared to 1994

Higher education institutions in 1987 by state/territory indicating mergers to be	Student load 1987	Higher education institutions in 1994 by state/territory following completion of mergers	Student load 1994
	EFTSU		EFTSU
New South Wales			
University of Sydney	16 140	University of Sydney	26 231
Sydney CAE	4 829		
Cumberland Coll. of Health Sci.	1 829		
Sydney College of the Arts	851		
NSW Conservatorium of Music	430		
University of NSW	14 518	University of NSW[c]	21 777
Aust. Defence Force Academy	857	Aust. Defence Force Academy	1 177
Macquarie University[b]	7 647	Macquarie University[b]	11 623
University of New England	5 685	University of New England	8 211
Armidale CAE	1 178		
Orange Agricultural College	378		
University of Newcastle	4 610	University of Newcastle	11 853
Newcastle CAE	2 234		
University of Wollongong	4 554	University of Wollongong	9 095
NSW Institute of Technology	7 057	University of Tech., Sydney	15 492
Kuring-gai CAE	2 324		
Nepean CAE	2 376	University of Western Sydney	16 625
Macarthur Inst. of Higher Ed.	2 014		
Hawkesbury Agricultural Coll.	1 369		
Mitchell CAE	2 955	Charles Sturt University	10 543
Riverina-Murray Inst. of HE	3 599		
Northern Rivers CAE	1 460	Southern Cross University	4 733
Nat'l Institute of Dramatic Art	120	Nat'l Institute of Dramatic Art	126
Victoria			
University of Melbourne	13 853	University of Melbourne	25 041
Melbourne CAE	3 955		
Hawthorn Inst. of Tech.	1 034		
Victorian College of the Arts	583		
Monash University	11 812	Monash University	28 681
Chisholm Inst. of Technology	5 196		
Gippsland Inst. of Adv. Ed.	1 818		
Victorian Coll. of Pharmacy	385		
La Trobe University	7 879	La Trobe University	16 918
Bendigo CAE	1 756		
Lincoln Inst. of Health Sciences	1 927		
Deakin University	3 781	Deakin University	17 190
Victoria College	5 698		
Warrnambool Inst. of Adv. Ed.	1 171		
RMIT	8 313	RMIT	18 619
Phillip Institute of Technology	3 977		
Footscray Institute of Technology	3 581	Victoria University of Technology	10 306
Swinburne Limited	4 362	Swinburne Uni. of Technology[d]	6 859
Ballarat CAE	2 001	University of Ballarat	3 387

Queensland			
University of Queensland	14 180	University of Queensland	20 601
Queensland Agricultural College	1 165		
Griffith University	3 665	Griffith University	14 048
Gold Coast CAE	90		
Qld Conservatorium of Music	315		
James Cook Uni. of North Qld	2 495	James Cook Uni. of North Qld	6 707
Qld Institute of Technology	6 977	Queensland Uni. of Technology	19 492
Brisbane CAE	7 228		
Capricornia Inst. of Adv. Ed.	2 024	University of Central Queensland	5 477
Darling Downs Inst. of Adv. Ed.	3 864	University of Southern Queensland	7 776
Western Australia			
University of WA	8 222	University of WA	10 990
Murdoch University	2 884	Murdoch University	6 098
Curtin University of Technology	8 562	Curtin University of Technology	14 857
WA CAE	7 021	Edith Cowan University	11 513
South Australia			
University of Adelaide	7 034	University of Adelaide	11 242
Roseworthy Agricultural Coll.	533		
Flinders University of SA	4 359	Flinders University of SA[e]	7 923
SA CAE	7 772	University of South Australia	16 500
SA Institute of Technology	4 903		
Tasmania			
University of Tasmania	4 282	University of Tasmania	9 669
Tasmania State Inst. of Tech.	2 008		
Australian Maritime College	245	Australian Maritime College	392
ACT			
Australian National University	5 336	Australian National University	8 736
Canberra CAE	4 163	University of Canberra	6 695
Northern Territory			
—	—	Northern Territory University	2 699
Catholic Teachers' College		Australian Catholic University	6 302
Catholic Coll. of Educ. (NSW)	1 638		
Inst. of Catholic Education (Vic.)	1 383		
McAuley College (Qld)	445		
Signadou College (ACT)	201		

a does not include other private institutions; however funded, as these did not join the
   Commonwealth government's unified national system of higher education. All of these
   institutions (including two which received no government funding, Bond University and
   Notre Dame University Australia) were small.
b includes Australian Film, Television and Radio School.
c includes minor sites from advanced education.
d includes Prahran campus of the former Victoria College.
e includes Sturt campus of SA CAE.
Sources: John Dawkins, *Higher education: a discussion paper*, Canberra, 1987, pp. 118–121;
Department of Employment, Education and Training, *Selected higher education statistics*,
Canberra, 1995.

Once in place the White Paper provoked an orgy of courtships and marriages among suitor institutions (see table 2.1). Few wished to stand aside and risk missing out on the Dawkins dowry – the many thousands of new places to be allocated, and the variety of special payments, subsidies and capital grants. Most of the institutes of technology grasped the opportunity to declare themselves universities and rename their senior staff 'professor'. Frenetic bargaining took place among the CAEs which, with their humanities slant, were by now clearly at greatest risk of missing the new enterprise wave.[14] State ministers were drawn into negotiations and attempted to temper the Dawkins orthodoxy with certain local political concerns. Rarely was efficiency or consumer choice uppermost. For example it was taken as a virtual necessity that the major universities would simply absorb any CAE close to their main campus and that such institutions would quickly lose their identity and distinct purpose. These were real estate deals and little effort was made to disguise the fact.[15]

In the regions the logic of amalgamation saw both innovation and ineptitude. Southern Cross was born when unresolved resentment between the Northern Rivers CAE and the University of New England stopped a more obvious allocation of resources. In Victoria a suitable marriage between regional neighbours Deakin University, Ballarat CAE and Bendigo CAE fell apart when their separate insecurities were jokingly expressed in the suggestion that they might call themselves the 'Country and Western University'. Discussions soon broke down. Elsewhere established universities were left to 'pick and choose' among remaining debutants according to the personal inclination of vicechancellors, councils and very occasionally the veto power of academic boards. Few would afterwards argue that the allocations followed any pattern or served any wider purpose than the crude fact that the many were easily reduced to the few.

The process for deciding the shape of the new sector brought to light many of the weaknesses of the Dawkins approach. Obsessed with the 'big picture', his ministry provoked radical change in the governance of the sector without having any clear idea how that might end. Provided it looked business-like and took account of government policy, the minister feigned indifference to the consequences of his actions. But now that Pandora's box was opened there would be no going back. Universities were now more vulnerable to government policy and more indebted to Canberra for ideas on how to manage themselves. None dared try to reestablish an older model of academic independence for down that path lay the risk that government would turn its back and withhold the many discretionary payments which now made up the 'payments for results' regime established by Dawkins.

The new model of governance

The new model of federal governance is worth close examination for it soon informed the way universities would view their own futures. First and foremost, the method involved the assertion of management prerogative over all other interests. Only government policy should direct the major allocations within higher education and all else should follow the dictates of good management. Second, and equally important, to achieve efficiency local management should seek reorganisation within the system, breaking up old fiefdoms and subjecting subordinates to vigorous review. Finally, new systems of governance should focus upon a few major instruments of control, leaving day-to-day management in the hands of lower level operatives. Those controls should be based upon budgets and performance plans which regularly forced subordinates to compete for scarce marginal resources. In other words, underfunding plus discretionary payments added up to intimate influence.

As we shall see, this form of strategic control through management reorganisation soon came to dominate the cloisters of all higher education institutions, even if the particular application was apt to reflect the personality of the vice-chancellor and the current mood in Canberra. It constituted a shift in government thinking away from a policy-centred approach in which questions of participation, industry training and access were dominant, to one in which these were incorporated into a series of management techniques that had its greatest interest in the governance of these institutions.

Previous shifts at the Commonwealth level had provoked changes in the roles of vice-chancellors, the formation of unions and the creation of peak bodies. But it is nevertheless true to say that here for the first time was a regime which created comprehensive internal changes by the use of a relatively simple set of management gestures. It was a lesson learned well and one which university leaders soon began to practise upon their own institutions with all the vigour which Dawkins had brought to his attack upon them.

In the new model of governance, the legacy of Dawkins became more permanently embodied, and in more than one sense. Dawkins was to higher education what the then Treasurer Paul Keating was to financial deregulation, and the then Prime Minister Margaret Thatcher was to British politics: the model neo-liberal executive, forcing through a single-minded reform crusade with a mix of system planning, market rhetoric and the determination to crush all political opposition. The win–crush ambience of the Dawkins style was heady stuff. Dawkins implemented the policies of the Green and White papers almost to the letter, with an obvious disregard for vice-chancellorial opinion or the unique features of academic work. What the senior management of the universities could not avoid they plainly chose to imitate. Stronger executive pressure from Canberra begat enhanced executive control at home. University leaders used the Dawkins reforms as legitimation for an internal revolution which often copied Canberra's much reviled instruments of government: the efficiency saving, the strategic fund, the relative funding model and the central performance formula. Subsequently, the 'threats' of Coalition ministers Vanstone and Kemp were mobilised for internal purposes in much the same way.

Market-managerialism and the Howard government (1996)

In mid-1996 the recently elected conservative Coalition government led by John Howard handed a new review brief to former private school headmaster Roderick West. The consequent West Report, *Learning for life* (1998), marked the official arrival of a pervasive market-logic in the organisation of Australian higher education. Except for some residual regulation to maintain access by some disadvantaged students, the new orthodoxy placed economic choice at the centre of decision-making. Accordingly, the distribution of educational opportunity in the universities would obey signals sent by selective consumers and entrepreneurial organisations seeking fees and other income opportunities.

Central to the preference for a pseudo-market system was the claim that the existing arrangements were far too dependent upon central planning, implying bureaucratic management of targets and supply-oriented strategies by universities unwilling to reduce costs. While this commitment to pseudo-market choice lay at the heart of the report and its subsequent debate within the education policy community,[16] much of the detailed argument actually turned upon the way public funding might be employed in a deregulated environment. In other words the market envisaged was largely defined as a quasi-market or mimic-market between institutions in which tax funds would still be used as an incentive system to encourage the emergence of increased private spending on higher education. This *imaginary market* reflected government efforts in other policy sectors such as health, pharmaceuticals and welfare where experiments were taking place in the introduction of 'user fees', co-payments and the use of private fund raising. What were the substantive initiatives proposed by West and his colleagues and how do they position us to understand the policy environment which helps drive the emergence of the Enterprise University?

In essence the recommendations turned upon a belief that students (and their families) should play a greater role in determining the flow of funds, and thus the priorities of the higher education system. For such choice to be possible West recommended a number of basic structural changes. First, and most important of all, he viewed fees as the building block for the new structure. This move took the form of both a new form of encouragement to universities to extend full-fee courses, and a decision to extend fee-charging into the realm of government-funded places. The boundaries placed on this act of imagination were evident in the fact that West anticipated a cap to limit the charges universities demanded from places currently being funded through tax dollars. Even so, he saw this as a compromise 'in the first instance' and indicated that a more open play of so-called market forces might later allow all fees to be set by the interplay of demand and supply.

In like vein the West Report advised government to accredit private universities and to sanction a voucher or entitlement fund which any given student might take to the institution of their choice. Similarly, the public resources available to furnish student choice would be shaped by income-contingent loans. And extending the imagined framework into research, the West Report outlined the need for the same kind of incentives and competitive pressures to drive the search for new knowledge.

While the West Report undoubtedly sought a radicalism of approach which most governments might find difficult to implement, it was plain that much of the substance of the strategy fitted neatly into the cost-conscious ideology of a Howard government bent upon the restructure of public programs. In this sense it was but a further expression of cost-conscious intentions made explicit by their predecessors, the Hawke and Keating Labor governments of 1983 to 1996.

Market governance

This observation need not require that we see Dawkins and West as a single impulse. In fact their differences tell us just as much as their many similarities. In the latter case we can easily see that higher education moved from its broad role in public culture and its function in raising the level of participation of citizens to a new orthodoxy which favours business values and income generation. This is common to both parties and both of the bureaucratic regimes they established. But under Dawkins the degree of 'active steering' from Canberra increased substantially. In fact the very use of the Green and White paper strategy, rather than expert inquiry, signifies the stronger political hand. Labor wanted both the policy tools and the business logic, but the weight was still on the former. The Coalition evidently preferred the game of economic incentives to the more overt resort to policy directives and with that shift came a strengthened interest in governance matters. By this we mean that policy became far more embedded in the incentive structures of the new quasi-market for education.

The apparent indifference in this shift towards governance to matters of social 'grand policy' previously expressed in ministerial statements or special programs was but the surface of things. Underneath, this new 'game of incentives' carried its own powerfully implied commitments to small government, greater individual responsibility, increased business control of higher education, and more inequality between institutions, students and communities.

Canberra continued to be the main player in manipulating these incentives, but the various parts of the higher education industry increasingly needed to find their own version of a common strategy to find new funds, compete for international students and attract business support. This strategy quickly transformed the internal structures of these universities, making them subject to stronger external imperatives and more energetic executive direction by their own management elite. Governance became a new process by which the policy goals of politicians, business interests and other key groups became expressed as desirable transformations of the *modus vivendi* of university life. Administrative structures and routines became the chief venue for the working out of different conceptions of 'the good university', and thus of 'good scholarship'.

This was achieved not as a discussion about alternative futures and their consequences, but as debate or conjecture regarding the emergence of new committees, revised faculty and school structures, new international programs and revised funding formulae for research and teaching. That this was always the way most corporations gave voice to more subtle transformations of values and goals might have escaped the attention of many academics, but the convergence was no less striking.

In other words the shift from policy to governance constituted more than just another play in the game of feint and position that long structured the post-war universities' relations with their paymasters in government. That very connection had been broken open, and remade along new lines. In the process, both the external connections *and* internal life of the universities underwent a profound metamorphosis.

In the ten years after the Dawkins White Paper the government withdrew from much of the funding of the institutions, forcing them to open themselves up to a wide variety of external sources and obligations. Yet in the shift from policy to governance, Canberra was able to ensure that its 'hooks' into the universities could 'pull' as well as ever, and more so. Politicians and administrators found a new potency in pressure for internal reforms, in which the remaking of the universities was all the more effective because it was the voluntary achievement of autonomous bodies – on paper at least, universities and their leaders were more independent, more self-determining than before. The outcome was that university organisation changed more in the 1990s than in the previous 40 years.

Government alone did not accomplish this shift, and its demands on the universities were so effective only because they resonated at many points with the larger developments that were taking place. Even while the universities were being remade as sites of governance, the role of intellectual labour in the economy was expanding, bringing business and the ethic of enterprise into the universities in new ways. At the same time government itself was being remade under the auspices of global economics and cultural change, and of neo-liberal politics. And the growing global realm was working its way into the heart of the universities, which as sites of governance, rather than places apart from the world and protected by policy, had now been opened to direct global influence.

Chapter 3 looks more closely at how the universities changed in the 1990s, under the three-way and continuing effects of globalisation, the transition from policy to governance, and internal reform. It begins by reviewing recent interpretations of 'globalisation' in higher education, and proposing a counter-interpretation. The concept of globalisation has been over-used, and in some quarters given too great an explanatory force, so that the specific circumstances of each national higher education system and each individual university are too easily lost. Nevertheless, globalisation cannot be ignored, any more than the salience of the shift from policy to governance can be ignored.

In the process chapter 3 suggests that the changes in Australian universities are by no means unique, and that in a more global era these changes coincide at many points with changes taking place in other countries. Indeed, one effect of the shift from policy to governance has been to facilitate what appears as a 'natural' convergence between Australian institutions and their overseas counterparts, particularly American counterparts, and to entrench imitating behaviour in the organic life of the universities themselves.

3   Roots of the Enterprise University (2): From academy to global business

Globalisation and academic capitalism

Traditions in question

'British mathematicians have responded with fury to the news that a collection of rare books and manuscripts, donated to Keele University for the benefit of students, have been sold to a private collector in America', it was reported in December 1998. The collection, compiled over 50 years by British public servant Charles Turner, included the first three editions of Isaac Newton's *Principia Mathematica* and eight books from Newton's own library. But the cash-strapped university threw tradition aside, raising $1.6 million.

A few years earlier Syracuse University in the United States decided to abandon its time-hallowed university crest. Discarding the coat of arms and Latin motto, it replaced them with a new corporate logo. A little later Monash University in Australia made the same move. Its Italian motto *Ancora Imparo* (I am still learning), attributed to Michelangelo, was replaced by the more emphatic 'Australia's International University'.[1] University traditions are in jeopardy, it seems. But it is easy to illustrate an argument with selected anecdotes. How much should we make of incidents like these? How deep and how general is the transformation of university identity that they suggest? How much have universities really changed in the last decade, the decade of governance and globalisation?

There is a considerable literature on the changes taking place in universities, or The University as it is often described. 'The University' is a generic short-hand term for a vast number of institutions of higher education throughout the world, with a wide range of histories, cultures, roles and missions, but sharing features in common including functions of advanced professional training, doctoral courses, and research.

It must be said that many texts concerning universities are deficient in their capacity to explain the university, or anything else. Rather than provide us with insights into what is actually happening, most of this literature focuses on shifts in The University as an imagined abstraction, with only briefest reference to the realm of its concrete condition. Some authors are anxious about The University and defensive about its traditions, others want to advance the current changes more quickly, but both groups discuss the topic without reference to real life universities.

The university in ruins?

One widely read analysis is that of the late Bill Readings in *The university in ruins* (1996). Readings' book is in a long tradition of philosophically informed humanistic discussion about universities. He believes that the modern government-funded university is changing irretrievably under the pressure of globalisation. The core project of the modern university has been that of forming a national culture, and turning students into citizen subjects, the bearers of the national culture. Globalisation is seen as undermining the nation-state and with it, this cultural function of the university. In its place the university is turning into a 'transnational bureaucratic corporation' whose logic is corporate rather than cultural. Individual universities are breaking free of the social context that nurtured them.[2]

The nation understands itself as its own theme park, and that resolves the question of what it means to live in Italy: it is to have been Italian once. Meanwhile, the state is merely a large corporation to be entrusted to businessmen, a corporation that increasingly serves as a handmaiden to the penetration of transnational capital. The governmental structure of the nation-state is no longer the organising centre of the common existence of peoples across the planet, and the University of Excellence serves nothing other than itself, another corporation in a world of transnationally exchanged capital.[3]

As Readings sees it, in the new university the old cultural judgements, varying by field of knowledge, are replaced by a universal notion of 'excellence'. Excellence ('quality') is vacuous, but enables 'exhaustive' surveillance and accounting so that the university can be administered as a net of bureaucratic institutions. Here the central figure is not the professor but the administrator ('manager'). Students are becoming consumers rather than the political subjects of the nation-state, and the academic disciplines are breaking down under 'the pressure of market imperatives'. The argument owes something to the famous essay by Jean-François Lyotard on *The postmodern condition*.[4] In the face of these trends, Readings is determined to sustain the role of 'Thought', outside 'the restricted economy of calculation'. With an echo of critical theorist Jurgen Habermas, he asserts the role of communications and community in universities as the basis for making something better.[5]

While it is true that the evolution of the modern nation-state and the modern university are closely tied, on the whole we find Readings' argument too reductionist and pessimistic. He was writing from the University of Montreal, where the national project – both that of the Quebecois, and that of Canada after the formation of a North American free-trade zone – is in double jeopardy. Australian government and universities share some features of the Canadian predicament. On the other hand, in some other parts of the world the nation-state is more robust: for example in Japan, China, France. In the case of the United States, national policy-making, in synergy with global finance, is a key element in its continued global dominance; and the global forms contain a strong element of national culture.

While it is clear that in the global era the nation-state is changing, it is more complicated and controversial to claim that the national is being altogether *displaced* by the global, or that the economic has successfully substituted itself for the political. Readings' defines globalisation as 'Americanisation', and Americanisation as 'the generalisation of the rule of the cash nexus in place of the notion of national identity as determinant of all aspects of investment in social life (pp. 2–3)'. There are a number of problems with this. First, are global relationships *inevitably* American in character, or are there other traditions? Second, is globalisation wholly economic as Readings' account appears to suggest? Does it have cultural (and political) aspects? Or is Readings arguing that we can simply read cultural change as an 'effect' of an economic 'cause'? Third, arguments of this type are circular. Readings 'proves' that global economics replaces national government and culture, by defining globalisation as that which replaces national government and culture with global economics. In that line of reasoning, Readings paradoxically has something in common with many of the advocates of a world re-ordered on the basis of global financial markets.

This points to a deeper problem: Readings' failure to test the nature of the university *empirically*, to examine the evidence. His book draws heavily on other scholars but does not engage with actual universities very much. If he had considered globalisation and the university in empirical terms, we suspect that he would have found that the trends he talks about in abstract are more uneven in practice, and sometimes absent altogether. Those trends are also criss-crossed with counter-trends. The future is not already fixed.

Policy as propaganda

Nevertheless, Readings' book is more considered than much of the contemporary policy writing on higher education. Take one of the more influential policy texts prepared in Australia in recent years, 'Australian higher education in the era of mass customisation', a background paper

for the 1997–98 Commonwealth government review of higher education financing and policy, the West review. The paper was written not by
the government itself but by Global Alliance Limited, a Tokyo-based
investment bank specialising in cross-border transactions and the information technology and global educational services industries. It had a
direct effect in shaping the thinking and the proposals of the West
committee.[6]

The Global Alliance Limited combines hard-bitten 'realism' with
shock tactics as the means of softening the reader for a wholesale
commercialisation of universities. It takes for granted that there is an
irresistible trend to global free trade in education, regardless of national
traditions or goals, a trend which Global Alliance actively supports, perhaps because global trade in education is its own business. Specifically
national features based in government planning and 'the "public benefit"
of higher education', such as restrictions on the use of the title 'university', the allocation of government funding to selected domestic providers, and the use of higher education to achieve social benefits, are in
the end nothing more than obstacles to free trade. (Global Alliance places
public benefit in quotes and so opens the concept to doubt.) These
obstacles must be swept away if individual Australian institutions are to
become cost-competitive on the world scene. Government must 'open
the floodgates for new domestic and international entrants', creating 'a
level playing field for non-profit and for profit players'. Anyway, argues
Global Alliance, the development of communications technologies, virtual universities and a more active student consumer make it impossible
to stay the same. The global university market will dominate and any
attempt to cling to social or cultural objectives in education is akin to
producing Ford motor vehicles with a 1929 Detroit assembly line.[7]

In the global market imagined by Global Alliance, institutions will
need to search out specialist markets and there will be only a limited
number of spots for broad-based research universities (significantly, such
universities are described by Global Alliance using the concept 'Harvard
in Australia U', pointing to likely American domination of its kind of
world market, and the extinction of any other distinctively national forms
of doctoral research university). In many cases, the preferred strategy
will not be the 'Harvard in Australia' doctoral university, but a different
institution based in low-cost high-volume production, perhaps through
distance education. When the costs of research and of 'chalk and talk'
are 'stripped' from the teaching function, says Global Alliance, tuition
becomes more cost-competitive.

Whatever the niche each university occupies, it seems that government
policy should be designed so as to support 'winners in the international
marketplace', that is, it should be economically rather than educationally

directed.[8] Global Alliance says little about the long-term policy objectives of nation-building and the creation of equitable opportunities via education, or the effects on teaching quality or the striving for research excellence; and nothing about the fate of different academic disciplines in its imagined new world. The profit and loss statement is the guide to questions about preference and value.

The simplification is familiar and easy to grasp, the scale of the vision is cinematic: large screen, big picture and 3 millimetres deep. Grandiose as it is, and far removed as it is from the present reality of universities, Global Alliance's vision does not seem absurd or irrelevant: it resonates with imaginings of the global that are now commonplace. Global Alliance has pitched it right for the times, one reason why it secured such a hold on the West committee. Of course there is an element of ambit claim here. We can assume that Global Alliance would be happy to see at least some moves towards commercial fee-charging and the opening up of public subsidies and the title 'university' to international for-profit providers, the companies that are its clients. But we want to draw attention not only to the content of the argument, but to its method. Global Alliance's approach is not grounded in actual experience, but in the highly 'advertorial' approach of a long-shot company prospectus. In its 102 pages there is little room for analysis not already loaded with hard-sell. There is no detailed study of the actual Australian system, of past policies and present trends, only the deployment of selected facts that build a preferred case. As Global Alliance's 'should' slides into its 'must' and then its 'will', its argument for wholesale market deregulation becomes established. It seems that the future of universities is clear-cut and unstoppable, a future in which stand-alone full-fee-charging corporate universities will sink or swim by their own efforts, and functions of government policy-making will be taken over by global merchant bankers and investment advisers – such as Global Alliance itself.

The Global Alliance paper tells us much about the politics of university reform. There is no denying the influence exerted by normative and programmatic texts, in situations where such texts are joined to the authority of government, and fit with established corporate thinking. Where these futurist texts often miss their mark is that the grasp on the here-and-now is poor, or is absent altogether. In place of research data, they favour folkloric tales of failure and success from which lessons are drawn. They treat every university as if it is the same as every other, and its problems and their solution reducible to standard failings. There is only limited clarity about the larger context in which the universities are operating, and less clarity about the daily life of these complex institutions. Indeed, the closer that such exhortative texts move towards the real life of the universities as institutions, the more their vision falters, and insight is replaced by a new propaganda.

The Global Alliance paper is more audacious than most, but in its argument for commercialisation, the university-as-business and management-driven reform it has many cousins. The Industries Commission and Productivity Commission for example, have produced a succession of reports on reforming the public services, including education.[9] The Hoare Report on governance and resource management in higher education (1995) used a similar if less flamboyant method to argue for more corporate-style governing bodies.[10] Internationally there are many examples of this use of official reports as unbridled advocates for marketisation reforms, for example World Bank statements on higher education.[11] The approach has also shaped some academic commentary on higher education in Australia, such as Peter Coaldrake and Lawrence Stedman's *On the brink* (1998). Coaldrake and Stedman include a short historical account and make some references to sociological data on the universities, but their book, too, is overwhelmingly exhortative in tone. Their solution to all important problems is for the universities to become more business-like and competitive. Here commentary on higher education becomes a sub-set of the burgeoning 're-engineer or perish' literature of advice on business management.

Government and globalisation

In *Universities and globalisation* (1998) Jan Currie and Janice Newson also describe an unstoppable 'globalisation' and its tidal-wave force. Globalisation is defined as 'a material set of practices drawn from the world of business', combined with a neo-liberal 'market ideology'. This conflates changes in politics and government policy, trends in international economics, and changes in the university subsumed under the heading 'managerialism'. It is not very different to the way Global Alliance sets the terms of debate, except that where Global Alliance sees benefits, Currie and Newson identify disadvantages. They identify downside of contemporary trends, such as income inequalities,[12] and the impoverishment of university systems. They emphasise the need to examine claims about globalisation critically, and draw attention to the role of 'agency', that is, the capacity of people to question and reject contemporary reforms to the university.[13]

However, by giving globalisation so much analytical clout the authors rob the very notion of agency they wish to assert. How much scope can there be for a different kind of university, when government, economics and organisational behaviour are all pulling uniformly in the same direction and with, it seems, the force of a tidal wave? If the character of university organisation in one country can be simply read off powerful exterior trends generated far away, what scope can there be for different university cultures? Is globalisation a 'given', or are global relationships grounded in history and able to be altered? Are universities victims of global forces, or themselves one of the agents of global changes, having scope to choose their own take on the global? Has the world been thoroughly integrated into one American world by globalisation, or has it rather been united in certain ways but with continuing gaps, dislocations, differences and 'others'?[14]

Ours is not a book primarily about globalisation. Nevertheless it is useful to set down what we mean by the term, which is occupying much attention at present, to help situate the changes in universities and to explain why we have focused on university governance.

Here it is necessary to distinguish between two factors shaping the contemporary university: first, changes in the character of government and politics; second, those changes in economy and culture which point to greater global convergence, the formation of global systems in the strict meaning of the term. Though it is true that the two sets of changes have become associated, and affect each other, we cannot read one entirely from the other. Globalisation is only *one* of the factors shaping the changes in the nature of government and hence in policy on higher education. And there is more to globalisation than neo-liberal ideas about the primacy of market economies and the minimisation of democratic politics. In some respects, globalisation is not necessarily neo-liberal at all. There is nothing inherently neo-liberal about faster transport or better communications.

The changes in the public sector and in policy on higher education include the decline of the old framework of government policy, the Keynesian mixed economy with its public programs in education, health and welfare; the rise of a neo-liberal policy of small government and the growing influence of business goals and models in public administration; and the emergence of new systems of governance in which autonomous public institutions are 'steered from the distance' by product specifications, and market-type incentives and competitive pressures. The notion of social capital has slipped from favour. The government-financed production of a non-market kind, in education, research and other sectors, is often seen not as social investment but as waste. The time horizons of public policy have shrunk. Short-term returns and short-term costs are increasingly important, as in the private sector. As Yeatman puts it:

Patterns of cooperation or collaboration are driven by the competitive dynamics of private utility maximisation. This is a very different conception of the work of government than that offered by the idea of a policy process which is located within a public sector oriented to public values and public goods.[15]

Although levels of government spending have fallen relative to need, in relation to domestic policies such as education the role of the nation-state and the effectiveness of its governing organs have *not* declined. Where governments are more constrained than in the earlier period is in relation to the external settings. A deregulated global financial system sets shifting limits on economic and social policies. International 'best practice' – mostly US practice – is transmitted instantaneously on computer screens, and attempts to colonise the thinking of government officials and politicians. The Internet creates an unprecedented level of instant interaction. In this environment commercial, technological and organisational innovation have become greatly intensified, and one policy objective is to increase the rate of social and technological change itself. Some governments (and universities) are destabilised, losing a sense of their own project. Others are able to rework that project in the more complex and volatile global setting.

'Globalisation' refers to the growing impact of world systems of finance and economic life, transport, communications and media, language and symbols. It is as much about the cross-global movement of people and ideas as about markets and money, and more about networks than about patterns of commodity trade or off-shore production.[16] David Harvey refers to 'time-space compression' whereby 'the time horizons of both private and public decision-making have shrunk', while communications and transport costs make it possible 'to spread those decisions immediately over an ever wider and variegated space'.[17]

The term 'borderlessness' is sometimes used to describe the trend to the global, but this is misleading. National and cultural boundaries have not disappeared, though they are crossed at many points. In the global environment, national institutions co-exist with global ones, and different national traditions become mixed, a process fuelled by tourism and migration, facilitated by cheapening air travel and the explosion of communications, and sustained by market-driven media images. Cultural symbols undergo a continuing process of reinvention and hybridity (the combination of previously separate attributes). All forms of identity become more unstable. In this context, cultural institutions such as universities – which are already affected by the partial withdrawal of governmental commitment to the earlier form of public sector nation-building – are opened up to strategies of reinvention, whether of an economic, organisational or cultural kind, or all three together.

Universities and globalisation

Universities are affected by the destabilisation and renewal in all cultural institutions and all institutions of public production, in an environment in which globalisation and neo-liberal government coincide.[18] They are also being remade by globalisation in other ways. First, universities are in

the forefront of the communications revolution. They were early users of
the Internet and e-mail, which are media for international collaboration
in research and teaching, and the site of a new kind of teaching, the web-
based 'virtual' course. In that sense the universities are one of the causes
of globalisation as well as an effect of it, and the developmental strategies
of some of the larger universities are likely to have a profound effect in
shaping the emerging new world. At the same time, electronically based
distance education and virtual campuses might become a major new
strand alongside conventional higher education. This option has been
slower to develop than some have predicted (or feared) but Micro-
soft, Disney, Time-Warner and other communications companies are
exploring ways of developing these forms of higher education, often in
conjunction with leading 'brand name' American universities. More
immediately, a 'no-frills' brand of corporate-based continuing education,
produced on a for-profit basis, is gathering ground in the United States,
and beginning to spread abroad.[19]

Second, the universities are the site of one of the growing global
markets, a market that is people centred and culturally based, and itself
one of the causes and carriers of global change: the market in the education of international students. Throughout the world there are now
about two million students who travel abroad each year to study. In
Australian universities international student numbers have grown very
rapidly, reaching 72 183 in 1998, 4 per cent of the global market. Australia's share has doubled in the last decade, and its number of enrolled
international students has tripled. These students are generating a billion
dollars in direct revenues each year, and as yet unmapped changes in
curricula and university cultures. As this suggests, most Australian universities now operate as global businesses, whether through global
distance education or through off-shore campuses, collaborative projects
with international universities and governments, or deals to franchise
courses and enter 'twinning' and 'feeder' arrangements. And as we shall
see, the new business practices and executive functions associated with
work in the global realm are now among the drivers of organisational
change inside the universities.[20]

Third, the impact of the global is still broader in that it is reshaping the
universities as a place of work and a way of life. Higher education has
become irretrievably communications heavy, travel based, marketing
dependent. External relationships are now vital to its continued susten-
ance. Constant international engagement is necessary in order to sustain
a role in the forefront of academic fields and stay abreast of the changes
in the university as an institution; as well as to recruit students, sign
exchange agreements and establish and carry through research and consultancy projects funded by international agencies. Not only the world

academic community, but also the *local* community has become larger and closer to hand, and in that sense more 'global' in nature. In less than a decade electronic mail has become the vehicle for a wide range of purposes including talk between teachers and students, the preparation of collaborative documents, course designs and organisational plans. It enables rapid problem-solving and the equally rapid transfer of a problem from one desk to another. As a medium it is highly malleable in terms of relationships, enabling a wide range of 'voice' tones from the formal to the intimate. Compared to a meeting or exchange of papers, it is highly efficient in the instrumental sense, shutting out all but the task-demand itself. It also makes it easier to step-up work rates and work surveillance.

The ever-growing volume of electronic mail – whether it is derived from the external demands on the university, intensified accountability pressures within, or the spread of global-style communication itself – foregrounds short-term responses and short-term gains at the expense of long-term projects and agendas. As Harvey remarks, in this setting, 'learning to play the volatility right is just as important as accelerating turnover time'.[21] In a networked environment, 'flexibility' is the principal organisational virtue. In practice, flexibility boils down to the ever more user-friendly dispatch of the ever-growing number of immediate tasks that are transmitted to every person's computer screen.

Academic capitalism

The new impact of the global on university life has yet to be chronicled empirically. In that respect practice is running ahead of research.[22] However, an associated trend has been examined. That is the growing role of business and industry in university life, and the shift of science-based research into a more entrepreneurial mode. These topics are taken up by Sheila Slaughter and Larry Leslie in their important book *Academic capitalism: politics, policies and the entrepreneurial university* (1997).[23]

Academic capitalism begins by analysing the impact of global economic competition on national education policies and the funding of higher education. It uses resource dependency theory to explain changes in national systems and in the pattern of incentives that shape the behaviour of universities, presenting data on the United States, Australia, Canada and the United Kingdom. The changes are broadly common to all four countries, but vary in detail, timing and extent. Resource dependency theory suggests that universities will do whatever is necessary to maintain the flow of revenues, and to maximise institutional prestige. In the empirical core of the book, the focus shifts to case studies at institutional level. These were conducted in the first half of the 1990s, mostly in Australia. Slaughter and Leslie examine the response of academic staff and managers to the (then) new opportunities and pressures to generate revenues. They are particularly interested in one form of entrepreneurial activity, technology transfer, the movement of research findings and product prototypes from university to industry. They explore changing norms and beliefs as academics (or 'faculty' in US nomenclature) grapple with the intersection between entrepreneurial goals and traditional commitments to teaching and research. The conclusion discusses changes in the character of academic work, noting that disciplines and institutions closest to the market are undergoing the greatest transformations.

Slaughter and Leslie argue that it was in the 1980s academic work was fundamentally altered. In 1980 the American government transferred ownership of the patents generated in federally funded research programs from government to the universities, encouraging the universities to themselves become 'capitalist' enterprises. The model of government-funded research in the sciences began to shift, from long-term programs of 'pure' research under academic control, to university–industry partnerships in which the direction of research was directly shaped by potential commercial applications. Research in biomedicine and biotechnology exemplified these changes. As the universities became more incorporated in industry, and their ethos partly shifted from the client welfare of their students to the economic bottom-line, this undercut the tacit social contract whereby universities had been treated as unique institutions, accelerating the shift from full public funding to partial dependence on market sources of income. External revenue targets – if not a fully fledged profit motive – began to shape the work in decisive fashion.

To maintain or expand resources, faculty had to compete increasingly for external dollars that were tied to market-related research, which was referred to variously as applied, commercial, strategic, and targeted research, whether these moneys were in the form of research grants and contracts, service contracts, partnerships with industry and government, technology transfer, or the recruitment of more and higher fee-paying students. We call institutional and professorial market or marketlike efforts to secure external moneys *academic capitalism*.[24]

There is no doubt about the growth of activities of this kind. In Australia in 1997, higher education institutions earned 15 per cent of their incomes from various kinds of fees and charges, compared to less than 3 per cent a decade before. Revenue from international student fees constituted almost 8 per cent of all revenues, while revenue from non-government-funded research grants and contracts was almost 5 per cent. In some universities, the level of entrepreneurial income was higher. For example at the University of NSW, revenues from fees, charges, and non-government research grants and contracts, amounted to $138 million in 1997, almost 26 per cent of total university income.[25]

Slaughter and Leslie find that in effect, some academics and administrators are now 'state-subsidised entrepreneurs'. If they have lost some of the old academic autonomy they have gained a new form of economic freedom in research centres engaged in technology transfer. The experience is not universal. One effect of academic capitalism is to fragment the unity of what has always been a loosely linked academic profession. For example academics in biomedicine, engineering, computing and business have more extensive market opportunities (and obligations) than those in mathematics and physics, or history and languages. Often, the strongest protagonists for entrepreneurship are the general staff who make it happen, and who are sometimes impatient with the niceties of collegial academic life.

Academic capitalism and the Enterprise University

As Slaughter and Leslie are careful to point out, in the new era universities are not entirely driven by profits. Academic prestige remains important, as a magnet for commercial income and as an end in itself. Universities are both profit maximisers and 'prestige maximisers', in terms of their social weight (their positional value)[26] and in terms of their academic qualities. Cultural values might be contested by accountants but they remain a potent factor, particularly in older universities with more deeply rooted academic cultures. As noted in chapter 1, because universities – or at least most universities – have not become purely profit driven in the manner of a business firm, in which the product itself is unimportant, the term 'academic capitalism' has problems. It implies a fully profit-driven corporation. We prefer Enterprise University because it captures the new institutional personality of the universities, while enabling a broader understanding of what drives them. It allows us to imagine the new spirit of 'enterprise' as driven not only by money, but also by the desire for institutional status, and by more engaging academic cultures and by the requirements of government.

This is not a criticism of Slaughter and Leslie, for their solid location in the empirical allows the full range of motivations to emerge. Another strength of *Academic capitalism* is the focus on university personnel as active agents in the remaking of their work. In contrast to a host of analyts who argue that external imperatives are enforcing, or should enforce, *automatic* changes on the universities, to Slaughter and Leslie the 'inner' personality of universities remains important. Thus they describe the role of external factors not, as often argued by those defending university traditions, as the subversion of autonomy. Rather, in their account academic work remains autonomous but is transformed. In their view, universities can still determine their own destiny, within historical limits.

At the same time they note that universities have become more externally engaged, being tethered to the market, and their motivations have altered.

It may be that this inter-penetration of economic capital and university education constitutes a major turning point in the history of the university, akin to its fusion with the nation-building role of the state in the late nineteenth and twentieth centuries, or the rise of the research university after world war two, or the transformation of elite higher education into mass higher education throughout the world between the 1960s and the 1980s. Notions of the 'knowledge economy' are an attempt to capture the emergence of forms of economic life in which knowledge and reflexive changes in knowledge are central to work practices and industrial evolution. The historian Fernand Braudel refers to the manner in which the rise of new epochal movements of an economic and sociocultural kind becomes expressed in changing institutional missions and organisational structures.[27] It is perhaps too soon to be sure whether 'academic capitalism' and the 'enterprise university' constitute a new epoch in the history of the university, or are less fundamental but still important additions to the multiple roles that universities already perform (though we find the former interpretation persuasive). What is clear is that in the encounter between the world of the academy and the world of business and industry, institutional missions and structures have changed.

Like Slaughter and Leslie, Burton Clark has produced work on where universities are heading which has a strong empirical foundation[28] (though he joins this to exhortations for entrepreneurial and market-based institutions that are somewhat less convincing). We will discuss Clark's empirical work in the concluding chapter. Here we note his argument that universities have been pushed towards internal change because there is 'a deepening asymmetry between environmental demand and institutional capacity to respond'. This 'imbalance' leads to 'institutional insufficiency'. Traditional ways become inadequate. In the new context universities need to develop a capacity in selective and flexible response. Universities successful in this period are doing so.[29] This highlights issues of governance.

Slaughter and Leslie discuss questions of structure and organisation only briefly, for example when referring to shifts from collegial to entrepreneurial styles of devolution. We do not feel the need to go over the ground that Slaughter and Leslie cover. In our account, their discussion of the rise of the entrepreneurial element in universities can be taken as given. But whereas their focus is on the political economy of the relationship between universities and external business firms, ours is with the incorporation of elements of corporate practice into the government of the university itself. Slaughter and Lesie are concerned with both the external environment and with academic cultures, but the mediation between the two is missing. Their discussion of changes in economic incentives, research practices and aspects of academic work needs to be complemented by the study of universities as institutions. The missing elements are governance and management.

Changes to governance have been potent in mediating the relationship between 'inner' and 'outer' worlds of the universities, and in reorganising, repositioning and reinventing them on more business-like lines – in making possible the external relationships that Slaughter and Leslie have mapped. This is where *The Enterprise University* comes in. However, before examining the new forms of governance in detail, we need to look more closely at the context of Australian higher education: the size and growth of the sector, recent shifts in funding and resources, and the rise of professional management.

Corporatism in Australia

The Australian zone

Universities in Australia have been shaped by British educational practices from the time of the first colonial foundation, the University of Sydney in 1851. More recently they have been affected by the American higher education institutions that have educated many Australian leaders. Both sets of influences remain strong. Australian universities also have established relationships with universities in Canada, and a continual exchange with the smaller group of similar institutions across the Tasman in New Zealand. There are also marginal influences from universities in Germany, France and other Western European nations.

Within the larger Anglo-American tradition, Australian universities have adopted certain distinctive features. First, throughout their history Australian universities have been more state-dependent than universities in the USA or even in Britain. It was inevitable that the early colonial universities, devised to fashion a settler-state bourgeoisie, would be financed by the colonial governments rather than the nascent bourgeoisie, which hardly saw itself as a central interest in education debates. Public dependence persisted after the new nation began in 1901 and was reinforced by the great increase in government investment triggered by the human capital revolution in educational thinking at the end of the 1950s, and the emergence of mass higher education and the democratisation of access in decades that followed. Just as the nineteenth-century universities in Sydney, Melbourne, Adelaide and Hobart were instruments of early colonial state-building, so in the 1960s and 1970s, with a reprise in the late 1980s, higher education was at the core of the nation-building projects of the modern period. Government planning determined the number and location of universities. Student fees played a minor financial role. One university, Western Australia, was free of tuition charges for most of its history.

Second, expectations of higher education in Australia have always been markedly utilitarian, in contrast with universities in many other nations – as commentators from time to time remark.[30] The liberal curriculum was imported from Britain to Australia in the nineteenth century, and 'pure' research in the sciences was supported by the publicly funded research programs that flourished between the 1960s and the 1980s. Nevertheless, notions of knowledge or of personal cultivation as ends in themselves were less deeply rooted. The acquisition of literature, philosophy and even languages in what was until recently a monocultural Australia were treated largely as signs of social position. Successive governments justified their spending on 'pure' science only because it augmented the potential for applied science. It is significant that in Australia there have been many more distinguished medical researchers and other applied scientists than world leaders in arts and humanities.

In these limitations we see the effects of a derivative educational tradition without strong local foundations, and a settler-state's pre-occupation with upward social mobility. One outcome of the utilitarian legacy is that Australian universities tend to treat international education as a revenue-raising exercise rather than a process of international exchange or person formation, in contrast with many East and South-East Asian student families for whom respect for education as a cultural process is strong. Another outcome of the pervasive utilitarianism is that it makes the universities unusually vulnerable to the argument that their functions can be discharged more efficiently. When public finance per student is reduced, the argument that fundamental disciplines are under threat receives less public sympathy in Australia than in some other nations.

Third, neo-liberal policies have been enforced with greater rigour in Australia than in the USA. Fiscal constraints have been tighter, and competition reform has been driven harder. The neo-liberal regime has been more readily enforced by international finance because of Australia's continuing dependence on foreign capital, commodity exports and foreign debt. Public institutions created during the Keynesian policy era – not only the universities, but the public utilities, public broadcasting, and the public hospital and school systems – have been under extreme pressure to corporatise their operations. In all of this Australia has much in common with other developed nations on the economic and cultural periphery of the Anglo-American world, including New Zealand (where neo-liberal policies have been even more harsh) and Canada. It also shares something with Argentina and Chile in Latin America. Precisely because of Australia's peripheral location, its national traditions are less strong and more vulnerable to arguments based on global best practice. At the same time Australia's executive-dominant political system ensures that neo-liberal reform has met little effective resistance. It is almost as if public policies in Australia, New Zealand and similar nations have been fashioned as zones of neo-liberal experiment, testing economic outcomes and political reactions before the application of those policies to the global metropolises of the United States and Europe.

Nation-building in a global environment

It is not an auspicious time for institutions of nation-building to be weakened and national identity to falter. This is because, paradoxically, success in the global environment rests partly on *local* identity, on the qualities that a nation brings into that global environment. Harvey notes:

The shrinkage of space that brings diverse communities in competition with each other implies localised competitive strategies and a heightened sense of what makes a place special and gives it a competitive advantage. This kind of reaction looks much more strongly to the identification of place, the building and signalling of its unique qualities in an increasingly homogenous but fragmented world.[31]

The weakening of fiscal capacity undermines both the nation and the university sector in the face of the challenge to devise a successful role in the global environment. In the absence of a wealthy American-style private sector, and given the traditional Australian dependence on the state as provider, public funding reductions simply weaken the capacity of those universities to devise services and activities that are able to express 'unique qualities' based on the place-identity of Australia. With capacity weakened, and risk margins accordingly reduced, the too-easy way out, for the government-managed system and for the individual universities themselves, lies in strategies of imitation and a drift towards American models.

Structural changes

The great growth of global connections and effects, the expanding economic and social functions of higher education, the rise of neo-liberalism, the reworking of policy as governance: these are more than changes in the rhetoric about 'The University'. There have been marked shifts in the political economy and sociology of higher education, shifts visible in the statistics, in which these larger historical movements can be discerned.

In the decade since Dawkins published his Green and White papers, there have been immense structural changes in Australian higher education. Between 1987 and 1998 the number of students in publicly funded universities grew from 393 734 to 671 853. The number of sectors of higher education fell from two (universities and colleges of advanced education, CAEs) to one (universities). After the centrally driven period of 'consolidation' during which the Australian government provided strong incentives for institutions to merge into larger units, the number of publicly funded institutions fell from 60 universities and CAEs of varying size and function in 1987, to 37 large-scale universities in 1998, each covering all or most available fields of study, plus a handful of small specialist institutions.

There have also been changes in the composition of the student body. Between 1987 and 1998 the proportion of students who were women rose from 50.1 to 54.7 per cent, there was a relative growth in older students and the proportion of students who were enrolled in distance education mode, and a great expansion in the number of postgraduate students, in both research higher degrees and vocational programs. The number of students studying at Masters and doctoral level reached 87 978 in 1998, increasing more than three times in little more than ten years, a remarkable rate of growth (see table 3.1).

The funding structure of higher education has undergone even greater changes. The proportion of the total funding of higher education derived from governments has fallen from 85 per cent in 1987 to 54 per cent in 1997. The proportion of funding in the form of fees, charges and non-government research and contracts has risen from about 3 to 20 per cent. The number of international students has risen from 17 248 in 1987, most of whom were partly subsidised by the Australian government and subject to quotas on numbers, to 72 183 students in 1998, nearly all of whom paid full fees directly to the universities concerned, with no limitations on enrolments. In 1998 almost one-quarter of all international students enrolled in Australian universities were located in countries outside Australia (off-shore), either in distance education mode, in institutions collaborating with Australian universities, or in an off-shore Australian campus.

In what had previously been a system free of tuition charges (1974–88),[32] a fee-paying postgraduate sector and continuing vocational education sector has also emerged, and undergraduate students and some postgraduate students incur a deferred 'user charge' under the Higher Education Contribution Scheme (HECS). For most students,

Table 3.1 Some changes in Australian higher education: 1998 compared to 1987

	1987	1998
Number of enrolled students in Australian higher education	393 734	671 853
Number of government-funded institutions	72	41*
Average number of students per institution	5 469	16 796
Number of international students	17 248	72 183
Number of higher degree students (Masters and doctorate)	27 968	87 978
Proportion of all funds from government (%)	85	55
Proportion of all funds from fees and charges (%)	2	15

*Includes 37 comprehensive universities (average size 18 601 students) and 4 small institutions.
Sources: Various Commonwealth Government education agencies; for 1998 data, the Department of Education, Training and Youth Affairs (DETYA).

the HECS debt is payable after the time of study when their incomes reach the threshold point of $21 334 per annum (1999), softening its impact. Nevertheless, the level of charge has steadily increased and by 1997 the annual HECS obligation constituted more than 100 per cent of the actual costs of provision in some courses, for example in under-graduate law. By world standards this was a relatively high tuition cost. Many students in Australian universities incurred higher charges than their counterparts in the American state university sector.

Although funding had been partly privatised, the sector-location of higher education had not. This period saw the emergence of an unfunded private university sector but it enrolled less than 2 per cent of students. The main private institution, Bond University on the Gold Coast in Queensland, had achieved successful courses in law and business but struggled in other areas. Because private institutions were not eligible for government subsidies, because public institutions were relatively accessible and until recently, fairly well funded by international standards, and because the institutions used by the social elite were in the public sector, an American-style private sector had not developed.[33]

Managing scarcity

The higher education system in Australian remains government sub-sidised for just over half its costs. Unlike private businesses, higher education institutions are not subject to the ultimate market sanction, bankruptcy. In other words, universities mix market and non-market elements in a jumbled fashion, with a trend towards the market side of the equation. Market economics plays its role in system–competition between institutions, in selected areas not subsidised by government which operate along commercial lines – international education, research and consultancy for industry and so on – and in the cultivation of entre-preneurial attitudes. In the United States the shift towards markets has been fostered by a strong private sector and by transferring part of the government subsidy of public universities away from direct financing of the institutions into needs-based student aid, encouraging students to become mobile consumers.[34] In Australia the trend to markets ('market-isation') has been a function of government system-setting and the targeted deregulation of aspects of university operation, especially fee-charging. This has been a centrally regulated deregulation, which of course is in keeping with the state-dependent tradition. But in Australia, as in the UK and many other countries, the main contribution of govern-ment to marketisation has been to squeeze the level of fiscal support, forcing institutional managers to pursue private dollars wherever they can be found.

Until 1996 the total level of government ('public') funding was not reduced in absolute terms, unlike the UK in the early 1980s, though in the context of the rapid expansion after 1987, public funding declined relative to the number of students, and costs of provision. The decline in levels of support per student accelerated from 1997 onwards. This was triggered by three decisions in the 1996 federal budget. First, the incoming Coalition government reduced direct grants in real terms by 5 per cent over the next three years. Second, and more importantly, it confirmed the 1995 decision of the previous Labor government not to supplement government grants to universities for the cost of salary increases. This policy stance has been maintained for three subsequent budgets, costing universities another 15 per cent in public funding, a sharp reduction in their position. Third, the Coalition introduced funded 'over-enrolment', whereby institutions receive partial official support for student numbers exceeding agreed levels of publicly funded student load. Institutions could now recoup part of the marginal cost of these extra places, at the price of crowding already over-full classes, while the government evaded its normal share of the costs of growth. The device had been copied from the UK.[35]

These changes accelerated the long-term resource decline of under-graduate education. They suddenly weakened further the position of those fields of study, such as many of the basic disciplines in the humanities and natural sciences, that were not strong income earners in fee-based markets. They strengthened the drive towards entrepreneurial incomes. In some institutions, especially those newer universities with little in usable assets or in private income of a non-market kind, the entrepreneurial drive began to take on a distinctly desperate feel. The 1996 budget changes also further increased student–staff ratios.

Staffing decline

Between 1975 and 1985 the average student–staff ratio in Australian higher education was just under 12:1. In 1987 it reached 13:1. By 1996 it had jumped to 16 equivalent full-time students per equivalent full-time academic staff member across higher education as a whole, and in some institutions was much higher (table 3.2). Since 1996 it has risen further, though at the time of writing complete post-1996 data were yet to be released.

A rising student–staff ratio leads to more large lecture groups with less opportunity for interactive or individualised learning, less small group teaching (in many subjects tutorials have been abolished, and laboratory work in the sciences has been curtailed), fewer new books in the library, academics whose research time is squeezed by the demands of increased teaching, and the growing use of educational technologies as substitutes for – rather than complements to – the face-to-face relationship between academic and student.

Over the same period there have been similar trends in many countries, due to the expansion of enrolments in the context of the neo-liberal induced scarcity, and the use of technologies in on-site student instruction and in distance education as a substitute for face-to-face teaching. In Germany, Teichler reports that between 1965 and the early 1990s average student–staff ratios increased from 9:1 to 17:1, a larger change than in Australia.[36]

Management fundamentalism

Since the Dawkins reforms, it has been a primary governmental objective to foster more business-like university organisation. Dawkins outlayed specific funding for reviews of executive structure and organisational systems, and professional training for middle-level managers. He also created what was to become a recurring rhetoric.

In July 1988 the White Paper said that the key to reform was to imagine the university as a corporation in its own right. 'Many institutions are extremely large and their budgets are equivalent to those of large business organisations.' The White Paper was punctuated with images of speed, strength and aggression. It demanded 'strong managerial modes of operation' and more 'streamlined decision-making processes ... with

Table 3.2 Student–staff ratios and financial dependence on the Commonwealth, institutions in this study, 1996

Institution by category of institution[a], including state/territory where not otherwise indicated in title	Total number of enrolled students (1998)	Student–staff ratio[b] in Mathematics/ Computing	Student–staff ratio[c] in Business	Proportion of university income from Commonwealth[d] (%)
University of Sydney [NSW]	33 587	13	19	55.5
University of Queensland	28 431	10	20	56.1
University of Adelaide [SA]	13 605	13	23	60.3
University of Western Australia	12 979	17	23	43.8
University of Tasmania	11 839	15	24	67.3
Redbricks				
Monash University [Vic.]	39 742	17	24	49.0
University of New South Wales	28 323	14	22	57.4
Gumtrees				
Deakin University [Vic.]	27 586	21	25	55.0
Griffith University [Qld]	21 514	16	20	56.6
University of Newcastle [NSW]	18 463	19	19	58.6
Flinders University of South Australia	11 017	16	21	58.6
James Cook University of North Queensland	9 147	11	18	64.6
Unitechs				
Queensland University of Technology	31 235	20	27	60.7
University of Technology, Sydney [NSW]	22 976	22	23	58.4
New Universities				
Edith Cowan University [WA]	19 055	21	25	56.6
Central Queensland University	12 031	30	35	57.0
Southern Cross University [NSW]	9 067	n.a.	25	66.0
National mean		*17*	*22*	*56.7*

n.a. means not applicable.

a For detailed discussion of the categories used here, see chapter 7.

b Number of equivalent full-time students per equivalent full-time academic staff.

c Included Business, Administration, Economics and Law.

d Proportion of all institutional incomes that was derived from Commonwealth Government operating grants for the funding of agreed student load, excluding student contributions under the Higher Education Contribution Scheme, plus the research quantum (see chapter 6). Does *not* include other income from the Commonwealth such as that deriving from research contracts.

Source: DETYA 1998, pp. 132, 137 and 148.

minimal timelag between making and implementing decisions'. It complained that governing councils were too large, and academic structures too committed to representative politics rather than corporate efficiency.[37] Towards the end of the Labor period the Hoare Report (1995) focused specifically on Canberra's objective of smaller governing councils that would more closely resemble corporate boards in form and function (chapter 5). In 1998, a decade after the Dawkins White Paper, the West committee found that 'outdated governance arrangements' were still hampering management.[38] Universities must adjust to the real world of business, or face decline, or worse. Remarkably, the fact that the universities *had* adjusted their systems of organisation – indeed, they had changed immensely in the decade since Dawkins – was not acknowledged by the West committee.

In this incessant hectoring for the reorganisation of the universities we see not only the normative style of policy-making discussed above, but a form of fundamentalism that always finds fault with any and every aspect of universities which is different from corporations. This fundamentalism looks for shareholders, stockholders and stakeholders and finds instead a world of scholars, students, unions, industry and community representatives and administrators. Whether these groups constitute a system of 'opportunity providers' or are in fact 'vested interests' bleeding the public purse remains open to doubt, according to this view.

Of course this fundamentalism is neither new nor original. Its proponents call it 'organisational economics' and its two central projects are known as 'agency theory' and 'transaction cost analysis'.[39] Together these provide a withering critique of the behaviour of all large organisations. Agency theory asserts that a central tendency for all managers is to seek self-interested strategies to cheat the owners or principals of the organisation. The more remote the owners, the greater the distortion. Transaction cost theory suggests, *inter alia*, that senior managers tend to lose control of lower level functions in large organisations and that this results in middle-level personnel doing to them exactly the kinds of things which they are prone to do to the principals – substitute their own goals for those of the corporation. The answer is to create an organisational system in which senior managers control middle managers, while devolving financial reponsibilities to them, and the actions of senior managers themselves are rendered transparent to corporate boards. The fact that the governing bodies of universities have a different history, membership and purpose is irrelevant to this view.

When legitimate debate about the best and most efficient means to achieve a diversity of scholarly purposes becomes an orthodoxy regarding 'one true path' to greatness we have left the world of discourse and entered the gravitational pull of ideology. In this we see the legacy of the notion that good management is, in Yeatman's words, 'context indif-ferent',[40] that it finds its own fundamentals in every time and place, that the rules of operation of a finance company in New York must displace the university's own history and its hard-won lessons learned, and that those rules apply whatever the mission of the institution, and whatever the academic discipline that is being taught or researched.

We are forced to conclude from this persistent application of a medi-cine which appears redundant that it is not a disease which is under assault, but the patient! Nevertheless, the potency of the message is plain. Resource shortage has been its great ally. Governing councils are only one element of the overhaul. Like the plastic pastel anterooms of modern offices and airport lounges, all different and all the same, the central arms of universities and their academic units, the resource and services divisions on one hand and the departments, schools and centres on the other, are all being repatterned along similar lines.

Executive power

The growth of the executive layer of universities is a spectacular sign that the policy message has struck home. Here the rise of executive power coincides with, and is mutually constitutive of, the growing role of market exchange and economic competition.[41] The precise form of manage-ment system, the number of leader-managers, the configuration of their different responsibilities, varies between universities and seems to be reinvented each time that a new vice-chancellor takes the helm. Yet, in every case it is 'executive centred governance'[42] rather than a council or a professoriate that defines the character of the institution to the new world of markets and corporate mandates. Its priorities are expressed in budgets, planning doctrines and targets for income earning, rather than scholarship, or the public interest.

Executive dominance, explicitly corporate in form and substance, has become part and parcel of every university. The new systems of exe-cutive governance are focused almost exclusively upon the office of the vice-chancellor. More decentralised posts in faculties, schools, depart-ments and research centres tend increasingly to reflect the agendas of executive governance. The rise of executive power has coincided with, and is mutually dependent on, the expansion of certain general man-agement functions including finance, marketing, private investment and international programs. The new systems of central oversight and planning are also supported by regimes of data standardisation similar to those pioneered by DEETYA including workloads, student load, average cost, funding mix and throughput. The development of these technical tools of command has permitted the elimination of most of the intermediate steps in the old university hierarchy and enabled the tighter clustering of management power at the executive level. This has been reflected in a growth in senior management portfolios. Table 3.3 illustrates the growth in the size of one key group, the DVCs and PVCs, in our sample of universities.

Some of the DVCs and PVCs were drawn from the ranks of public corporations and departments, and a smaller group from the private sector. The majority had risen from the academic ranks, and academic credibility was still reckoned necessary for vice-chancellors.

In the quantitative expansion in the executive group we can trace one effect of the increased sophistication of university organisation and

Table 3.3 The vice-chancellor's office: 1998 compared to 1987

University and category of university	Total number of deputy vice-chancellors and pro vice-chancellors[a], in	
	1987	1998
Sandstones		
University of Sydney	4	8
University of Queensland	0	4
University of Adelaide	2	2
University of Western Australia	2	2
University of Tasmania	0	3
Redbricks		
Monash University	2	5
University of New South Wales	2	4
Gumtrees		
Deakin University	2	3
Griffith University	2	8
University of Newcastle	1	5
Flinders University of South Australia	1	3
James Cook University of North Queensland	1	4
Unitechs		
Queensland University of Technology	...	4
University of Technology, Sydney	...	4
New Universities		
Edith Cowan University	...	4
Central Queensland University	...	3
Southern Cross University	...	3

... indicates that institution was not a university in mid-1987.
a Total number of positions, not people: some positions were vacant in 1998.
Sources: Data gathered during research for this book, using individual universities' Internet sites, published reports and personal communications. The various sources often conflicted, so that these data are likely to be subject to some debate.

systems. In many cases the expansion has also reflected a period of rapid growth and merger in which council, academic board, faculty and departmental institutions have had their settled purposes radically disturbed. For a period of several years many of these universities were simply 'joined at the top' and detached below, further increasing the role of executive level leaders.

Beyond the extensions in function, already on the public record, there are the qualitative changes in the economy and culture of the universities – changes intertwined in complex ways with the trends to growth, merger, non-government funding and the reworking of university missions. Some such qualitative changes are the inevitable corollary of modernisation, for example the adoption of standardised enrolment systems and standardised data collection systems. Some are the results of more contingent extensions of power, such as the drift of key decisions into a vice-chancellor's advisory group. Whatever the precise genesis in each case, and the degree of external dependence does appear to vary quite a bit, in all cases it is now executive management which defines the university. It is increasingly decisive in articulating the purposes of the universities and the character of the academy itself. More and more, it determines the boundaries of what is possible in a university, the outer limits of what can be taught and researched.

Managers versus academics

In most Australian universities the new style of executive management had its first impact right at the top and centre, and then spread downwards and outwards to the academic units. Faculties, departments, schools and centres have been reorganised as discrete budgetary units with partial responsibility for their own funding, staffing and performance, often competing with other or similar units inside the university for part of their resources.[43] This process of downwards-moving corporate reform is never quite complete. Not only does the extent of corporate reform vary between (and within) universities, here executive re-engineering runs up against a heterogeneous tradition. Far from integrating grass-roots academic cultures seamlessly into a larger plan, managerialism often finds itself at one end of a polarity. The fault-line between managers and academics falls somewhere between faculty dean and individual staff member. Heads of department often face divided loyalties.

The academic/management polarity is deeply felt, as numerous surveys of academic attitudes attest.[44] Zealous modern managers find in the academic resistance to performance modelling and resource redeployment little more than the expression of 'the retarded time of recalcitrant forms of social organisation', as Harvey puts it.[45] Meek and Wood found in their study of management and governance in Australia higher education that 42 per cent of senior executives believed that academic staff resistance to change was an 'impediment to effective management'.[46] Yet for many academics committed to disciplinary learning, the world of plans and targets is the antithesis of what a university is meant to be. This is not a conflict of symmetrical forces. Academics lack weapons and they find it hard to sustain collegial forms in the face of the growing scarcity of time and money. At the same time, they are the people who carry out the core business, and their consent is vital. The managers hover around the edges, but they own the means of action. In recent years they have held the advantage, especially in newer universities. As one vice-chancellor remarked in a conference paper in 1997:

Australian universities have both a strong managerial tradition and a strong collegial rhetoric, and the two are always potentially in conflict. On the whole, collegiality operates to stop things happening rather than to prompt innovations, so a vice-chancellor looks for managerial levers to get things done. These levers lie in the power of the budget, the power of the imagination and the increasingly general expectation that a vice-chancellor is there to do things.[47]

Meek and Wood asked the same questions of three groups in a sample of universities: senior executives, faculty deans, and heads of departments. There was a marked variation in views. Though 71 per cent of executive leaders felt that academic staff had 'adequate' opportunity to participate in the formation of the university mission and strategic plan, only 43 per cent of the heads of department agreed. While 33 per cent of executives believed that the overall management style was top-down decision-making, 53 per cent of deans and 71 of heads agreed. Heads perceived a trend to centralisation, but senior executives mostly did not. Collegial governance had little senior level support (19 per cent), but majority support among heads (61 per cent). Whereas the middle managers acknowledged the presence of conflicts of values, senior managers did not.[48] Table 3.4 provides details.

Tactics often dictate that academic values must be side-stepped rather than confronted directly. The lingering idea of the collegial is surprisingly strong, to the extent that executive managers state that collegial values are not under threat. Yet in almost the same breath the executives admit they want to drive those collegial values out. Here the main limitation on managers is the continued existence of academic tenure, the not-quite-secure regime of permanent employment traditional to universities. Meek and Wood noted that the majority of executive officers found that tenure was an obstacle when attempting to set 'new directions' for their

Table 3.4 Attitudes to issues of university organisation: senior and middle managers

	Executive officers (%)	Deans (%)	Heads of department (%)	All groups (%)
Q. The trend in this institution is towards central management authority at the expense of collegial processes				
agree/ strongly agree	27.8	45.3	67.7	59.1
not sure	7.8	12.4	10.1	10.2
disagree/ strongly disagree	64.4	42.3	22.2	30.7
Q. The values of academic staff and the goals of management are often in conflict				
agree/ strongly agree	29.5	47.4	64.9	58.2
not sure	17.0	12.4	15.4	14.9
disagree/ strongly disagree	53.4	40.1	19.7	26.9
Q. At this institution, collegial decision making should take precedence over executive management				
agree/ strongly agree	19.3	41.9	60.6	52.5
not sure	18.2	20.6	17.9	18.3
disagree/ strongly disagree	62.5	37.5	21.5	29.2

Source: V. Lynn Meek and Fiona Q. Wood, *Higher education governance and management, an Australian study*, 1997, p. 79.

universities.[49] Among the universities studied in this book, the proportion of academic staff with tenure was high at UNSW (59 per cent), Central Queensland (58 per cent), James Cook (57 per cent) and Newcastle (56 per cent); and relatively low at Queensland (39 per cent), Monash and Edith Cowan (42 per cent), Western Australia (43 per cent) and Southern Cross (44 per cent).

Yet for academic staff, dependence on tenure as a source of power is not a strength. One 'side' (management) has room to manoeuvre; the other (collegial academics) is caught in a defensive posture and does not. In this environment, the capacity of the academic profession to reinvent itself as an organisational player is limited. Its demographics have not helped. In 1998, 33 per cent of Australian academic staff were aged more than 50 years, and no less than 68 per cent were aged more than 40 years – though Queensland, Western Australia and Monash have relatively high proportions of staff under 30 years.[50] A fixed and ageing staff both retards the strategic options and intellectual elan of the academic profession, and points managers towards other forms of developmental investment.

A recent study of the American academic profession by Gary Rhoades finds that increasingly, tenured 'faculty' have been bypassed by managers when it comes to strategic decisions about resource deployment, course delivery and the use of instructional technologies in the classroom and course delivery.[51] Increasingly, general staff labour, and non-tenure track part-time academic labour, are replacing tenured faculty in developmental areas. Technology has been used as a substitute for collegial practices rather than an adjunct to them, with the acquiescence of an often technology-shy academic profession. Capital investment is now at the core of modernisation and restructuring in universities just as it is in many parts of industry. It is likely that a study in Australia would show similar trends. Meek and Wood found that no less than 73 per cent of executives believed that traditional teaching in lectures and laboratories was being replaced by technology-based teaching. Only 42 per cent of the heads of department agreed with this assessment, suggesting a rate of change that is rather slower than managers hope.

The balance of the literature suggests that in higher education the expanding sway of management is being achieved *at the expense of* academics, almost as if corporate reform and modernisation *necessarily* imply a weakening of academic authority and independence. This suggests that the relation between institutional organisation and academic cultures tends to be a zero-sum relationship. If so, academic sensibilities are having a diminishing influence in the development of universities, those who argue that the universities should be treated as 'just another business' are getting their way, and the university imagination is increasingly a managerial imagination. As chapters 4–6 show, our empirical findings are generally consistent with the trends mapped in the literature, though the journey from college to corporation is not (despite the more alarmist claims) complete.

4   Territories and strategies:
Executive power in the Enterprise University

The best game in town

In the weekend papers around Australia at the end of June 1997 a small university in Queensland made its pitch for a place among the elite. Claims for excellence, quality and a role in the international market were signed off over the name of a senior executive who carried the title of both vice-chancellor and president of the university. In a sector where symbols are the currency of power, titles are coin of the realm. Double-barrel titles therefore announce a certain amount of insecurity, but perhaps also a youngest siblings' clearer vision of the future. Vice-chancellors are, after all, a titled artefact from an older world, not unlike governors-general. No one outside the British protectorate really can tell the difference between the vice- and the full chancellor. Presidents, on the other hand, are unambiguous, especially to outsiders.

The small Queensland university is not alone: other vice-chancellors, too, now flourish a Napoleonic 'president' on the business card, with its fleeting images of modernism, power, strategic verve and international reach. Of course the process of modernisation which is implied in new titles may also be a means to obliterate the very cultural specificity which made the institution strong in its previous form. According to this paradoxical imperative, the would-be consumers of 'Sandstone status' might actually seek out the distinctive 'old world' reputation of these institutions. As Bourdieu notes, the act of merchandising, where it actually changes meanings, is apt to alter this economy of tastes.[1]

Presidency is plainly a thing to both inspire confidence abroad and instil respect at home, and the one is not at all distinct from the other. Indeed we find that 'external' moves being made by university leaders begin to inform the 'internal' world of the university to a greater and greater extent. Eventually they exceed the more regularised actions of leaders acting out their 'normal' work as administrators. This is not to say that the external becomes part of the internal life of the academy. Far from it. Rather there are some actors who are able to travel between the two (unions, executives, council members) and of this group the executive management of the university is most able to use such mobility to refashion its own role. Moreover, the new role permitted for VCs is such that the roles around it are required to change.

I haven't had much experience in what they call the real world but the obvious thing at universities is the enormous authority of a dynamic VC. They can virtually do what they like. My VC could say 'today is Tuesday' if he wanted to. I am directly responsible to the VC, so are all the other staff, and it's his budget. (Dean, Gumtree university, interview conducted on a Monday)[2]

In the game of names we see the tensions and opportunities in the new, modern university – an executive authority earnestly and publicly reworking its territory, a minor institution pitching an improbable line to an unspecified audience, and an industry announcing that its most important quality was that it could and should be appreciated and understood in a new language of executive power.

In this study of the nature of the new Australian university we are seeking to explain the experience of power and authority, its ordinary life, as it were. We see this as a local achievement, but one which is accomplished in reference to a number of national and international imperatives. This local manifestation of new forms of authority and influence is seen as being at least as important as the more geometric properties and proportions of power, or its formal ideology.

What is it like to try to work within the executive level of a contemporary Australian university? Do changes in job titles signify new purposes, new pressures? How do those in authority speak to one another and to their institutions about the future they hope to share? How do they imagine themselves dealing with the new world of higher education? What position do university leaders adopt in regard to others in the university sector, and particularly within their own organisations? What things are shared, what things invite conflict or tension?

The fact that such questions now resonate at all levels of the higher education system tells us that significant and widespread patterns of transformation are taking place. Older certainties are being questioned, new projects and perspectives are demanding attention. At issue is the central purpose of the new university. Because such issues are never decided on normative grounds alone, participants press their claims through new forms of governance which direct and filter the resources and values through which institutions enact new futures.

In this chapter we report the views of those who exercise ultimate academic power – not Nobel Prize winners or poets, not even surgeons or professors of law, but vice-chancellors. To make this story compelling it is necessary to look at the other elements of the executive structures of modern universities – deputy vice-chancellors, executive committees and chief administrators. This necessarily complicates the narrative of university authority. We are obviously not just speaking of individuals wielding a common power, but of individuals seeking to use existing positions of influence to advance a view, their view, of the future of the university.

The position itself has to be constructed and in the art of construction we see the chief executive's double play – his or her reflexivity perhaps – an executive strategy to advance a cause must also find a new way to secure the position of the individual who sponsors it.[3] It is our hypothesis that the various new forms of executive power evident in Australian universities are principally concerned with building a new form of executive authority inside the university. While this is often linked to specific goals and projects for any given institution, these purposes are generally much less salient for those involved than are the larger tasks of reinvention.

As a further bend in the refracted currents of university power we also deal directly with the fact that VCs are themselves academics, or former academics and that in this role they seek to engage directly with the power issue, and thus with the issue of their own new significance. The vice-chancellor of the University of Queensland, John Hay, for example, told a conference in 1994 that the modern vice-chancellor had to contend with a university which was bound together 'in the first instance, by specialist languages rather than by such general macroscopic notions as the pursuit of truth'.[4] This not only 'relativises' the claims of academics, but establishes a significant capacity for these chief executives to shape and deflect critical attention.

We see a continuous dialogue between executives building their positions and executives dealing with practical strategies concerning markets, enrolments, fund-raising and the like. At its most expansive this reflexivity establishes a gap in the structure of the university. Person and position become too tightly merged. Structures and institutions do not support agreed strategies, but exist to extend the reach of particular executives, committees and incumbents. Put in brutally simple terms, no other institutional agency in the university is competent to challenge and check the more energetic forms of executive authority.

This may not be a problem in all universities but it is a bigger problem than it once was and it may soon become a modern hallmark. Closely allied with this divide is a discernible failure of reformed universities to replace older forms of professorial collegiality with a genuine, competent alternative. In short, the new breed of vice-chancellor may be resorting to executive symbol-building precisely because universities have so far failed to find any other means by which to harness the administrative and academic identities which shape university behaviours. In other words executive centralisation may become the best game in town primarily because it is the only game.

Government intervention

A key element in the mix of things which now shape executive authority in the university is the role of federal government policy intervention. Again, our hypothesis is that as governmental pressures on universities have increased and become more critical of local traditions and differences, so too vice-chancellors have adopted a 'mirror' strategy to increase their own common controls over otherwise diverse internal traditions. Beginning with the Dawkins reforms, governments have provided explicit and implicit incentives for vice-chancellors to centralise authority and capture internal resources. A typical example of an explicit incentive was the Dawkins Green Paper's sarcastic remarks about the practice of electing key office-bearers such as deans. Once this was officially ridiculed as a naive and inappropriate means for selecting university leaders, institutions quickly moved to abandon the practice.

An instance of implicit incentives is provided by the government's practice during the late 1980s and early 1990s of funding some higher education reforms by retaining a percentage of annual budget allocations as a 'strategic fund' to which universities might apply. Even small 'hold backs' of 2 to 5 per cent quickly impact at the margins of all major programs, multiplying the points of dependency upon central policy-makers. Having suffered this outrage against their autonomy, most university leaders then moved to practise the art in their own dealings with deans and other budget holders. These comparatively small 'hold-backs' grant central leaders enormous power over all new programs. Indeed they often appear to create a bidding war from below in which faculties seek to please central budget holders with proposals for major new undertakings, in order to maintain funds for existing commitments.

And finally university leaders have emulated the agendas of their Canberra referees by seeking to use internal reorganisation as a means to loosen traditions and break up established alliances. Everywhere around the system we see VCs claiming for their office a unique authority to define new university structures, to initiate new ventures from the top down, to invent new positions and to annex new territories both local and international. The new generation of vice-chancellors seek novelty, either in their own creations or in the opportunities created by governments. In their discussions of their own power they return again and again to the winds of change blowing through the 1980s and 1990s. Far from wanting to stand firm against the storms, they almost always bend forward, pulling their institutions behind, running with the wind.

Governance 'outside-in'

Territories

Table 4.1 lists the executive officers in our sample. We found that executive power in the university is now far less about managing an organisation and its programs and far more a matter of imperial politics and diplomacy. At its most complex the authority of the new executive structures reaches into other higher educational institutions within Australia, and into foreign lands which are defined as markets. The 1980s saw the boundaries of institutions breached by government rational- isation and a 'land rush' by the larger universities. This both propelled vice-chancellors into the business of territorial politics and legitimised their new role as principal agents of a more external definition of univer- sity identity. Institutions created out of mergers tended to be either of two types: powerful existing universities which annexed new territories, or conglomerate institutions composed of part old, part new higher education bodies.

The strategic choices themselves, and the very existence of such choice, were a novel experience for university leaders. Trade-offs between smaller versus larger, higher cut-off scores or lower, geographically dispersed or concentrated campuses had to be calculated quickly and often without extensive consultation. Senior executives faced their key constituencies – staff, council and students – with momentous decisions already made. Once decided, these new institutions had to be tamed, structured and administered and here again the still point in a turning world was provided by vice-chancellors and their closest advisers.

This imperial role continued to grow. A number of senior institutions established themselves as leaders of local networks. In this sense also central executives have lifted themselves into an exemplar realm. The University of NSW, for example, has such an avuncular role at Charles Sturt. The University of Melbourne has had a similar relationship with the University of Ballarat. And outside the national borders the senior officials of universities have developed a significant continuing role. They regularly go abroad to sign agreements with foreign governments, to open new campuses and to visit their equivalent of the expatriate minorities – the foreign alumni. In sober newspaper reflections they speak of new lands of opportunity in Asia, of competition for foreign gold, and of this or that country already being 'fished out'. Increasingly power at home is furthered and established as a direct consequence of potency abroad:

Table 4.1 Chief executives who were interviewed, from the sample group of universities

University and date	Position	Held by
Queensland 26 June 1995	Acting Vice-chancellor	Ted Brown
QUT 29 June 1995	Vice-chancellor	Denis Gibson
Griffith 3 July 1995	Vice-chancellor	Roy Webb
James Cook 28/29 Aug. 1995	Vice-chancellor	Ray Golding
Central Queensland 31 Aug. 1995	Vice-chancellor	Geoff Wilson
Newcastle 23 Oct. 1995	Deputy Vice-chancellor	Keith Lester
Southern Cross 27 Oct. 1995	Vice-chancellor	Barry Coynygham
Flinders 3 Nov. 1995	Vice-chancellor	Ian Chubb
Adelaide 31 Oct. 1995	Vice-chancellor	Gavin Brown
UWA 13 Nov. 1995	Vice-chancellor	Fay Gale
Edith Cowan 17 Nov. 1995	Deputy Vice-chancellor (Staffing)	Leonie Still
	Deputy Vice-chancellor (Academic)	Brian Lawrence
Tasmania 22 Nov. 1995	Vice-chancellor	Alan Gilbert
Monash 31 May 1996	Vice-chancellor	Mal Logan
Sydney 3 June 1996	Acting Deputy Vice-chancellor	Ken Eltis
New South Wales 6 June 1996	Vice-chancellor	John Niland
Deakin 22 July 1996	Vice-chancellor	Geoff Wilson
UTS 1 Dec. 1996	Vice-chancellor	Tony Blake

Without being melodramatic. I don't think the institution will survive unless it internationalises.

The new leaders see themselves as players on this larger stage. As the University of Canberra's Don Aitkin told a conference in 1997 the vice-chancellor is not only the prime minister but the minister for foreign affairs (and some act as treasurer as well).[5] One VC lamented the fact that Australia has not developed a provost role which would allow him to adopt a more American presidentialism, which he defined as an external focus free of too much internal competition.

I told the Council that we wanted a Deputy who would be a senior Deputy, a kind of Provost on the American model, responsible for the day-to-day activities of the entire university... When you talk of Provosts, say at Stanford, that person has no ambition other than to run the day-to-day activities of Stanford ... but will never become a president and has no ambition to become a president ... It's a different career structure altogether and I just think that's what an Australian university system has got to have. I think management is falling in a heap in Australia.

There are ironies here, because many US provosts aspire to the presidency and some of them make it. A chief executive who focuses too much on foreign affairs might cut himself adrift from his own institution. The street-smart VC, it seems, is one who holds her university at arm's length, yet maintains effective control.

Another answered a question about what it is that defines the VC's role by saying 'A large part of the VC's job is being able to have an overview of the territory' and listing among his key reforms the transformation of the physical environment of the university.

Strategies

This new strategic power places the VC at the centre of new definitions of the university role in a changed world. VCs are less the representatives of their institutions than they are arbiter and measure of the new VC role. They speak on behalf of the whole institution when they say there must be fees, there must be special relationships with industry, and so on. In the past this power was more likely to be confined to decisions concerning new buildings and senior appointments. This was above all an administrative power. Universities were settled institutions with certain purposes. The new breed are critical of this old world in which leaders had 'tremendous authority and no power ... Everything [was] achieved by negotiation or persuasion or cunning, or whatever you've got'.

The new power is far more to do with the creation and use of strategic choice. The idea of the university was not always open for strategic choice. Now it is, evidently. Chief executives help create this idea of possibility, but they do so most often as a kind of geographic impulse. They speak of 'where we are going' rather than 'what we are' and this continually opens up their institutions to fundamental change. The new opportunities for universities become a new space which VCs define for their own organisations and which they then occupy with their own account of a preferred future.

The signs of this new role are found in numerous places. One that we noticed right away was the tendency for new VCs to speak of themselves as having a kind of political 'honeymoon' period in which to capture the attention of their new institution, to set a new agenda, and to convince others that their vision had to be taken seriously. This is both more overtly political than it once might have been, and at the same time more brittle.

I think universities are driven by myths ... once you get a reputation for being a hard worker, once you establish that, you can take off two days a week and no one will ever [notice].

If you don't use your honeymoon period to differentiate your period ... you're never going to be a change agent ...

Strategic authority is not supported by a common formal process or collegial values. It relies instead upon the maintenance of institutional momentum, a suitable external environment and reasonable levels of internal compliance. Too much bad publicity, a bad report card from the Department of Employment, Education, Training and Youth Affairs (DEETYA), or protracted disputes in committee, see executive authority collapse with breath-taking speed.

And biographically the decline of the VC as academic also reflects a stronger management-centred reality. They feel the pressure to maintain academic credibility, to keep some attachment to their disciplines. But they recognise that administration at all levels forces VCs and DVCs away from academic work and into management work:

I think at the dean level you should be able to manage a reasonable amount but once you get up to this level it's very difficult ... Of course I've also moved into the administrative side of the discipline as well ... So you move into management in all ways, rather than just one.

These introductory observations conceal a great deal of diversity within institutions and between them. But what is remarkable is the fact of strikingly similar deployments of executive authority across the sector. All the VCs we interviewed, and most of the other senior staff who described the imperatives of the senior role for us, pointed towards a certain *will to power*, expressed as a singularity, a solo purpose, and a relative detachment from the institutional structures around them.

Having said that, we also saw this common power focused in several ways. We detected 'Domestic leaders', 'Rationalisers', 'Entrepreneurs', and 'Facilitators': the features exhibited by leaders in each category are described below. The categories are not water-tight, and some leaders combined the features of more than one. To anticipate for a moment the institutional typology set down in chapter 7, we did not find any particular correlation between leadership type and university type, except that the vice-chancellors of newer ('Dawkins') universities were rarely Entrepreneurs and more likely to be Domestic leaders or Rationalisers. Entrepreneurs can afford to cut loose from the activities around them, making selective forays back into the internal politics of their institutions to achieve particular objectives. Entrepreneurs were mostly found at the older 'Sandstone' universities or the first wave of post-war universities, the Redbricks. Vice-chancellors of newer universities have less to draw them away, and more internal spade-work to do: mostly, theirs is an administrative stewardship. They find it difficult to let go.

Will to power

Domestic leaders

Power is not only the style of influence of the CEO, but also the primary terrain on which this executive action takes place. In the 'domestic' case the field is kept deliberately focused. There are fewer grand gestures towards Harvard and the global order. Less mention too of research quantum and tertiary entrance scores. These are 'localists' in the sense that they seek to define a future for themselves and their organisations which is outside the Sandstone paradigm, shielded from unreasonable demands.

Let's be different ... the tradition of this place is essentially industry linked. Applied. Very foreign to me in a way. But in fact that is the strength of this place. So I thought the interdisciplinary is responsive. It's survival. I use the term feral university. You really want to be out there ...

In this former institute of technology we see the hallmark concerns of these VCs working with new structures and the opportunities they provide to deploy power and establish a purpose. The world of amalgamation is one above all of opportunity for executives to build their own world anew. There is a strong sense of 'like it or not' determination and a willingness to dismiss other structures of influence – shown clearly in the off-hand contempt for unions. Most strongly felt of all, however, is the idea that only the VC sees all that is to be seen. Council and board, deans and staff are condemned to partiality, it seems. There are no titans of industry to challenge and no shareholders either.

I came here with the amalgamation ... The most significant thing was the amalgamation because it raised some fundamental questions about the structure of the new creature ... We've looked pretty comprehensively at management practices hand in glove with structure.

Evidently, the processes of merger and amalgamation open up opportunities for executives to extend their view of the right structure of their institutions. More than anything, this period is recalled as a time of *comprehensive* attention to detail. In place of the usual patterns of tinkering and mutual adjustment, vice-chancellors and their close advisers remember a period in which old structures were shaken loose and they could contemplate control of the university on something approaching a clean sheet. This was never seen as a joint project, but rather one in which their own views would need to prevail through sustained justification:

I'm happy to be responsible for the decision if people feel that the whole process is transparent. They may not like it but they understand the reasons for which it was taken.

Such open acknowledgement of the singularity of executive power echoes through many interviews and is often defined as a clear distinction between things which the VC must do, and roles which others may play. Separations, distinctions and clear hierarchies are emphasised. Yet many VCs still wish to retain the idea that they act on behalf of all parties, and should not be defined as 'management':

I find the dichotomy of management and others rather offensive for a university ... The union may say: you may have consulted with the rank and file at the university committee but you haven't formally engaged in consultation with us. I'm being required to mend my ways in certain areas.

The ambivalence of the older forms of university authority becomes clearly apparent when VCs speak of their relationships with academic boards, university councils and their various committees. Considerable effort is being made to tame these otherwise wayward interests, making them consistent with newer principles of management solidarity:

If I don't agree with a decision of Academic Board I'm happy to let University Council know that ... However, Academic Board has no accountability for some of the resource issues of the institution and I wouldn't expect Academic Board to feel I would go along with everything they said in that area.

Academic Board hasn't been involved in strategic planning ... I'm a bit cautious about getting Council too involved with activities that might involve considerable expenditure.

The stance taken by the domestic 'keep it simple' approach is to avoid excessive competition with Sandstone universities which far outrank his own university's research record, tertiary entrance scores and fee income. Instead the emphasis is upon a kind of 'no fuss' professionalism. Shielded from odious comparisons, and free of strong pressure by council, business and academic board, these VCs are clearly the paramount point at which the organisation exercises control over its possible futures.

In some of these cases the geography of power is regional, rather than international. Smaller institutions emulate the international position-taking of the older metropolitan universities by defining their own different realm:

We have no pretensions to being a major research institution.

We don't have a Smorgon or a Pratt on our Council... Business is not having a big impact into some of the big decisions we're taking or the direction we're going ...

Extending the executive role into a given territory is more likely to be expressed as a struggle to manage separate campuses within a region than it is to project power into a national or international system. Regional campuses generate strong centrifugal pressures. Schools and faculties which cross campuses provide continual friction for libraries, appointments and budgets. VCs and their deputies devote much larger parts of their time to fixing broken fences and repairing communication systems. The 'localists' find an unending puzzle in the search for appropriate internal structures, either because they lack strong discipline-based departments, or because the ones they have are too few in number to create a balance of forces at the university level.

Below the faculties we're looking at having a series of schools. At the moment this place has centres and it drives me up the wall because everything is a centre. They hated departments because departments were so compartmentalised that nobody talked to anybody else. So they went to this thing called 'centre' and now everything's a centre – it does not matter whether it does research or teaching. But where you're looking at going back to schools which are somewhat larger than the current centres ... we'll be looking at amalgamating centres and programs. It's a matter of persuading people that this is the right structure.

Still, VCs also gain power of a different kind in multi-campus settings, the power of aggregation and integration, the power of all-too-necessary coalescence in an institution whose identity is readily fragmented. They have all the decisive strategic advantages of the universalist in charge of a bunch of regionalists. To intervene effectively in university affairs, the regionalist must put together an unstable coalition from issue to issue. The university leader, free to move in every direction, is always there or thereabouts.

Set on a larger stage the assertive version of domestic confidence emerges as a corporate language and symbolism spoken with one voice. Equally centred on its own authority, this approach to executive power is far more energised by the need to wrestle with management complexity. Less can be assumed than before, and power is always in need of better and clearer amplification. Again the chance to make a 'new institution' assumes an almost passionate, heroic purpose. These are the chances that might not come again, it seems:

I arrived with what was a new university.

We couldn't even graduate a student without sitting down and developing a structure.

It means you can sit down and think about the idea of the university and how you want your role translated into reality.

Rationalisers

For another group, the rationalisers, there is an unending list of budget, personnel and information technology software waiting to be tried. The arguments put forward are those of the private sector CEO intent upon lifting the company performance by dint of management improvement. And central to that vision is the idea of a single, unified hierarchy of decision-making inside the university:

One of the most fundamental management principles was to make a partnership and the other was to avoid federalism at all costs ... It is a totally unified structure ...

The performance plan has to have real solid practical consequences. If you get that system in place, you do find there is real coherence ... that stretches from the top of the university right down to the departments.

I really went there wanting to place a great emphasis on planning and planning of a budget.

I took a lot of interest in quality management approaches from about 1990 and it's an area I've actually given papers at conferences. I suppose in a way it's what happens when you become obsessed with a new area. I was far too theoretical and probably talked about management principles too much, but it was – I'm still very excited ...

This vision is just as distinctive in regard to what it excludes. Not only are federal structures seen as too open to diversity and alternate sources of loyalty and authority, but collegiality is also roundly condemned:

collegiality in Australian universities ... has been essentially a negative force.

What the new rationalisers seek most is simplicity of command. The simple but dramatic purposes imposed by territorial influence beyond the university's borders have inspired widespread pressure among these VCs for structural simplicity within. Interestingly, this runs counter to organisational theories which predict 'expert systems' to evolve towards complexity.[6]

Collegiality might be viewed as an obstacle to this highly focused purpose in so far as it empowers a wide range of academic voices to speak to issues of governance from the high status afforded by the norms of peer respect. However, only the least confident VCs would have reason to fear that form of solidarity, given how muted such claims had become even before the top-down revolutions of the 1980s and 1990s. An alternative interpretation of the slight on collegiality is its capacity to buttress a more dangerous power, the power of disciplines.

In many of the institutions we surveyed, VCs and their executive advisers described a general shift towards limiting the semi-independent authority of deans who preside over faculties with discipline-based mandates. The common strategy they define is twofold. First, deans are being drawn upwards to sit on executive, budget and planning bodies responsible for the university's overall strategy. This is viewed as a means to curb the powers of 'independent fiefdoms' and 'robber baron' empires. The new central planning committees typically require deans and other budget holders to submit to a process of 'performance-against-planning' in which faculty priorities are subsumed under a set of priorities established by the VC and his or her executive. In many cases we also see a more exacting system of performance evaluation of deans in which individuals are measured against their progress towards meeting such central targets and objectives.

and it's now clear that the merger will see the executive simply become the deans.

the perception that power is not a zero-sum, that you actually can increase the quantum by giving away as long as you can harness it for the whole organisation again.

So you've got to somehow bring the deans home again ... obliging the deans to come in and be the central managers of planning and management resource in the university ... they're ready to be corporatised.

Second there are reforms aimed at changing the line of responsibility within faculties by breaking up disciplinary constituencies in favour of a more management-centred definition of these middle level university structures. Deans no longer enjoy an authority derived from a wide base in the traditional disciplines of engineering, arts or law, but instead become 'executive deans' appointed to manage a diverse collection of programs and priorities. In some cases the faculty nomenclature is replaced by the less independent vocabulary of 'schools':

there are seven schools ... run by the executive deans and the ordinances which they run make it clear that, whereas the Faculty is an Athenian type entity in which every academic in the coordinating departments bonds [sic], a school is not like that ... They are in line management to the dean, the dean is their supervisor so everyone in the university has a supervisor.

... the beauty of that [school executive] is that it's a small group of people and it's people who do actually have management authority and budget control.

This new set of structures is seen by VCs as being more open from above and thus less likely to be captured from below. Lacking a precise history in the traditions of a given profession or discipline such units must deal with the executive power of the university on terms it is well placed to dominate. Tradition, purpose and academic culture are subservient to a far more simple and direct set of incentives based almost exclusively on the power of the budget:

that really does change the culture pretty fast. The only way to change culture in the university is to link budget in with it ... then you get a reaction the first year it's introduced.

So you start off simply allocating to schools exactly what they would have got next year if this year's proportion is obtained ... Then we take five percent off the top ... and it goes to strategic planning fund. ...We then make determinations about their capacity to add value to where the university is going ... Normally you don't move the five percent around but you do normally move one and a half, two percent. So everyone, obviously, has to get something ...

This drive for simplicity is also evident in the relationships being forged between an enhanced central executive authority located in the VC's office and other key actors such as the university council and the port-folios of deputy vice-chancellors and pro-vice-chancellors. Many of the VCs interviewed expressed a desire to define and limit these other potential sources of authority.

Council ... worries me a bit because I'm not sure all governing bodies are competent enough to bear the load ... If they've got the right chief executive, he or she is not going to let them manage hands on.

An effective Vice-Chancellor can lead a strong Council in an environment of change.

DVCs: I'd actually like a system where they didn't have parentheses after their names ... you want a very strong executive team that you can't sort of put a cigarette paper in between in the meantime ...

The new dominance of central definitions of the purpose of the university also extends to attitudes to student participation. The most energetic rationalisers lament the tendency of student activists to see their priorities as something other than the shouldering of official res-ponsibilities:

Students want to do NUS things, they want to get involved in peripheral activities. It's really an interesting task to get them involved in the core activities in the university.

In another version of the same style we see the VC of a large metro-politan university refer to himself as 'a one-person cabinet'. This partly has to do with the mix of functions which most CEOs experience. However, paradoxically, it also speaks of a degree of complexity which sees this VC defining his role not with reference to the public domain, but as a variant of something imagined (probably wrongly) as being 'only found in organisations like BHP'. The purposeful elements of this style are evident in both the environmental geography of power already discussed, as well as in a longer and greater sense of the time-space to be used.

These kinds of VC are more likely to speak of their mission in terms of ten- and fifteen-year horizons, even though they make no obvious claim to be expecting this as their own period of tenure. The impact of the office is larger than the real time elapsing. There is a claim being made for bigger historical impacts and larger than career purposes. There is something of the missionary in this rationalising style and it is interesting to hear a number of senior administrators refer to the University of NSW as a recognised caste of corporate leaders, capable of propagating such a common system.

For example, one observes without being asked, that four of the current eight VCs in the so-called 'Great Eight' are former University of NSW staff who 'often come back to University of NSW' for their policy. To call it a mission may be too strong, for the language is something less than evangelical. Typically the rationalist vision is defined by budgets and resource management strategies: 'my decision was not to restructure the university through faculty reorganisation, but to restructure through budget design'. What this refers to is a new world of financial incentives.

If you look to see how you should structure a Social Sciences area, you've probably got five models around the country, and some work and some don't. ... it's a matter of taste that you should have economics in the faculty of commerce rather than the faculty of arts ... those things don't seem to make much difference to me. What makes a difference is three or four principles that flow through the budget and that's where the changes were brought through.

The rationalising VC wants to step back from specific battles over funding projects ('the place is too big and too complex for me to be able to make the best decision about that') and to focus upon a smaller number of defining incentives. Deans are motivated by annual targets and personal performance reviews. Academic board is confined to curriculum decisions. The VC's own small executive group, which includes the senior budget officer, is mostly interested in 'money and policy'. Faculties accept that their dean is part of the central university plan, and not 'a warrior who comes once a week to do good battle for faculty'. And the 'other things that become important are mundane things like the excellence of the accounting system', *mundane* being a description which neatly cauterises academic passions.

The rationalisers are also keen allies in a struggle to bring measurement into play as a means to motivate and demonstrate success:

if you have a PVC of Finance, to have an accountant rather than an academic is probably a reasonable thing to do ... where you have a DVC who is looking at academic procedures or research it's probably still worth having an academic in that position.

These distinctions reflect a practical recognition of different forms of knowledge, but they also suggest a stronger division of labour and a clearer hierarchy within those knowledges than was once thought necessary.

And the measures quickly move into areas others view as essentially academic, reformulating the academic project of the university. Asked about industry relationships, one leading exponent of this approach offered the observation that 'most universities value their links with industry', but fail the test of measured performance: 'One way to test it would be to see how many honorary degrees they've given out in the last five years'.

Entrepreneurs

Perhaps no single style so well encompasses the mood of the post-Dawkins decade than that of the buccaneer virtue of the entrepreneurial VCs. Queensland, La Trobe and Monash each had travelling potentates as often away as at home, and more comfortable in Canberra than in committee. Unlike the rationalisers, this group remain sceptical of the role of comprehensive internal systems which they fear might limit their own options:

A lot of things you just let happen and a bit of freewheeling is not necessarily a bad thing.

High on the list of attributes favoured by such leaders is executive discretion. They like structures which work for them, which are quick and confidential and which keep accountability to a residual of limited financial indicators. In short, they choose their administrative order the way they might select an airline or a bank. And being entrepreneurs they mostly like to extend their influence through their own visions of a new university standing tall in an external world of competitors, collaborators, allies and adversaries. Far less weight is given to plans and formal structures. Sharing power with deans and DVCs is apt to lead to counter-claims or the need for lengthy negotiation. Consequently this type is less interested in delegation than are the rationalisers who see this as a means to extend a central system downwards:

We devolved an awful lot to Deans of Faculties and I've tried to claw back some of that responsibility.

The entrepreneurs define structures as good and bad according to how flexible they are in allowing new projects to be defined and enacted from the top. Entrepreneurs prefer some distance between their institutional positions and the formal machinery of university governance. They favour support over planning, advice rather than review.

Q. What are the strengths and weaknesses of your senior management structure?
A. It's a model I feel comfortable with and that's probably important ... My job would be to convince them [deans] of the correctness of this university-wide policy. Rather than get them too heavily involved in questioning the wisdom of that.
Q. [Your approach] on the international side?
A. We decided to put the international stuff in a separate company where I chair the Board and in that context, the overall policy is never really questioned.

The success of the university led by this kind of VC is entirely linked to the personal power of the incumbent rather than the elegance of the process or the comprehensive sweep of the resource management system. Progress is defined by particular projects and initiatives undertaken at the top. Other actors inside the university are invited to 'come on board', but little time is expended on establishing high levels of general involvement.

It's not for me to invent a role for the academic board, it's for the academic board to find a role in the system.

I'm identified very much with that Asian push and I'm known through the region by my interest in it ... I think quite a bit of it is linked to my name.

The consequence of this form of governance is a shift to a more overtly political process of agenda setting. VCs use their power to force the pace, requiring other groups to run to catch up. They also use their more comprehensive control of information and news-making to keep other institutions inside the university guessing. While playful, the style is openly coercive:

My style has been one of putting the toe in the water. When we first started the [name of initiative] ... which has not come to fruition yet, but the way I acted was just to indicate to the Academic Board that this is something that was in the wind ... and in due course I kept informing them and so on. I did the same with the Council so they all got used to the idea. I could say to them when the deal came to fruition a bit: we started talking about this 12 months ago and none of you raised any objection at the time. We've been able to deliver it ...

I do it that way. It's terribly important in an academic community quite early in the process letting people know what's on your mind ... But you don't invite debate: You say this is on our agenda.

Those who wish to maintain their influence at the top table are required to find a means to assist with new ideas, often without clear information about the resources and constraints involved. Criticism and counter-planning are anathema to such forms of governance and these VCs have clear ideas about whether or not their subordinates are playing a constructive role:

My style was to clear it with the committee of deans and they'd identify difficulties, rather than opportunities, because that's the way they think ... It's a bit like the fee thing now: I can't tell them what's on my mind but when the Academic Board meets I'll soften them up a bit and say 'We've got to generate some damn money somehow' and 'Where would *you* get it from'? Maybe fees are on the agenda: we don't know but I've got to look after the university, and so on ... I wouldn't distribute a paper: it'd be an oral report.

The search for structures which support such a style is complicated by the fact that universities retain a legislative core which seeks deliberation, debate and a staged hierarchy of authoritative decisions. Not surprisingly then, the entrepreneurs often favour strategies to circle round existing structures, to augment or replace them with private companies and independent funding sources, and to focus key decisions on small groups such as the VC's informal executive and the council's budget subcommittee.

A. At the end of the day the VC is accountable to the finance committee of Council ... I think there's going to be more [use of private company structures]: the sheer ease and getting out of process. If you want to kill anything you get into process.

Q. Is that mainly speed or confidentiality?

A. The main one is being able to do something quickly and also you don't want everyone to know.

Where existing authority holders below the level of the VC seek their own structured role, these VCs and their supporters may simply elect to go on about their business, confident that any important decisions will gravitate back towards them. Other groups may attempt to define separate agendas and articulate a different set of interests but they lack the authority to generate their own entrepreneurial power.

Deans? Yes, a bit of tension has evolved over the years ... the Deans feel, though they don't say it, that my relationship with them has diminished because of the importance of the executive around me. We used to meet every two weeks and now we meet every three weeks. They've started meeting by themselves because of that [laughs].

Facilitators

There also is a characteristic form of governance which follows an internal attention to detail. In this case the interest lies in reorganising the decision-making systems of the university to achieve a comprehensive and agreed set of outcomes. This style favours group over grid, to borrow Mary Douglas' famous formulation. When asked about bigger issues such as relations with industry, one of our VCs names some initiatives but then says what really counts is the old values – getting a bigger share of the best school-leaver market! These are targets the whole organisation can agree upon and which bind the disciplines together.

One such VC has decided to establish a senate in order to reach a larger number of academics, especially professors. He feels there are probably too many layers of administration, but does not see this as a simple problem to solve:

I bet if you went into any university in Australia and walked into the department of chemistry, you would find something like a laboratory manager, depending on the size a couple of other people. You go into the faculty office, you'd find that there would be a few more people shadowing what goes on in the chemistry department, shadowing what goes on in the administration and all they do is squabble over whose numbers are right. That gives plenty of opportunity to pass the buck: it's not my problem, kick it upstairs.

Asked if better training of managers would help, he seems unimpressed: 'I don't know what we could get out of spending a huge amount of money on it, doing a course set up by some management consultant to tell me how to run the show.'

'I'm a great believer in guided collegiality', he says. What he means by this is not perfectly clear, although he does see great benefit in any system of participation which gives him access to more information about what staff think. In another case, a recently appointed VC lamented the over-enthusiasm for rationalist executive institutions:

I think that in terms of the flavour of the management/worker relationship it's just a little too far in the direction of being managerial and there's a danger that this senior management group is isolated a bit.

In this account the pathologies of the older style governance systems were based on 'stagnant' consensus-seeking in which every group had the

power to slow or veto decisions. This diagnosis is not far from the
rationaliser's guide to the university. But where it parts company is in a
softer line on collegiality. In place of previous forms of negative authority,
this group-based style aims for 'what's often called the learning organisation with employee empowerment', not only among academics, but for
middle level administrators as well:

I think that in the academic community at large there is this problem about the
confusion between formal consensus, collegial decisions ... and decision making
involving consultation.

The group style is more concerned than any other with the achievement of common purposes across the university. This is less a matter of
planning and legislation than about shared values and purposes: 'So
you've got to get that vision understood and accepted ... the more that
level of vision stretches, the more effective' you can be. These leaders
place greater emphasis upon drawing administrators and academics into
common projects. They are critical of many established university structures such as academic boards and faculty committees on the grounds
that they divide these two parts of the university community:

That's one of the things that worries me about the Academic Board reinventing
itself ... there's a degree of academic vis-à-vis general staff snobbery around this
institution.

Executive structures

Consequent to the emerging role of the VCs as the pre-eminent influence
within their institutions, most of the universities we surveyed have
developed new, semi-formal decision-making groups to support the VC's
vision and reach. Most have no formal status and are not defined by
statute. Most have no direct reporting relationship to other university
bodies such as council or academic board. Many do not keep minutes
nor publish their recommendations. Instead their purpose is to keep the
VC informed of university crises and emerging challenges. They also act
as a means to bind key executive actors to a common strategy which
supports the VC's position on all matters of general debate. Key items
about to come before other committees are discussed and a caucus
position is developed. Meeting weekly and convened whenever the VC
seeks advice and support, these 'kitchen cabinets' (see table 4.2) underline the shift of power towards less formal, less open patterns of university
governance. They are as flexible as needs be: changeable in role, agenda,
members and *modus operandi*, but united by a common interest in the
pragmatics of power and career. They are composed of people who, for
the most part, need each other.

Table 4.2 Vice-chancellors' executive groups ('kitchen cabinets'), 1995–96

University and case study date	'Kitchen cabinet'	Membership	Pattern of meetings
Adelaide October–November 1995	Senior Management Group	VC, DVC (Academic), DVC (Research), Registrar [about to add six 'superdean' divisional heads]	Formal weekly meetings, increasingly important vis-à-vis academic board
Central Queensland August–September 1995	Executive Group	VC, PVC (Academic), PVC (Research), PVC (Operations and Resources), Registrar	Meets 'fairly often but not regularly' (VC), constant informal contact
Deakin July 1996	Not explicit	VC, DVC, Vice-President (Academic), Vice-President (Administration), PVC (Research), PVC (Development)	
Edith Cowan November 1995	Vice-Chancellor's Executive	VC, DVC (Academic), DVC (Staffing), PVC, six faculty Deans	
Flinders November 1995	Vice-Chancellor's Advisory Committee	VC, DVC, PVC (Academic), PVC (Research), Director of Administration, two senior women	In addition to meetings, most members in frequent informal contact
Griffith July 1995		VC, DVC (Staffing), DVC (Research), PVC (Administration), PVC (Information and International Services), PVC (Equity), PVC (Quality), PVC (Gold Coast)	Meets regularly, informal contact between most members of the group located near each other
James Cook August 1995	Executive Group	VC, DVC (Administration), DVC (Humanities/Social Sciences), DVC (Science/ Engineering), DVC (Research), Chair Academic Board	Informal body, but meets weekly and seen as determining in university

Monash May–June 1996	Vice-Chancellor's Executive	VC, 2 generalist DVCs, DVC (Research and Development), PVC International, PVC Business	Informal meetings, major impact on financial decisions, deans excluded
New South Wales June 1996	The Executive	VC, DVC (Academic Affairs), DVC (Research and International), PVC (Development), three vice-presidents (Registrar, Executive Director Finance and Business, Director Information Systems), President of Academic Board	Weekly meetings, every second week joined by 12 deans to form Vice-Chancellor's Advisory Committee. Also Budget Committee of VC, two DVCs, Executive Director of Finance and Business.
Newcastle October 1995	Senior Executive Group	VC, DVC, University Secretary and Registrar, Executive Director of Finance and Property, PVC (Research and IT), PVC (External Relations), PVC (Development)	Tensions, with some members of group in close contact with others, some more isolated
Queensland June 1995		Informal group of DVC, Secretary and Registrar, PVC (External Affairs)	17-member University Resources and Planning Committee with senior managers, superdeans and staff and students is key body, but the small group more likely to make big decisions, particularly in the absence of VC
QUT June–July 1995		VC, DVC, Director of Planning and Budget; two PVCs (Research and Academic) are excluded	Meets informally, regularity unclear but a powerful group at QUT

continued on next page

University and case study date	'Kitchen cabinet'	Membership	Pattern of meetings
Southern Cross October 1995	Executive Committee	VC, DVC, Executive Director of Administration, Director of Coff's Harbour Campus, six faculty deans	Meets monthly, seems to be no small 'inner' group
Sydney June 1996	Vice-Chancellor's Advisory Group	VC, senior managers including DVCs and PVCs, excludes deans	
UTS December 1996	The Friday Morning Group	VC, DVC (Academic), DVC (Administration), PVC (Research), PVC (External Affairs), Executive Director of Administration	Weekly meetings, supplements decisions made in 30-member Vice-Chancellor's Committee, which includes deans
Tasmania November 1995	University Budget and Planning Committee	VC, DVC, PVC (Research), two deputy principals, Chair of Academic Senate, executive deans	Meets monthly, monitors faculty budgets
Western Australia November 1995	a. VC's Advisory Group b. Small informal executive group	a. VC, DVC, PVC (Research), eight executive deans b. VC, DVC, PVC (Research), Registrar and Vice-Principal	b. Meets every Friday morning

Note: the information in this table was current at the time of the respective case studies, though subject even then to various interpretations. Particularly in the case of more informal bodies, practices not only varied over time but were understood variously by different informants. Details such as frequency of meetings, transparency and even lines of accountability were often impossible to pin down. Precisely because these 'kitchen cabinets' are used as flexible and malleable mechanisms, they are rarely codified and difficult to define. This does not detract from their often key role within executive power systems: the contrary is the case.
Source: Data compiled during the course of the research.

The subject matter of these bodies overlaps with that of another new committee system, the central budget and planning groups established by system rationalisers. Decisions concerning who attends the informal group and who participates in central executives vary according to the strategy adopted by different VCs. It is widely accepted that it is in the VC's gift to decide his or her personal support system, further reinforcing the pattern of positional discretion evident elsewhere. Typically deans are included in the formal executive but not in the advisory meetings. The same is generally true of presidents of academic boards.

At the University of Sydney, for example, the Vice-chancellor's Advisory Committee is composed of senior officials but not deans. A similar structure exists at Flinders where the Advisory Committee also explicitly includes two senior women. At the University of Western Australia and the University of Technology Sydney, the Advisory Group meets informally each Friday morning and is composed of the VC, the DVCs and PVCs, as well as the registrar and vice-principal, or executive Director of Administration.

The formal planning and budget committees tend to be larger and have as their base membership the same participants as are found in the 'kitchen cabinet', plus deans, academic board presidents, directors of some administrative units such as information systems and any directors of separate campuses. There is little evidence of the wider constituency of the university being included in either type of executive grouping, with the University of Queensland being one of a very small number to allow student representation. No case was found in which academic staff enjoyed rights of participation.

Free to deal

Independent positioning

The new exercise of executive power is as varied in style but less diverse in purpose than one might expect in so complex a set of institutions. None of those we interviewed appears strongly tied to council[7] or academic board, none of the VCs interviewed saw his or her executive structure as more than a means to extend the reach of a unified management prerogative. None spoke strongly of the binding traditions or conventions established by their predecessors or of the need to fashion an executive structure which obeyed local imperatives. All condemned notions of collegiality which suggested a separate source of authority. All remained deeply suspicious of the disciplines and the faculty structures which once nourished them.

Also common to type was the sense that they made their own choices about the structures they worked in. One prefers informality, another

wants an executive, another a senate. So this is what they arrange for
themselves. This is their right and to some degree the sign of their power
over the university. Ruling effectively is defined as the establishment of a
system of internal and external flexibility which allows the most senior
managers to answer directly to the VC's vision of future opportunities.

Each VC seeks some way to articulate a common view which others are
invited to acknowledge. Rather than viewing their power as an extension
of a known repertoire of administrative practices and decisions, the
modern VC is primarily an almost independent authority who takes
positions on behalf of his or her interpretation of the university's identity.
They 'position' their university in a wider space of public appreciation.
How they do it will vary. To some it is a matter of capturing good
students, to others a question of using Asian empires as leverage on
Australian minds. Positioning plainly takes a good deal of their time. But
the process appears to vary as much as the means. We see planners and
those who repudiate plans. We found consultants, as well as those who
avoided consulting wherever they could. If one generalisation could be
made from this sample of approximately half the current Australian
university leadership, it would be the obvious one that those working
hardest on an international profile probably paid least attention to internal
processes of discussion. But that may also be a scale and age effect – in
large old universities VCs are least concerned to build alliances with staff
and more interested in instrumental tactics to advance their cause.

Also striking is the sense they all wish to project of being 'free to deal'
with a new environment of threats and opportunities. The new habit
of 'tough talk' about the changed world of higher education is usually
directed at requiring others to accept top-down change and frequently it
is directed at soft targets such as deans and trade unions. More interesting than the targets, however, is the idea that this attribute is now
somehow central to the cause of the university. Most telling is the idea
that culture is simply an artefact of budgets – 'the only way to change the
culture of the university is to link the budget with it'. While this *realpolitik*
speaks loudly for the changed character of executive rule, it also raises
questions, as powers concentrated at this level extend with fewer checks
or constraints than ever before. Certainly the VCs would claim that this
is what is called for in the times in which we live, but given their capacity
to shape the way we discuss and appreciate such opportunities, there is
considerable scope for senior management to become self-referential and
limited only by the personal energies and interests of incumbents.

More than once we heard deputies and PVCs assess the future of their
institutions in terms of the changing attention and focus of their current
VC, rather than the enduring missions and strengths of their wider
constituencies. Variations in the style of individuals and in their personal

networks of influence in Canberra, Asia and in the business community count heavily and impose risks which the formal decision-making structures of these institutions are less able to mediate. This might be considered a simple matter of evolutionary pressure necessitated by the new environments of financial uncertainty and external competition. But it is equally credible to suppose that the general patterns of executive centralisation and discretionary power indicate a more hazardous, error-prone world. Rather than representing and reflecting the character of the institutions they govern, such VCs may come closer to the model of the ever risky professional football coach or the private-sector CEO.

The frequent observation by subordinates that their VCs travel much more than they once did suggests something other than better airline schedules. The role itself has plainly become larger and more flexible. As such their performance is always somewhat separate from the character of the institutions they lead and they are regularly seen to fail just as often as others succeed. Moreover the consequences of success and failure at the top are far more decisive for their organisations. In such an environment the role of the VC now resembles a 'double or nothing' dynamic where greater circulation of people through positions, shorter appointment horizons, larger expectations and fewer counter-balances within the organisation promise higher risks along with fewer riches.

Centralisation and detachment

We take these observations as evidence of the uneven emergence of new forms of executive authority in the university. From the perspective of those inside the institutions, these new forms appear to be both more concentrated and more strategic than before. Executive power is less interested in the wide range of legislative actions and educational moves being made by academics and instead appears to focus its considerable new authority upon a chosen repertoire of projects. This might be expressed as a tendency for all the VCs we interviewed to see themselves as having a particular mandate, or cause for which they already hoped to be remembered by future generations of leaders, or at least to be valued by the selection committee at the next university to which they aspired to be appointed.

The key to this new strategising and the observed concentrations of power appears to be a significant reshaping of the executive territory in which VCs act. Within the university this takes three basic forms. First is the emergence of smaller executive committees which have unrestricted agendas, no formal minutes and no direct accountability, except through the VC's own line of responsibility to council. These bodies express the fact that the VC's role is extended by him or her, at will. Those chosen to come to such executive meetings are there at the VC's discretion and enjoy special access to central policy-making at his or her 'gift'. The fact that others in the university know that such meetings of the 'kitchen cabinet' exist, are decisive in shaping policy, and express one's centrality (and marginality) to the university's political process only serves to strengthen their function as an extension of executive authority. The fact that the meetings cannot be observed, may fail to record their decisions and are formally accountable to no one does nothing to diminish their authority.

A second form of centralisation emerges from the general (though not universal) tendency for VCs to redefine deans as middle level executives, rather than discipline leaders in their own right. While in many places we found this shift to be less than complete, there was much effort being made at the top to recast the role of faculty leaders. Typically the new approach to executive management seeks to define the more independent deans as 'robber barons' and owners of warring fiefdoms. This language was almost universal, suggesting that the same set of management consultants or the same Australian Vice-Chancellors' Committee (AVCC) sub-committee had popularised this cause. The common strategies for achieving this incorporation of the deans' role were two. In some smaller universities PVCs dedicated to one or two faculties were used to hold resources firmly at the centre. Deans retained educational responsibility and continued to chair a faculty level board, but without funds such structures lacked real authority. The second stratagem was to create a central planning committee and bring deans onto that, along with their budgets. By this means the central leadership of the university aimed to exercise direct influence over resources formerly held at faculty level, and to employ faculty-based incentives (teaching loads, research plans, etc.) as a means to promote university-wide objectives. In some cases this second stratagem was also accompanied by the creation of so-called 'superdeans'.

These executive managers are placed over a larger grouping of faculties or schools and are identified as general managers of operational activities at this level. This further dilutes the disciplinary authority of deanship, reduces the capacity of discipline-based departments and their professors to treat the deanship as an extension of shared authority and, most importantly, cuts the previous tie between the dean's role and the authority of faculty boards and committees.

The third aspect of executive centralisation which we observe is that concerning external territorial power. The arena in which many new influences are expressed is one which is closed to most inside the university. The policy world in Canberra, the marketplace and the new international system are the three overlapping circuits of such influence. Paradoxically, the more universities become dependent upon such environments, the more powerful and the more centralised do their executive structures become. At its most dramatic this new power dynamic is expressed as the almost universal fact that Canberra-imposed budget cuts grant VCs and their close advisers unique power to reshape the profile of their institutions.

Threats, rapidly emerging crises, invidious comparisons, perceptions and judgements of would-be investors, and interpretations of likely future policy settings all rank high in the determination of new university projects and in the fate of existing commitments. Fewer and fewer academics, students and community members of council are equipped to interpret these signals. While these new territories are unquestionably important and real, they also lack the substance of earlier signals. As a result the new VCs must call upon a form of symbolic politics to create direction and commitment, and in so doing must lift their own roles outside the normal administrative line. This detachment is evident in the new travelling lifestyle of the modern VC, in their diplomatic missions to titular protectorates, and in the experiments with 'provost'-style deputies seen in some cases.

However we also observed a number of limitations and complications in this general pattern of centralisation and detachment. Chief among these is the confused roles of DVCs and PVCs. While the lack of a clear functional mandate undoubtedly serves to make such officials more dependent upon the VC's own authority, the cost is increased second-guessing and duplication. Many of the institutions observed here were in the grip of some form of instability at this level. DVCs gave conflicting testimony about their functions, VCs wished to do less administration while holding onto final sign-off rights on almost all matters, and professional administrators were neither subordinate to the DVC or PVC who owned their portfolio, nor transparently accountable in their own right. In other words, while VCs had accomplished significant change in their own roles as detached, strategic leaders, they had often left those around them in some confusion about their own functions. This appeared to indicate that improved strategising was being paid for at the cost of clarity and accountable administration.

5   College and corporation: Institutional power in the Enterprise University

Rachel Boston

Good-bye to all that

Once universities were able to temper the effects of sudden change and deflect many of its pressures. They understood themselves as centres of collegiate decision-making, derived from ancient tradition and embodied in statute: a legislative world of registrars, calendars and careful deliberations. The transition from policy to governance has enabled – if not demanded – major changes in the collegial decision-making structures of universities, altering the character of their constituency (their 'stakeholders'), and transforming their inherited culture. The most obvious reason for this is that the universities are increasingly exposed to commercial pressures. But this is only one part of the transformation.

The Enterprise University is less cumbersome than previous forms, less open to veto and inertia within, and generally more capable of articulating a single, defining strategy for its own 'reinvention' during times of extreme turbulence in its environment. The logic of corporate decision-making is more freely embraced than before and collegial values are more frequently subordinated to central purposes.

The exercise of management power in the Enterprise University is in this sense more 'transparent' and perhaps more effective. By combining strong central direction with sophisticated displacements of decision-making away from councils and academic boards and into informal negotiations between a network of key players inside and outside the university, power is simplified. This power is also openly 'transparent', linking the executive authority holders to key government stakeholders and a small caste of external business interests and international target groups. It is power in parentheses, since the formal authority of legislative bodies such as council and academic board is now bracketed by *ad hoc* committees and semi-formal consultations which have no mandated authority, yet exercise significant responsibility.

In creating the Enterprise University, the formal institutions have been extensively restructured, and this process has been both deliberate, and achieved without apparent difficulty. A common pattern emerged at virtually all the universities we examined. Empowered by an agenda set in response to outside imperatives, executive management has sought to refocus the representative functions of councils and to define, and sometimes confine, their roles to that of supporters of a single corporate mission. Oversight of the administration of the university has been transferred from councils to the university executive in general and to the VC's office in particular. Academic board has had its role narrowed to procedural and curriculum matters which have little proactive impact upon external mission, and even less on the flow of resources.

In the Enterprise University it is seen as important that everyone is kept informed, that financial and statistical information is available, that strategic plans are drawn up and the university executive is charting a course for the uncertain future. In an era of reduced per capita public expenditure on education, clear strategic directives and a marketable corporate image have a critical function in maintaining the internal political coherence of the university. 'Planning', creating an ethos of involvement (though not consensus), is the hallmark of a new system of decision-making and communication that is fast gaining ground on older 'representative' committees, marginalising them and sometimes replacing them altogether.

A host of new corporate structures have also emerged as an alternative or 'shadow' institutional process for the raising and spending of resources. Most of these lie outside the direct control of the university's traditional legislative process and instead reflect the priorities of executive management and its new constituency at home and abroad. These firms and foundations run parallel to collegial decision-making, linking entrepreneurial academics and their sponsors to new central objectives. Little if any of this 'soft money' economy is visible to those not directly involved and decisions appear to be made faster and in this sense more efficiently than before.

Those at the level of dean and below are drawn into new strategies through processes of budgeting and semi-formal consultation which emphasise information and accountability, but not autonomy. Only where such 'middle level' institutions include new planning committees did we see a significant sharing of the enhanced power of the university's formal process of decision-making. Here we mostly observed increased pressure for such bodies to honour the implementation of established priorities, rather than to act as a source of innovation.

Some find in all of these changes the clear signs of decay in the 'Idea of a University': where the typical pattern of reform is joined to a bothersome central bureaucracy, there the grumbles are loudest. Yet by no means all academics are unhappy with the changes, and middle administrators are often strong supporters. Often we found a sense of relief that things were so much better than they were under an autocratic manager of the past, an older inefficient and unworkable system, a previous era of 'god professors' and privilege.

At the same time higher level bureaucrats like the new arrangements because they spike the powers of previous 'amateur' structures and heavily regulated collegial processes. For one extremely busy senior academic manager it is clear that policy formulation, strategic thinking and planning, and better access to financial and statistical data have become crucial elements in her management style. A woman integrally involved in committees and projects, she spoke damningly of past ineptitudes, poorly informed decisions and conservative agendas and networks which had left the university largely to 'manage itself'. In this context, governance and management in the form of 'grace and favour' at council and an executive committee of academic board responsible for handing out funding are 'old boy', 'ad hoc' and 'old hat'. A more systematic, explicitly planned and procedural and more transparent form of management is emerging, and it has its point.

Similarly, traditions of morning teas, tenure and time for interaction within departments and faculties are challenged by managers offended by time-wasting committees, 'dead wood' on the payroll, and boring collegial debate, which they often parody as diatribes on the intricacies of parking on campus. Directives from above, with clear and transparent goals and processes, are often viewed as secure and relevant, a welcome relief from the stagnant democracy of committee systems. The 'insiders' of the new processes have grown to prefer a more limited 'consultative' form of input which is channelled through strategic planning processes and communication strategies.

Governance and management

University councils

In the membership composition of university councils (which here include senates) lies official recognition of those sectors of community, government and the university with the greatest interests in the university. Pre-1986 universities evolved a standard form of council which, especially in older institutions, could be quite large. The standard council included representatives of academic and general staff, students, parliamentarians, members of university convocations, executive management, and a few co-opted members from business, law, community and the arts. In the 1990s this standard council has been under consistent pressure to become less of an internal reflection of established university directions and more a projection of its new self-image, and thus more amenable to (even enthusiastic about) projects of reinvention. Reviews of councils have proposed to more effectively encompass the 'community' by reworking council membership. There is the same kind of message in a number of state and Commonwealth government reports.

Being in touch with the 'community' has been an increasing part of councils' role since the growth of public expenditure on universities in the 1960s. Mediating accountability for public monies, and monitoring the broader educational activities of universities within their geo-political region have long been central tasks for governing bodies. Nevertheless, it seems that 'community' interest is no longer adequately fulfilled by representatives of the professions and mainstream non-government organisations. Councils are moving towards more exclusive reliance on business representatives, and often those parts of business with a vested interest in higher education. The Enterprise University seeks to embody a definition of 'community' which is explicitly business oriented, if not business dominated.

The impact of the business model of organisation is not confined to the membership of councils: it goes also to their roles and to their *modus operandi*. The Dawkins Green and White papers saw the representative character of councils as a barrier to be overcome. The 1988 White Paper recommended that the councils be reduced in size and changed in role, while institutional management and executive leadership was strengthened. The council was ear-marked for a university version of the corporate board of directors, to supervise and provide a check to the more muscular CEO that the government envisaged. In other words the council was to imitate the proprietorial interests of shareholders seeking to hold executive management responsible for the profit performance of the company. The attempt to create boards of directors where no shareholding actually exists appeared as a means to legitimise profit-taking and institutional/ corporate self-interest, but without any other effective replacement for the shareholder's bottom-line or dividend.

The new system created by the Dawkins reforms also brought with it a complex policy and reporting framework enabling devolution of corporate financial responsibility to the universities. Governing bodies are even now still adjusting to the increased accountability of university finances to government, and their own greater autonomy in capital expenditures. The post-Dawkins amalgamations provided historic opportunities for executive managers and the more energetic outsiders on councils, and led to a range of changes in the framework of governance, including new constitutions with new governing bodies (for example at Tasmania), and cases where parts of subordinate institutions were absorbed into a larger conglomerate so that new members were added to governing bodies.

'Downsizing' the council

In this atmosphere of uncertainty, in which governing structures were clearly far more malleable than hitherto, the Commonwealth's Hoare committee,[1] and committees on university governance established by Liberal governments in South Australia and Victoria, all produced reports which argued that in the light of the intensified fiscal duties of post-Dawkins, councils were undefined in their roles and needed rationalisation (see table 5.1).[2]

Again, the underlying assumption was that councils were too representative of the views of broader community interests and of those who work and study in the university, and not representative enough of business. All three committees concluded that the governing bodies of Australian higher education institutions were too large with too many 'internal' staff and student members. All three produced ideal compositions for smaller tighter councils, with a greater proportion of appointed members from industry and commerce.

The Hoare committee recommended that the states amend their enabling legislation to favour governing bodies of 10–15 members, with 'external independent members' outnumbering internal members. In other words, external legislative change should be used to force internal reform. The state reviews in South Australia and Victoria proposed similar models. These reports also attempted to refocus the councils through membership changes and through delineation of the council's role in relation to executive management.

The recommendations concerning overall numbers have resulted in legislative change to South Australian university councils. Numbers on the governing bodies of the University of Adelaide and Flinders

Table 5.1 Three governmental reviews of university councils

Report	Recommended size	Proportion external	Proportion internal
Commonwealth's Hoare report, December 1995	10–15	majority	minority
South Australia, *Balancing Town and Gown*, February 1996	ideally 10–15; no greater than 20	two-thirds	one-third
Victoria, *University governance in Victoria*, June 1997	21	two-thirds	one-third

University have dropped from 35 to 20, and there is a majority of external nominees. This suggests greater focus on a single vision expressed through the executive management, the more so because council members are not, as in a public corporation, shareholders themselves. It also suggests a lesser degree of internal determination of the character of the university.

It has taken some time for the change in South Australia to be achieved, indicating that the 1980s shift in governmental thinking about universities has had a significant but delayed impact on council structures. Indeed, we found that while the reform mood is widespread, other cases are less clear-cut, and there have been a variety of approaches. The size and membership of councils still owes something to the traditional formulation of councils as a committee of representatives and officeholders concerned with the overall direction of the institution. In some cases total numbers have grown in the wake of institutional mergers, rather than shrunk. The argument that 'successful institutions don't correspond to the Hoare recommendations' was voiced by many of our interviewees. The impact of the Victorian *University governance* report is less apparent than that of its counterpart in South Australia. Throughout Australia many councils have redefined their roles, but often less in relation to external pressures and more in relation to restructuring within the university, the rationalisation of committees, and management's search for a preferred internal structure.

The University of New South Wales (UNSW) was the first university to reduce the numbers on its council in line with the Dawkins recommendations. In 1988 the size dropped from 40 to 21, and council committee interaction with executive management was formalised. This is a small council by national measure. One member pointed out that it could not be smaller, since all the committees have to have a minimal membership. Executive leaders characterise the most recent stage in the council's evolution as a 'defining period' and council members have participated in retreats to assess and review their role.

In contrast, the Monash Council is one of the largest governing bodies in Australian universities with a current membership of 39. It provides a good example of tensions which exist across the sector. The size of the council is partly the result of the amalgamation which added campus representatives from Chisholm Institute of Technology at Caulfield and Frankston, and the Gippsland Institute of Advanced Education. Some interviewees indicated that the inclusion of the new campus representatives was 'encouraging parochialism on Council'. However, interviewees also said that the Monash Council was like a board of management on which stakeholders had a representative role that could not be avoided. It was too well entrenched.

Council functions

Monash has undergone a remarkable expansion, and has been relatively successful in attracting funds through internationalisation and applied research. Evidently the size and character of the council has not been a huge barrier to that success. However we encountered criticism of the Monash Council, concerning executive management's manipulation of the agenda and the 'selected information flow', with the last minute tabling of confidential documents, or the delivery of confidential information in verbal form at the meeting. Reportedly, the enormous size of the formal agenda and the sheer quantity of detail made it difficult for council members to intercede, or to articulate alternatives.

Similar kinds of criticisms are made of councils across Australia, whatever their size and composition. Councils are involved in matters of importance and complexity in which executive management may want to move quickly. Policy issues may include the choice of a new campus, restructuring and investment in university-owned companies, community services policy, and even book-selling, as in one meeting of the University of Queensland Senate immediately prior to our visit there in 1995. Having already considered the issues, executive managers are often unwilling to revisit basic assumptions at this final stage. In the case studies we found the executive power to pre-empt council evident everywhere.

Despite the many differences between the various university councils, all of them share responsibility for the appointment of vice-chancellors (often it is here that a chancellor leaves her or his deepest mark on the institution). The council also holds fiscal and legal responsibility for the operations of the university, as universities are not incorporated bodies. The council operates internally as the place of appeal within the university, and externally as the body responsible for overall success or failure. Some councils have become explicitly involved in industrial matters by overseeing enterprise bargaining negotiations. Potentially, and to some extent actually as well, councils remain important parts of the Enterprise University, in contrast to many of the academic boards.

In addition to the appointment of vice-chancellors, it is the control of capital funds which establishes the locus of power for most of these governing bodies. Some institutions have high-powered, often informal executive groups that direct planning, investment and maintenance of capital funds. However, the councils themselves often become significantly involved in decisions concerning capital investment, and not only at the universities with the 'hollow logs', property ownership and large sums of investment capital.

In some cases corporate structures deploy funds away from direct view of the council. For example, at Monash the Monash Foundation is a separate, wholly owned, investment company focusing on the investment of capital funds. Similarly, a recent phenomenon at Queensland University of Technology is the investment in capital works of funds derived from international students. However, most governing bodies sign off on detailed capital spending programs which are devised and managed by a council committee. Vice-chancellors are almost always members of these committees.

Here again we see the emergence of an imitation board of directors. The appointment of the CEO and approval of capital programs, together with ultimate legal accountability, define the council's role. Omitted from the new picture is the idea of the council as a legislative or deliberative body devised to represent the university to itself and its community.

Governance by other means

With strong and growing incentives to engage in entrepreneurial activities and the drive for 'first mover' advantage in relation to their competitors, executive managers everywhere have developed a range of university-owned business enterprises able to move quickly and operate with commercial secrecy. Characteristically these companies are largely outside the ambit of council control despite annual reporting mechanisms. More and more activities are now being conducted through separate corporate structures and international offices. As a result councils' accountability to government and the community is mediated and redefined. Again, the definition of community has grown more specific, more corporate, and less representative of any publicly argued notion of 'public interest'.

Since the 1960s universities have been involved with company structures, particularly in relation to the exploitation of intellectual property generated in research. However, since the late 1980s the creation of independent university-owned companies has become a standard mechanism for establishing new areas of university activity, or expanding already established areas while restructuring. There has been a marked growth of company structures relating to research, investment of capital funds, information technology services, delivery of educational services to the corporate sector, language education, international education, and domestic fee-paying markets, notably via business schools.

Executive managers find several advantages in company structures. Our interviewees noted quicker response to market opportunities, the ability to 'set up an office in Hong Kong' and take risks in international markets. The establishment of a corporate identity creates financial and legal potential and is an effective marketing tool. It also provides a flexible instrument that is subject to immediate executive direction.

In these companies the three-way relationship between company, university executive, and university governing structure can vary. Often company personnel overlap significantly with the university's senior executive group. Vice-chancellors become directors. DVCs and PVCs are also found as managing directors. However, in most cases senior executive leader-managers do not take the role of hands-on company manager, preferring to appoint specialist managers with outside backgrounds. In these wholly owned companies, annual financial reporting is required: beyond that, in the relationship between university and company a variety of arrangements have emerged.

A common structure used to bridge the gap between the company and the university's legislative structure is that of a 'clearinghouse' body, for example as used at Queensland. Typically this is a committee with executive management representation, with input into the strategic direction of the company. In some cases these bodies are informal, or they are transitional and short-lived, established at the beginning of the life of the company to ensure that the company and its activities are locked into the governance and managerial structures of the university. Of course the more informal such company–university links, the better. After all, the purpose of establishing a company structure, rather than conducting activities through the existing organisational structures such as faculties, schools and departments, is to secure autonomy and to conceal activity from the conventional university decision-making structures.

In this manner, the use of corporate structures in Australian universities has effectively moved large areas of activity to outside the ambit of governing bodies. Often it is those areas growing most quickly or otherwise strategically significant – international activity, technological developments, industry links – that are involved.

Governing managers – or managing governance?

When we interviewed members of councils and senior administrators and managers, across the higher education sector, one thing about councils became clear: there are as many ways to 'manage' the council as there are formulae for the ideal governing body. Whether executives are adopting the recommendations of Commonwealth and state reviews, or they are reviewing their own councils in the light of these documents and the debates surrounding them, they are all aware of the need for strategies for defining their council as a more effective and flexible body. This awareness also includes barely concealed criticism of the council's competence. As one vice-chancellor put it:

The governing body simply has to become a custodian of the strategic direction set by the university. They also have to take their auditing role seriously, not just in the financial sense but in auditing in a quality assurance sense. This means really serious attention has to be given to the professional development of council members ... to training them in understanding the distinction between sovereignty and competence. To seriously bring them in to strategic planning, and *seriously keep them out of attempting to manage.*

At the start of the year at one Sandstone, council members participate in a retreat and induction. They are provided with reports from executive management and exposed to a rigorous preparation. The focus is on 'audit' as part of strategic planning.

We're not inviting council actually to interfere and manage these things. But keeping them informed ... and they will change overall direction if they want to and they will sign off on ... the integrity of performance against plan and operational plan against strategic plan ... It means that all the business that comes from the council during the remainder of the year, they understand the context of very well.

Keeping the council 'informed' is a minimum requirement which can be made into a strategic operation. An internally generated framework, a planning document, is used as the basis for council's evaluation and oversight of university activities. At best, the well informed council sits back and absorbs, questions its executives and satisfies itself that all is in accordance with plan. At worst, the rhetoric of planning muffles discontent and ensures that council has no role in dealing with matters of urgency unforeseen by strategic directives. Implicit in the example is the idea that council governance really should be separate from executive management. It is often a difficult line to draw, but the principle is shared by many senior executive managers. As one said:

There is a clear division between the executive function and management of the university and the governance function of the council.

This tendentious separation between executive management and council, this 'clear division', is maintained by the way in which managers actively manage the council, the procedures they adopt, and the communication strategies they employ to keep council informed about, but insulated from, the actual management of the university. A common distinction refers to actual management as 'day to day' as though this were merely an implementation stage of previous strategic decisions. In practice our interviewees used 'day to day' as code for all but the most generic executive decisions (and generic scene-setting deliberations of governing bodies were mostly framed by 'day-to-day' managers). The tension was evident throughout the study, conducted at a time when the role of council was under review at a large number of institutions. Some such as Tasmania and NSW are strong on methods that clearly define and quarantine the role of council members. Others, if complaints are to be believed, effectively keep Council members out of decisions. Several leading executives also believe that co-opting people with experience on corporate boards of directors helps to confine the scope of council activity as exterior to 'management'.

The incidence of councils controlling management is less common, though it does exist. Sydney is often quoted as a paradigm case, one to be avoided. More commonly, the council provides a forum for review of managerial prerogative; a role guaranteed by the generally public nature of council proceedings. Ironically, this is a guarántee that belongs more to the representative council than the corporate council; and in the new era, it probably restricts a more vigorous Council questioning of senior management.

Despite the fact that the debate over the composition of councils reflects a conception of universities as most appropriately governed by a majority of 'independent' and 'external' interests, as yet the representative aspect of many governing bodies is little changed. Only the legislatively driven changes in the South Australian universities have substantially altered student and staff representation. What has changed more significantly is the role of council and its committees in relation to management. With the increased entrepreneurial activities and the use of corporate structures to compartmentalise university activities, the governing body – aside from its participation in this restructuring – is left with a hybrid structure of continuing authority. In many other ways council is less involved with day-to-day or urgent matters, and more engaged with the formulation of strategic directions, planning for capital expenditure (in some cases) and financial and quality-related audit.

It is the style and prerogatives of executive management which dictate the role of the council more effectively than do 'policy drivers' and review documents. We found evidence of the 'management' of council through the streamlining of committees, retreats and induction procedures, executive reporting, and, equally, through inefficiency, informality and obfuscation. The governing body is a location of power within universities which at times is hotly contested and at others, quietly and cleverly manoeuvred around.

Reworking council committees

Much of the useful work of councils is done through committees, yet the 'constipation' of information flow through committees is a problem for a large number of institutions. Outdated or redundant committees litter the books and are the first thing to be rationalised at review time. This is largely due to the development of operationally focused advisory committees advising the vice-chancellor. In many universities, this is now where the work is being done. Complex committee systems of council which 'shadow' the management functions of the university hierarchy are no longer seen to be required. Here the tensions between managerial decision-making and council governance are being reworked by rationalising the council committees and by shifting most of the council decision-making into a more centralised executive committee or group of committees.

The council has sixteen committees that report to it at the moment, so you can imagine that the council thinks it's a management committee but it isn't. So we've knocked all that off and now there'll be three: there's an audit committee, an academic senate and a resources committee and underneath that, a planning and development advisory committee. (vice-chancellor)

At Flinders, the university council has been reduced in size, not only to tip the balance away from internal members but to streamline activities by reducing the areas of day-to-day business on the agenda. There is a neat fit here between reduced size and redefined function: on smaller councils there are just not enough members to put on all the old sub-committees. The role of council in strategic issues – financial accountability, broad policy and operational finance – has been preserved, perhaps strengthened. These changes have coincided with the early work of a new vice-chancellor. Council's three-committee structure of audit, academic senate and resources seems stark, the bare bones at the beginning of a new stewardship. While such a structure could easily grow another committee or two (albeit likely to be committees of limited duration), the point is that daily decision-making has been centred on the VC and the VC's management committee.

The management committee needed no formal process of review or statutory amendment to immediately appoint two of the university's most active and senior women academic managers to its ranks, a laudable act of benevolence and a nimble management move. In this manner the vice-chancellor was able to capitalise on the talents of these women managers, mark a clear point of difference with a previous administration, and take a personal stand on affirmative action. While some would argue with the reduced number of academic staff on council (down from eight to two), and the preponderance of 'external' appointments which left no space on council for even the DVC, few would question the wisdom of vice-chancellor's impeccably modern discretionary appointment of extra senior women onto the central management committee. They might, however, notice the increased strategic power of the VC to define the character of this and any other form of representation.

The role of councils or senates also depends on the effective role of other bodies such as academic boards, which we discuss below. At the University of Western Australia (UWA), restructuring of the academic board to create an academic council has affected the policy development role of the senate. Importantly, the senate has delegated resource allocation and budgets to the academic council. While the UWA senate still has ultimate legislative responsibility for finance, investment and endowments, staffing and buildings, through its standing committees, the UWA academic council has an enhanced role in the preparation of budgets and the provision of advice to senate. As at Flinders, the effect is to create another decision-making body brought close to the vice-chancellor to deal with significant day-to-day decision-making in policy and financial matters. Not coincidentally, we find again that the hand of the vice-chancellor has been strengthened.

Bored at the board

Collegial and post-collegial

The collegial tradition imported from Britain to the colonial Australian universities was based on self-governing academic units. Administration was minimal and there were recurring financial crises. Despite moments when governing councils or governments interfered, sometimes spectacularly and controversially, in the pure form of the model the universities were dominated by a small coterie of professors who determined their own incentives and objectives. The fact that external interference was readily defined as 'exceptional' underlines the strength of the self-referencing collegial tradition. Professors were subject only to peer validation, and they had few peers. Universities functioned in effect as a private club. Entry was closely guarded. Administrators and junior teachers were the servants, 'managers' were unknown. Thus the early forms of 'institutional autonomy' and 'academic freedom' were shaped.

By the late 1950s, amid public funding, mass enrolment, modernisation and a professional service ethos, the limitations of god-professordom and amateur organisation were apparent. Collegial organisation was fading. Yet the collegial ideal and some of its practical manifestations outlasted its pure institutional form. The notion that the true heart of the university lay with its tenured scholars persisted in the academic practices of many, perhaps most, of those scholars themselves. The newer universities created in the 1950s, 1960s and 1970s all replicated the structure of professorial board-cum-academic board and faculty assemblies, in which slow, conservative academic decision-making jostled with administrative logic. Even the post-1986 universities felt obliged to invent for themselves an academic board to be the apex of both scholarly decision-making and collegial identity.

At the turn of the new century Australian universities are strung out at different points on a continuum from collegial governance to managed corporation. Some are making the full journey, others have paused somewhere in between. In certain new universities, academic cultures are weak, and the organisational logic so centre-controlled that 'collegial' forms such as academic boards are little better than imitations, signs that the university is a university, like the coat-of-arms and crest. It is in the oldest Sandstone universities that distinctively academic institutions are most obvious. In part this is a function of collegial survival, in part it derives from the intrinsic strength of their academic cultures, located somewhere between collegiality and post-collegiality.

Institutional academic cultures

Research focused on governance and its leading practitioners is less well equipped to discern variations in the cultures grounded in the disciplines themselves. We interviewed a number of grass-roots academics, but not enough to develop a complete picture. More readily detected, given our focus on institution-level phenomena, was the outcome of the fusion of the disciplinary cultures of each particular institution, the singular (or fractured) *institutional* 'academic culture' that had resulted. Here the academic culture was observed as often indirectly as directly, through the lens of middle or senior management. Much could be discerned from the language of senior managers, from their particular sensitivities to their own university environment, from the codes and the absences they found it necessary to employ. In this manner, from a combination of the case studies and prior knowledge, certain variations in academic cultures and academic–management mix emerged. These variations are summarised in table 5.2.

In the faculties of a modern Sandstone such as Queensland, work is subject to academic control, but within the larger setting of a performance culture and a post-collegial commitment to fund-raising and external responsiveness. (Melbourne, outside the study, shares these characteristics.) Here collegiality seems to be becoming something else, but these are not pure corporations, they are hybrid corporate–academic institutions. Research remains central to their prestige, and scholarly indicators are important. The culture is not so much collegial as academic–professional, in which the service roles of academic staff assume the dignified authority associated with medicine or law. At Queensland management is overt and sometimes entrepreneurial, but it has been undeniably successful and this contributes to a strong confidence evident

Table 5.2 Principal institutional academic cultures: universities in this study

Collegial	Professional service	Corporate	Entrepreneurial
Sydney	Queensland	UNSW	*Deakin*
Adelaide	Western Australia	Monash	*Monash*
Tasmania			*Central Queensland*
	Newcastle	UTS	
Monash	Griffith	QUT	
Newcastle	James Cook		
Flinders	Flinders	Deakin	
	UNSW	Southern Cross	
	Monash	Central Queensland	
	Deakin	Edith Cowan	

Note that there is much internal variation between disciplines. *Italics* indicate important secondary strand.

across the institution. Collegial melancholy is minimal. Western Australia is on the same path, combining relatively low-key central offices and a highly academic ambience with a reformed organisational system, and an effective entrepreneurial relationship with industry and the international market.

In contrast, at Adelaide and particularly at the University of Sydney, these processes of modernisation and hybridisation are less complete. The fit between management and academic practice is not as 'seamless'. Genuine collegial vestiges survive, and overt management–collegial tensions are in the air.

Memories of a high-collegial culture at Sydney are still very recent. One senior female executive at a new university, formerly located at Sydney as a middle-level academic, remembers that university in club-like terms. The positive side of exclusivity was that once you were accepted as a 'member', you were looked after very well:

The University's manner of managerial largesse was open to the traditional kinship links amongst the staff, be they professional links or blood links. A lot of people at Sydney University had been there all their lives, knew each other and married each other ... People invested a lot in the workplace and a lot of their lives were lived out in the workplace. And Sydney University was very benign in its approach to its own.

Club members who were sick or unproductive were protected. Sometimes they spent a year longer on full pay than they were entitled to. Members looked after in this way were usually older men, rather than women, and young people could find it hard going. On the other hand, she found the vice-chancellor's door was open whenever she wanted. There is a plain contrast between collegial Sydney and the more corporate institution that she now inhabits. In the latter the historical depth is missing. Relationships are negotiated on 'more dispassionate and instrumental grounds'. People are more mobile and do not bond lifelong with one place. Formal industrial relations and modernised management systems cut across the collegial tradition. A tight fiscal climate reinforces this. There is clearly some ambivalence here. It seems that collegiality had its pros and cons.

Other recollections of high-collegial Sydney are less benign. One female professor now an academic manager recalls that under vice-chancellors of the past:

A lot of what is now done in committee was done behind the scenes through personal contacts. Individuals who wanted something, either singly or in groups, went to see the VC informally and talked about it. Grace and favour. This was a major mode of operation at this institution. In many respects it was retrograde. ... To whomever the VC was well disposed, did well. It led to a lot of behind the scenes politicking, which is not to say that doesn't happen now, but the mechanisms are different.

Another female leader in a post-1986 university recalls that at the Sandstone she knew, collegial academic culture was associated with a collegial governance practised by a cabal of senior men with academic pedigrees. Non-academic administrators were treated badly. She is much happier in her present institution. The climate is meritocratic, and if it is gendered in favour of men, it is more open:

We've never had a hierarchy up at the top like UNSW or Sydney, or perhaps Melbourne, which was a network of isolated scholarly men. (I don't want to say that the VC isn't scholarly, right.) Men who'd done particularly well in their own academic careers and formed the top management tier ... I've never felt that here. It's always been much more of an open system.

Meanwhile, back at Sydney, the university is changing. Though collegial traditionalists survive, increasingly they find themselves at loggerheads with professional managers and with managerialist academic peers. The conflict is messy and often unresolved. One contemporary observer at Sydney notes:

The top people are looking to go forward in a much more corporatist way whereas those from the more old fashioned collegiate approach think that if you're a professor you should be able to do what you want. The people who've taken up the corporate approach are amateurs. My impression is that at Melbourne they [the University's leaders] have been a lot more successful in drawing people together round key bits of rhetoric, whereas here, there's resistance.

Such conflicts at Sydney and elsewhere are often played out on the basis of trifling pretexts, in which old academic licence or institutional habits are at stake – whether the university should abandon its Latin motto, whether a new round of forms has to be filled in. Traditional ambience still survives at Adelaide. While Sydney-style dramas are less in evidence, managerial–collegial tension is apparent, especially in academic board politics. One academic with little sympathy for collegial tradition notes that

The major cleavage in the institution ... is between the senior management group and the managers per se, and academics on the other, particularly professors, departments, disciplines, faculties. All those epistemological categories sit very uneasily with administrative categories like student services, computing services, student information and particularly the registrar's kingdom.

He notes that still, in many academic departments at Adelaide:

There's an assumption that because they [the departments] exist and have been maintained in reasonable comfort in the past, why should they not maintain that? Modernising influences in some of the faculties are prepared to grapple with managerial issues and accept the [performance] criteria for what they are and work to meet them. But that is seen as somehow letting down the side. You're playing the Dawkins game, the administrators' game, all of which is most regrettable in the eyes of an influential and highly placed minority.

Most of the newer pre-1986 universities (the Gumtrees) exhibit something like the academic-service culture of Queensland/WA, if more frayed and with varying confidence in institutional management. In these universities, symbolic academic–managerial conflicts still take place. One faculty head at a 1970s-founded university defends the traditional morning tea from management proposals for user-pays costing. Students and junior staff may not come if they have to pay $1.50 instead of the traditional 20 cents a cup. In this case the tradition is not that of a club of senior academics, it is that of an egalitarian and interdisciplinary environment in which staff mix freely with each other, and with students.

In contrast, at Redbrick Monash and NSW and also at Gumtree Deakin, there is a more overtly corporate strain. Often scholarly goals are subordinated to the bottom-line of university income and prestige. NSW and Monash are mature research universities but they have something in common with the Unitechs and New Universities in our study. In all these institutions, academic staff seem more performance- and institution-conscious than elsewhere (of the Sandstones, Queensland is closest). NSW· is profoundly interested in academic performance, and uses top-down control to secure it. It is also decentralised in the corporate manner. Top-down control is decisive. Performance drivers have been installed throughout as its leaders were keen to point out during the study. Monash is more complex. It is decentralised in the old collegial manner: faculties control their inner life and centrally controlled performance measures are weaker than in many other places. Yet both corporate goals and the entrepreneurial spirit are strong in business, computing and to a lesser extent engineering. In the period of the study, the VC's office was another important point of entrepreneurial activity. Monash's secondary strand is a residual collegial culture, especially in arts, in a state of subterranean resentment against the university's manager-leaders. Deakin's entrepreneurial spirit is expressed in its commercial training arm, Deakin Australia. Again, during the period of study the VC was another source of entrepreneurship.

Integration of the academic cultures

The differing academic cultures are configured with management cultures and systems in often complex ways. In some institutions, dynamic and autonomous academic cultures have shaped the historic terrain on which management works. More uncertainly, they continue to affect its evolution (arguably, Sydney's academic cultures have retarded the emergence of the strong executive apparent everywhere else). In some new universities, academic cultures are weak: they are not only controlled by management, they owe their existence to it. In certain institutions management has evolved so as to complement academic culture, fitting it like a glove. In others, the management systems seem to have been designed in opposition to academic cultures, functioning more like a blanket. Nevertheless, in every university, regardless of its age and the state of scholarship, the secular trend is for management to increase its determining force.

Some management cultures are more low key, such as Western Australia's, or their role is simply less well developed, as at James Cook and perhaps Newcastle. Monash's executive is distinctly entrepreneurial, typified by leadership flamboyance and big picture politics, risk-taking, the drive to expand functions and market share (and willingness to leave the details to others). The entrepreneurial leadership avoids disaster because it is joined to tight corporate administration. Central Queensland is also notable for leadership-driven initiative, for example in the creation of its new sites outside Rockhampton. Entrepreneurial strands run through parts of Queensland and James Cook, for example in commercial research. In contrast the UNSW style is typified by tight control of the detail all the way down, the careful weighing of risks, and the collective character of strategic judgements at the top. It is classically corporate.

It is in the varying styles of centralisation/devolution that strategies of integration are expressed. All such strategies bear the mark of local history, so that in the Sandstone universities devolution is more overtly academic than elsewhere. However, all universities have restructured the relationship between the centre and the parts, some more than once, and in every case the objective is to secure institutional coherence and managerial leverage.

Some universities are overtly integrated from the centre-top, for example QUT and less aggressively, NSW and Queensland. A softer form of integration, with greater emphasis on devolution, is practised in institutions such as Western Australia, Adelaide, Griffith and Flinders. In pre-1986 universities the typical path is from collegial devolution to a more corporate form of devolution, with resources passed downwards but constrained by centrally controlled systems, and the independent power of the professors decisively reduced. Says one VC, an enthusiast for the model:

Power is not a zero sum. You can actually increase the quantum by giving it away as long as you can somehow harness it for the whole organisation again. You've got to somehow bring the deans home again. If you devolve authority to the deans and that's all you do, you've got a problem ... [instead you] make them corporate citizens.

Inevitably, attention is focused on fashioning structures that will secure integration. Vice-chancellors' groups which include deans are one mechanism. Meta-disciplinary groupings are another. These do not always work. Like a number of institutions, Sydney has attempted to address the problem of size by devising larger groupings (super-faculties) under a PVC for funding and staffing purposes. However, the super-faculties lack an organic logic. As one observer puts it:

There's no identification with the academic groups. They don't function as a group, just as an arbitrary collection of things.

In some post-1986 universities, integration systems are still emerging. The University of Technology in Sydney is unusual. It combines a some-times corporate culture with almost post-Fordist institutional integration: an uneven mixture of bureaucracy and public service, vocationalism and industry focus, disciplinary experimentalism, entrepreneurial practice. UTS is sometimes tightly tethered, sometimes loosely coupled, mostly informal, and more networked than controlled. It is smaller than Sydney and NSW, which helps.

UTS's management recognises a plurality of purposes, interests and organisational forms, and tries to work that plurality as an asset. Most other manager-leaders drive instinctively towards a unitary form of organisational coherence. Still, try as it might, no management can quite overcome the situation of dual authority inherent in a modern educational institution resting on academic labour. Even the newest, most corporate university invests in academic systems where teacher-researchers carry the design and practice of teaching, and the execution (and at least some initiation) of research. The separation of resource decisions and educational decisions has weakened academic authority but not abolished it altogether. One dean says that:

We're caught between two models. The collegiate, egalitarian, quasi-medieval structure that involves faculties and the academic board in which the head of the academic board is a significant person, versus a managerial structure of people who are not academics as such but are managing targets all the time ... I'm not sure which in ethical or emotional terms that I prefer, but I know they're different.

Sometimes, as at Deakin, this structural duality appears as a sign of weakness, a fault line in the institution; in other cases it seems to demarcate a necessary separation between institutional organisation and academic creativity. Successful Sandstone universities exhibit dual structures, albeit organically joined at many points. Forcing a university into a unitary system, however logical on paper, runs the risk of decisively subordinating the academic to the managerial. At the same time, a dual structure in which one party is always becoming stronger is scarcely a recipe for stability.

Here the academic board, representing 'a traditional discourse of equals who are colleagues', as the same faculty dean puts it, is in the firing line. Heading the academic side of the dual structure, it is inevitably a site of symbolic tension. It is at the same time both the main structural relic of the collegial era, and the continuing repository of an academic authority in disciplinary matters that management always wants to subordinate but can never quite do without.

Academic boards

Like the governing bodies of universities, their academic boards (here the term includes academic councils and academic senates) are undergoing a period of extensive redefinition. The process is particularly fraught because of the central role played by the boards in the collegial universe.

The boards are sometimes transformed, but more often marginalised: most executives find it pragmatic to allow a shadow-form collegiality to survive, corresponding to its lingering ideological role, rather than to abolish it altogether.

The size, composition and function of academic boards vary considerably. In some universities all members of staff at the level of professor and above are ex-officio members of the board. In some an executive committee of the board may act as the main advisory body to executive management. Some chairs of academic boards have a role in executive decision-making, while in one university the vice-chancellor chairs the academic board. Perhaps the only universal feature of the boards is their role in the development and approval of curriculum and new courses. However, we found one university where a large part of this role had been devolved to a specialised committee; while in many institutions the academic board's role in setting academic policy seems to be largely irrelevant, given its lack of control over resources at a time when policy is often ruled by economics. Many managers and academics view their academic boards as confined to the role of 'rubber stamp' in decision-making, and 'safety valve' for harmless dissent. In some universities academic boards are seen as irrelevant, or near-irrelevant, with little or no impact on management decisions and on the direction of the institution. In others they can exercise a reactive input into strategic planning and policy issues as they arise: nevertheless, boards of this kind have no role in initiating or controlling major policy or financial decisions.

Despite academic boards' symbolic function of collegial exchange many interviewees lamented a lack of academic debate, and the irrelevance of contemporary board activity. Only one university in our sample, Edith Cowan University, uses a committee of academic board for producing the university's operating budget. Everywhere financial decision-making is shaped by formula funding and by executive-led committees with varying constituencies. There might be greater transparency but there is rarely any board input. The removal of financial decision-making from the ambit of the academic board seems to many a rational and democratic exercise. Obscure networks of 'god professors' dispensing 'grace and favour' on traditional academic board finance committees is a feature of collegiality that evoked little enthusiasm from any person that we interviewed. However, the boards' loss of role in financial decision-making, combined with the rise of executive leadership, has left most of these bodies in something of a quandary.

'Some of them are asleep'

In a small number of institutions whose traditions are rooted more in the pre-1987 college of advanced education sector than the university sector,

it seems that the peak academic body always lacked importance in
overall management.

It's too big, to start off with. Some of them are asleep, bored out of their senses.
A lot don't go. The same people always speak and say the same thing ... You
probably have to have an arena in which people have the right to speak and
present their grievances. The problems are not so much with the structures or the
philosophy behind the structures, more with how you involve large numbers of
people in decision-making processes (departmental head).

Compounding this, in places like QUT, a top-down management
structure guarantees that the academic board remains marginal. In cases
where the boards are very weak, the board can be sidelined even in
traditional areas of academic control such as curriculum development
and course approval, and the level of overall debate in the university can
be very low.

We've got a number of things that don't go near the academics at this University
... for example, the whole business of what courses you are going to run in two
years time. That never comes to the Academic Board of the Institution ... It goes
from the Executive to Council.

The VC will not allow new course work to be done there and he will not allow the
Academic Board to discuss resourcing ... You take staffing and resourcing out and
there is very little left ... No one would willingly go to this University's Academic
Board.

In such worst case scenarios the boards give final approval to courses
and academic policy, but the real decisions are made by senior managers
in consultation with deans or heads; and resource priorities often directly
shape course delivery.

Part of the problem was that the Academic Board had become irrelevant to some
extent from the point of view of the Deans. Let's say we were talking about off-
campus delivery. I would have that debate, probably as an individual with the VC,
then in the general academic planning group, then in the Dean's academic
planning group, then in my faculty executive, then in my faculty board. Eight
weeks later I would front up at the Academic Board and have the same damned
debate all over again. By the time we got to the Academic Board, all of the Deans
and VCs, PVCs and DVCs were totally bored with the whole issue and it was in
the past.

Inevitably the weakness of academic boards prompts laments from
some academics that professional collegial culture has been weakened. It
seems that as its instrumental role has declined the symbolic importance
of the board has grown, but as an absence rather than a presence. The
academic board in its most sidelined and irrelevant form symbolises

more than academic decision-making processes. It is seen as a part of an egalitarian and democratic fabric of university life, and linked to constructions of academic integrity, an integrity all too overshadowed if not altogether on the skids. In this highly dualistic world view, which is the mirror image of an extreme executive-centred view, academic and executive authority can never be compatible. The notion of academics having an effective input into decisions affecting their modes of teaching, the environment in which they teach and what they teach, is seen as the very antithesis of corporate management. Here the decline of the board becomes proof of the triumph of executive dominance.

'Downsizing' academic boards

Figure 5.1 graphs the size of the academic boards of 13 of the universities in the study. Not surprisingly, most boards in the sample had been reviewed recently or were currently facing review of their size, role, and composition. Many had been made more streamlined. The trends to reduced member numbers (traditional boards often had well over 100), and fewer committees, are among the more general patterns discernible in the higher education sector. At UNSW the academic board was restructured in 1988, at the same time as the council was reformed.

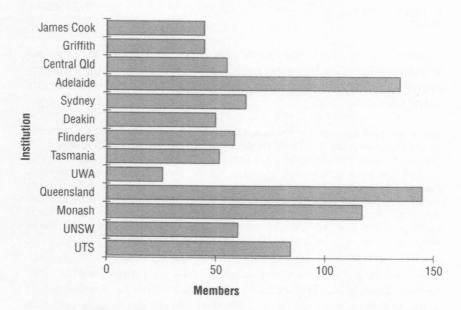

Figure 5.1 Academic board size

The board was changed from a professorial board of 140 to a broadly representative 60-member body with five major committees. Sydney's board, which once included nearly 400 members, now has 63 plus 10 non-voting observers. The old board structure has been preserved as an academic forum which acts as an electoral college for the functioning board, providing an interesting bridge between the old and the new world. Other large bodies, such as Adelaide's 134-member academic board, are the subject of discussion papers and are likely to be rationalised in membership and role. Review does not always lead to reduction. The 1996 review of the Queensland Academic Board left intact its membership of 143 members, with 60 per cent ex officio.

Recent reviews of the boards at the University of Sydney, James Cook and Queensland made formal the role of those academic boards as advisory bodies without authority over management or planning. At James Cook, following the review in September 1996, the words delineating responsibility for 'supervising and coordinating the activities of schools, faculties and departments' were deleted from the board statute. Other changes to the statute clarified the board's role as an advisory body focused on the creation of academic policy. The James Cook review also found that:

It is not practicable for the Board to seek to become the University's planning body. While it should be briefed regularly on the resource outlook of the University, its size and its lack of detailed knowledge of resource possibilities will not allow it, even with fewer members, to become the body actually doing the planning.[3]

In other words the reviews made it clear that the boards cannot *actually do* the planning or perform management functions, and from here they slide easily to the assertion that as a consequence, boards should not have any authoritative involvement.

In contrast to James Cook, the Queensland review of the academic senate, which took effect early in 1997, affirmed that the academic senate should advise on 'the academic aspects and content of the University's Strategic Plan'. The review also confirmed the role of the board as 'the principal independent source of advice to Senate and to the Vice-Chancellor on all educational and academic matters'. To all intents and purposes its traditional collegial role at the centre of the university continued, as 'a discourse of equals' as one Queensland dean put it. However, our research indicates that the role of the Queensland board had been circumscribed by the university executive, just like most of the rest. It has no role in resource allocation. Prior to 1983 resources were distributed indirectly through the academic board, but that year an 'Academic Resource Group' system was introduced. Resource allocation is now managed by the University's DVC and PVCs. This specific-ally 'advisory' role of the academic board expresses the separation of academic and resource responsibility evident throughout the structure of the University of Queensland.

The review of the Sydney's academic board[4] sought to formalise the role of the board as the 'primary academic policy advisory body' and to clarify its relationship with the senate, the vice-chancellor's committee and the major planning bodies. It was argued in the review report that 'the Board should have the right to proffer advice on the academic priorities and policies appropriate to the resource outlook of the Uni-versity'. These reviews often focus on attempts to find a new role for the board as an advisory committee within management-driven structures. Despite this there are some boards that end up effectively outside of management structures. Critics are alert to this trend:

Academic board has become a sort of advisory committee which is not in any chain of command. (union branch president)

Board chairs

How can an academic board be structured into the contemporary systems of tight senior management groups, informal power in the office of the vice-chancellors, and streamlined councils? One way is to bring the chair of academic board into the senior management group. We found the appointment of past and current chairs to PVC positions is becoming more common. It is a way of mediating the role of the academic board through a single senior academic. This also facilitates executive control of the board itself. The chair must juggle personal, representative, and corporate responsibilities. At the University of NSW the chair of academic board is a full-time executive officer and a member of the small executive management group, the other members of which are the vice-chancellor, two DVCs and one PVC. The board chair is also an ex-officio member of many council committees, including financial committees. It appeared that he 'self-limits' his role so as not to interfere with executive decisions. He assumes an observer/ neutral adviser status. In other institutions, some see a problem in the chair of academic board being part of senior management. One board chair comments that:

Sometimes decisions might need to be made that are contrary to the wishes of management and I think it would be difficult to be both a member of senior management and chair of a group that had a contrary view, especially in terms of the perceptions of members of Academic Board ... I personally think it is difficult to wear two hats at once and more importantly to be seen to be wearing clearly one hat or the other.

The identity of the chair can often determine the larger role of the board. At UTS, the appointment of a new chair in 1995 was associated with a change in the board's role. According to one participant, the academic board is 'becoming more proactive', engaging with and even initiating university debate on the development of 'responsive' policy, and the direction of the institution. During 1996 the board was involved in planning strategic directions, including UTS priorities in the face of government budget cuts. The result of discussion and debate across the university (including, crucially, at the academic board) was the identification of several key strengths that UTS will focus on up to the year 2000 including 'flexible learning'. However, the board is still criticised as 'filled up with busy work' with little time for 'rare passion'.

While its chair may sit on financial committees, the UNSW academic board has little role in formal budget decisions. However, it does comment on the previous year's budget. This is facilitated through the annual budget forum, an initiative of the UNSW senior management that is aimed at gaining feedback from academics.

They [the Academic Board] have nothing to do with resource allocation. That is clearly a function of the administration. They have no role in budget setting. What they do have is a budget forum, where they look at the current budget, not future budgets. They may make some recommendations. But you can't make budget decisions in a large group. The academic budget forum has a useful explanatory function: it's all on the table.

Both management and boards are casting round for ways to use a representative body in an advisory role, but such roles have limited scope in relation to resource allocation, and it is difficult to attract participation and legitimacy to bodies so far from the real action. The ultimately untenable separation of 'academic' policy and resource priorities is still the preferred solution of executive management.

Western Australia and Flinders

In a small number of cases something else is happening. Perhaps the most interesting change in systems of governance is the reshaping of a few boards as smaller – though still broadly representative – executive bodies, able to provide strong input into policy development, as well as curriculum development. In these cases the academic board is being reshaped as a positive presence, not to secure a resurgence of collegial decision-making but to better fit with the needs of executive managers interested in better feedback and consultation with academic staff. One vice-chancellor says that some people at his university still believe that the academic board should be 'the supreme governing entity', organising management itself. In this model 'the role of senior managers is to provide good papers for that body to ... inform its decision-making'. He has a different role in mind:

That is catapulting back to 1960s management style. What I see the Academic Board doing is providing additional input for consultation and policy advice [to those actually] ... implementing that policy.

The restructuring of the academic boards at Western Australia and at Flinders has led to a distinctive and new approach to the relationship between academic policy and institutional management. In both cases the boards have been restructured to form cohesive advisory bodies including deans/executive deans, ensuring a central place for the board in university policy development and strategic planning.

At UWA the 182 member academic board, largely a professorial board, used to meet monthly but now gathers only four times a year. An academic council, meeting monthly, functions as the executive arm of the academic board. It has 23 members with up to two additional co-opted members, and includes the deans, the senior executive managers, and student and staff representatives. It is chaired by the vice-chancellor. There are nine committees. The academic council provides advice on budgets and resource allocation to the university senate. It is the key committee at UWA, with a significant role in strategic planning, resource allocation and policy development. It seems to be the main engine of policy creation. Academic policy is still the province of the Academic Board, but decisions are made by the council on behalf of the board.

The Academic Board has always been all the professors and heads of department and whatnot, and it's still that, except that the Deans are on it ... It's there purely as an intercollegiate, interdepartmental, parliamentary-type thing for the Board to come and have a whinge if they want one: mostly they don't come any more ...

There used to be a standing subcommittee and a planning committee. We got rid of both of those and got an academic council which is the Deans and four people elected by the bodies, four by the Board ... It has the right of delegation from the Board, except that if anyone on the Board is unhappy about anything the Council has done, they can ask for a meeting before the Board.

The Academic Council is intended to straddle the functions of representation and of effective managerial decision-making, using a series of high level committees. However, most policy is *initiated* by the VC's advisory group – 'the Friday morning group' – the executive deans, the chair of the Academic Board and the PVC, DVC and VC.

At Flinders, the committee restructuring of 1995 replaced the Academic Board with the Academic Senate. The vice-chancellor (or nominee) chairs the Academic Senate, which has 58 members and meets monthly. It cross-consults with another major committee, the Resources Committee, on resource matters and the budget. There is no formal requirement for Academic Senate input into the budget process. However, the council has delegated to the Academic Senate the determination of principles for distribution of research funds, which is a resource distribution issue of major importance. Speaking prior to these changes, one senior executive explained them as follows:

We will have an Academic Senate which will deal with every aspect of policy concerned with the academic life of the University. There will be 12 professors and 12 academic staff, a number of general staff and ten students, and around 60 altogether. You need about that number and that sort of spread for it to be what it ought to be, which is a two way conduit. It tells the faculties what's happening in the University and it feeds back to the Senate stuff that the Senate ought to know about.

At both Flinders and UWA the changes are characterised by the central position of the reconstructed academic board in the executive-led decision-making. In both cases the new academic council or senate is chaired by the vice-chancellor or her/his nominee. In the case of Flinders, the vice-chancellor has the power to appoint up to five members of the Academic Senate. While Flinders' body is more than twice the size of the Academic Senate at UWA, the same principles of broad-based input into academic policy-making are in operation. The smaller UWA Senate enables more direct input into budget and resource allocation, while Flinders is pioneering notions of 'cross-consultation' between a major financial decision-making body, the Resource Committee, and the Academic Senate. Neither reconstruction attempts the widespread but problematic split between academic and resource responsibility. Both retain representation of the internal stakeholders: academic and administrative managers, academic and general staff, and students.

Reworking collegiality

Some academic boards have retained a traditional collegial character in the sense that through them certain academic leaders (as distinct from executive managers) retain an important role in institutional governance. Other boards have maintained their collegial character and broadly representative constituencies, but have been turned into consultative committees used by executive management. Policy initiatives are passed to the board for input prior to implementation. At still other institutions, the academic board is a formal structure utilised by executive management as an information channel within the university, a place to deliver updated visions of the future directions of the institution, a 'feedback loop', or with some styles of executive management, a bulletin board.

But you don't invite debate, you say 'This is on our agenda. I think it's essential for us to engage in this thing; it's going to take maybe two years and I'll keep you informed'. By and large I find academics will go along with that as long as you keep letting them know what's happening, where are we going, what are the difficulties ... they tend to accept that. Where they get cranky with you is that you just drop it on them all of a sudden and I think they're right. It's the whole way in which you introduce new ideas into an institution ... I would always put [those matters] under my report. I'd have ten or 12 items to tell them about.

In most institutions the role of the academic board as an advisory body has been partially supplanted by other decision-making bodies and communication strategies: maybe a broadly representative vice-chancellor's advisory group appointed by the VC; or ad hoc working groups that fulfil the need for consultation on specific matters as they arise. Often the academic boards become one advisory committee among the many utilised by management as part of its communication strategies. One VC argues that:

The big challenge in university ... is getting the right balance between collegiality in the positive sense and a stagnant spiral democracy.

Here the notion of collegiality is highly malleable. 'Collegiality in the positive sense' means a collegiality annexed to executive communication. Another VC:

Traditionally, collegiality in Australian universities, and I think in most western universities, has been essentially a negative force. It's been a very strong conservative engine in sub-cultures in which, if you can get one 'No' it's worth about one thousand 'Yes'. My view of that collegiality is it really is vital for the future of universities but we've got to somehow turn it into a positive force as well. Conservatism in universities has been one of the most important characteristics, it's helped them survive but they need to be creative as well ... the key to managing universities is to harness collegiality, to turn it into an agent for change.

In reworking collegiality, an artful management deploys external factors in its favour. Many saw the Dawkins mergers and other reforms as a process of strategic and financial centralisation. Against this background, the notion of collegiality as a democratic input into management can unite executives with their communities. This official 'collegiality'

– sometimes stretched to include consultation with external stakeholders – is translated into feedback, consultation, and in one vice-
chancellor's lexicon, 'guided collegiality':

I'm a great believer in guided collegiality. I think collegiality is just the synthesis
of the views of every individual who's prepared to speak.

This form of 'collegiality' negotiates 'consensual', 'consultative' and
'participatory' management. Another vice-chancellor saw the debates
about collegiality as exhibiting an inherent confusion between total
consensus management and consultative decision-making:

There is this problem about the confusion between formal consensus, collegial
... and decision-making involving consultation ... Always there will be a
substantial number of people who settle for nothing less than total consensus
government ... [if you have] some consensus in that situation ... you get a system
where most people are reasonably happy with the overall consultation process.

Note the shift between 'consensus' and 'consultation': the ambiguity
about whether it is the role of collegial interaction to provide a consensual agreement so as to achieve management decisions, or whether it
is enough for consultative mechanisms to be in place.
   While each university differs in the way these changes play out, executive management and many senior academics are sceptical of the role of
collegial decision-making. The twin pillars supporting such scepticism
are senior management's redefinition of 'collegial' to denote 'consultation', and the awareness by staff that the embodiment of collegial
decision-making – the academic board – no longer functions as a salient
source of institutional identity.

Networking downwards

Beyond collegiality

If boards and councils were once seen as bastions of 'collegiality', in the
Enterprise University the membership of the 'college' is transformed. In
many respects this is a transformation in the use of information, with
those at the centre seeking to communicate their plans and intentions
directly and informally to wider constituencies.
   In some places we found an invited group of people met regularly with
senior management, usually the VC, as a form of 'feedback' or a way in
which managers could keep in touch with certain sectors of the university
community. Large forums or mass meetings with lower level managers,
departmental or school heads, are now also common practice. University

communities are increasingly informed about executive decisions. In a few institutions executive managers actively encourage the participation of non-executive managers in executive decision-making, sometimes specifically including women.

There is an identifiable tendency for executive managers to create and recreate 'more effective' avenues of information dissemination and input into policy- and decision-making. Many of these initiatives are part of the personal management style of the new academic leader, most often a vice-chancellor, and serve as an initial (and often temporary) way of marking a difference in the functioning of an institution. In some institutions, what is important is having more representation from students, academic and general staff than is already provided. In others, the involvement of external representatives of business, industry and community is viewed as the crucial factor in 'good management'.

The search for appropriate internal structures is ongoing and relentless. From time to time, key questions are negotiated. Who has influence over resources? Who should influence, inform, or provide a check on management prerogative? What are the most appropriate forums? Should people be appointed or elected? These questions rarely stay on the agenda, but are resolved in local political strategies based on an executive reading of the terrain, so that no two universities are exactly alike in their internal workings. In each of these moments, the trend towards the marginalisation of academic boards (and some councils) is apparent.

It is partly to compensate for the 'thinning out' of the old representative role (boards) and character (councils) that management is developing new avenues of input. There is a significant overlap between the 'democratic' face of some communication strategies, and collegial notions of consultative or consensual decision-making. The new executive communication strategies negotiate a minefield of *realpolitik*: the need for those who work and study in universities to have an input, traditional notions of collegiality, and newer conceptions of the university as constituted by those with the greatest interest in its success.

We need a new committee!

One way in which executive managers invite participation is through *ad hoc* committees or groups focused on a specific area of work and deriving their membership from a selected cross-section of the university community. Sometimes this may signify a loss of faith in the capacity of more formal structures; at other times it is designed to bypass collegial systems. A vice-chancellor may set up a number of 'university' or vice-chancellor's committees to sit alongside already existing council and academic board committees. The University of Tasmania is one case in point, with parallel university, academic board and council committees. Temporary working groups with appointed members and specific functions are another way of getting the work done in a 'consultative' manner, a method of tapping expertise without creating or empowering a constituency. One DVC put it this way:

Tomorrow, the demands will be different and the structures will be in the way. The structures become more and more of an obstacle unless you have the [right] processes ...

We put groups together for specific purposes and I think that's very effective. It's essential to do things that way. For example, if you're building a building, you've got engineers, IT people, security ... They're always in different territories but if you are to produce the best buildings, they have to make joint decisions. There's one cable and everybody's using it.

Some institutions use existing committees to deal with new projects or demands: many are turning to *ad hoc* committees. Take the example of new buildings. Though most universities have committees that oversee capital expenditure, closely associated with the council, or kept close to the vice-chancellor, *ad hoc* working groups may be brought into being to oversee the implementation of specific capital expenditure. In response to the 1993–95 reviews by the Commonwealth Committee for Quality Assurance in Higher Education, many universities used working groups headed by senior academic managers to develop the institution's submissions and organise its system of internal quality assurance. In some cases a hand-picked group of trusted senior managers was used, because it enabled an informal and confidential style of operation. In other cases the quality reviews elicited a more public self-examination, and called up faculty-based representation.

These hand-picked groups of people perform a task limited by time or event, without leaving any residual formal committee structure in place. Involving the 'relevant people', in a blaze of internal publicity, working groups are a transparent consultative mechanism. There is the sense that constituent members of the university are participating directly in important management decisions. These managed informal processes, increasingly crucial to informed decision-making, are presented as 'collegial', but again the term is only partly appropriate:

What would be conventionally referred to as a collegiate approach is really a very important thing within an institution like this. I don't interpret it as meaning that decisions are all taken by consensus, but that people with an interest and insight into an issue ought to have an opportunity to engage in consultation and discussion. Where appropriate, I'm happy to be responsible for the decision if people feel that the whole process is transparent. They may not like it but they understand the reasons for which it was taken. (vice-chancellor)

Communicating power

Thus in the Enterprise University many advisory functions of council and academic boards and their committees are being displaced by new communication strategies; while formal bodies like the boards are used as a medium for more hierarchical information flow. Communication strategies become an important tool with a number of purposes: to keep management itself informed, to test the waters, to implement change, perhaps to lower resistance to otherwise problematic management moves.

It's not an entirely top-down situation. In a very large organisation, we've tried to put communication strategies in place. (DVC)

The University of NSW provides a strong example of the use of sophisticated information strategies to accompany formal decision-making. The deputy vice-chancellor (academic) meets with all the heads of school every two months, and the vice-chancellor holds a public meeting immediately prior to the meetings of Academic Board. There are also two to three other lunch-time meetings for all general and academic staff of the university. As noted there is an annual budget forum at which the previous year's budget is open to criticism from the university community. Though technically these meetings are outside formal decision-making processes, their timing is linked to formal meetings.

This mix of the formal and informal does not necessarily solve every management problem. The university has a clearly defined small executive, and a substantial number of deans (11), without super-faculties. Numerous administrative tasks have been devolved to smaller academic units, including departments. One problem facing executive managers, despite well-developed communication strategies, is 'silo management'.[5] This can occur when senior managers operate in different parts of a process. Stronger line responsibility, which is necessary for devolution, can obscure processes of university-wide importance. Communication strategies do not necessarily deal with this problem, as they may simply follow the lines of devolution.

An example of silo management problems is the organisation of enrolment. This involves a cross-section of administrators, and can require great input from staff of smaller academic units, departments and schools. Enrolment challenges the administrative and decision-making processes of any university, and it is one area where involving a cross-section of staff in policy and decision-making appears crucial. However, some managers are reluctant to expand committee structures to deal with it. As one UNSW executive put it:

Getting the performance of the functions across divisions to be as good as within our line management areas is something I don't know how to solve. You don't want to create additional committees and new structures ... because you become very inefficient.

Wanting decision-making to be understood by the university community can demand much of executive leaders. Many vice-chancellors embark on 'talk campaigns' within the institution as part of the communications necessary to effect organisational change, or simply as the management style required within a particular organisational culture. At one institution, consultative management is ingrained. The vice-chancellor reports that he sometimes feels that he is 'digging his grave with his teeth' in lunching and chatting with each group of deans and faculty representatives on a twice yearly basis. Each department has an advisory committee comprising representatives of industry and business: the VC also maintained contact with these groups on a twice yearly basis.

Apart from the formal interactions through academic board, the mixed committees and the VC's committees that I've set up, the whole informal thing is really important. As well as communicating, reinforcing a sense of community is very important for a place like this. We also do the same with student groups.

Some vice-chancellorial consultation and conversation is designed to prepare an institution for change, to get people on-side and let them know what to expect. In the Enterprise University 'communication' goes hand in hand with engineered consent.

Other VCs are involved in strategic planning processes comprehensive to their institutions. In universities that embrace strategic planning as a communication and consensus-building strategy, faculty plans are linked with overall university directions. Operational plans with specific targets become the basis for action in departments and schools. These are the styles we described in chapter 4 as the favoured repertoire of the rationalising executive. Both UTS and UNSW have adopted the strategic planning ethos and along with many others, invest serious time and money into the planning process. Conversely, there are universities where a VC or small senior management working group has written a vision statement which is simply another official publication on a shelf.

Clearly consultation is not the same as planning. But where strategic planning is successful, it not only constructs the objectives of the institution, it reconstructs the corporate purposes of the institution from within. Engaged in meetings and producing documents, those involved are part of a process of participatory management where a specific type of input is elicited. Often management consciously uses strategic planning-style initiatives to create a sense of community involvement in university directions. In the process, the constituent parts of the community are themselves reformulated, for example through the addition of external representation from industry and business.

Does this activity take place in academic boards? It does not, with the exception of the reconstructed boards that are now executive bodies (UWA, Flinders), or exceptional moments such as the allocation of budget cuts (UTS). Yet surely the representative constituency would have something to say about the direction of the university? After all, members of the board are often involved in implementing the outcomes of strategic planning activities, in new courses and the reformulation of disciplinary structures. But vice-chancellors prefer their own informal groups, never 'representative' in any formal sense, and always advisory. What can be the continuing relevance of flat collegial relations in the university when management constantly reinvests in temporary networks from above, these sounding-board advisory bodies and project-focused working groups?

I think that it's very difficult to articulate precisely because there's an interesting thing going on at the moment outside of the universities, the fashionable trend in management and communications and so on is to move more towards the learning organisation ... it's more like the collegial universities but, in fact, I think you'll find it's different because it isn't consensus management, it's a fairer sense of consultative interaction. (vice-chancellor)

But something is missing

The separation of 'management' activities such as budgeting and strategic planning from academic decision-making in faculty and academic board structures is not complete. As noted, there are institutions in which academic board members, sometimes the board itself, are integrally involved in certain strategic planning. More often than not, however, these activities are confined to one committee or are of limited duration.

For example, the Academic Board at UTS became involved in that institution's strategic response to changes in government policy, and this response had direct effects on the operating budget. At a time of fiscal crisis, the academic community was called on through the board to contribute to building a consensual response. Yet this was an exceptional moment, at UTS and in the system. The overall pattern is that of a growing divide between on one hand executive management, on the other traditional collegial policy-making, based on consensus among senior academics. The newer forms of consultative (rather than consensual/collegial) management – temporary forums, advisory groups, planning rounds, VCs' conversations – occupy this gap without filling it. Thus forms of consultation are very important to the Enterprise

University, and one of the keys to the transformations that it brings. The consensual decisions of the old academic boards legitimised academic networks within the framework of the international academic college, and protected the academic disciplines. The newer methods of communication and consultation are deployed to protect executive management and legitimate its decisions. They guarantee certain academic projects, but without ceding authority to the disciplines or to collegial bodies.

No doubt the new communication techniques are also motivated by the need for effective information flow, not to mention the legitimising appearance of same, as part of managing a community of intellectuals. They are also joined to processes of internal university image-making and 're-norming', in which management uses external pressures for change to secure acceptance of internal reforms. For example, strategic planning involving lower and middle level managers can be an effective way of using the intellectual power of the collective institution; it also enables the internal and external marketing of change. The plan might involve local units, and planning might fashion them as instruments of management, but the plan itself is never determined by them, except in its local operational details. Communication strategies in the Enterprise University are more interested in *how* things should be done than *what* should be done. The *what* is already embodied in the model of enterprise imported from abroad and managed from above. Consultation and information are crucial to the success of this new vision but thus far they have been circumscribed and defensive elements of the story of change.

Attempts by senior managers to stay in touch with the university community can enable more informed decisions at the top. However, there is little that those who are not themselves executive managers can do to influence the institutional agenda; and with the erosion of the importance of academic boards and the increased informality of managerial communication, there are fewer checks on the prerogatives of executive management. Communication strategies such as the DVC and VC meetings at UNSW are normally intended to inform others of decisions determined at the top and awaiting implementation.

The erosion of the power of academic boards and the limitations on the ambit of councils mean that the character of universities is now largely determined by executive management and key entrepreneurial individuals. This both limits and focuses the involvement of students, staff and managers at the level of deans and below. In the late 1990s what remained of collegial inputs were negotiated through remnant academic boards, the new communication and planning techniques, and far more informal networks of power. This power was conditional and was itself increasingly driven by fiscal imperatives and exercised its considerable discretion through new funding regimes and separate corporate structures.

While we found a degree of acceptance and compliance with these changes, managers and senior staff were rarely enthusiastic about the new structures. They were seen as inevitable rather than desirable. In the space between these two words lay an unspoken criticism: for all their nimble footwork and clever communication, reformers had yet to find a replacement for the power of collegial cultures to mobilise a more widely shared sense of collective identity or institutional purpose.

6   Economies of invention: Research power in the Enterprise University

Butterflies in formation

In 1995 we visited a Gumtree university of small-to-medium size with a good research reputation in delineated fields. The first interview was with the university's leading non-academic administrator. He talked fluently and at length about the strategic issues facing the institution, about its decision-making and financial systems, and the relations between its academic and administrative wings. This was straightforward enough. But when he began talking about research, the confident matter-of-fact tone gave way to a more distancing voice. There was a kind of diffidence, in a tone of respect, as if the world of research with its various secrets was a world that he as a manager could never completely grasp. Yet there was frustration, too. How could all that creative energy be harnessed so as to maximise the university's position? The problem – as he unselfconsciously and unforgettably put it – was 'to make the butterflies fly in formation'.

The ideal of formation flight captures the dilemmas of the management of research, from a certain, obvious perspective, dilemmas which management imposes on itself in the struggle for institutional advantage.[1] In a competitive higher education system, research (among other things) is a means of defining value and manufacturing symbols of excellence. It is a primary source of institutional prestige and income: in its most prosaic form, research is the pre-eminent 'numbers game' in the Enterprise University. Research management's objective is to succeed in that numbers game. By externalising a university's research it can be imagined as a single quantifiable system. Managers can count it, control it and give it shape. Despite the contemporary scepticism in government about 'picking winners', every funding agency and every research manager does this to an increasing extent. In the more objective systems of the Enterprise University it is achieved not through personal grace and favour, but by the systematic filtration of projects through a central university research plan and set of performance indicators.

Research is hallowed by university mission statements and in the policies and plans of research-as-management. The universal commitment to 'innovation' promises a generous shelter. Yet the offer can be deceptive. Here 'innovation' in science and scholarship is placed under the authority of 'innovation' in funding formulae, incentive systems and the devolution of decisions. Yes, the Enterprise University is committed to creativity, but *its* great discoveries are made in creative re-engineering of the organisational kind. There is no end to the creative organisational moves to be made, for everyone knows that research always falls short of what might be achieved. There is always room to do better, always scope for smarter management and for stronger performance pressures.

One source of this imagined unfilled potential lies in the mystery of research, its shadow-life beyond the scrutiny of managers. A focus on applied and commercial research generates the best income indicators, while competitive academic grants are guaranteed to warm the heart of any PVC (Research). However, research that leads to the best institutional performance according to conventional indicators may not be research that researchers want to do. They might prefer not the research with obvious social utilities, or the research most likely to win grants, but the most fundamental of all basic research: research that is driven by curiosity and discovery. And in the older universities, where such traditions have their strongest hold, it is hard for managers to breach disciplinary fortifications. The drivers of basic research, that desire to critique, to extend, to transform, to reconstruct, to leap-into-the-dark, can scarcely be modelled. It is clear that basic research can be of dubious economic potential, especially in its early years. Yet to complicate matters significantly, basic research breakthroughs can be associated with spin-offs for commercial research. How can all of this be factored into research plans and development strategies?

One strategic option is to follow in the slipstream of researcher-led innovation, using management systems to add value and protect intellectual property. But for the performance-driven research manager, the doubt remains. Can the university take the risk of leaving research to the researchers? Will this not lead to wasted income and missed opportunities? It seems to them far safer to use carrots and sticks and operating rules to prod research in predefined directions. In the older universities more latitude is given: the management of risk imposes unequal burdens upon our different institutional and intellectual traditions. Yet even in the older universities, research management is becoming more comprehensive and more indicator driven.

If independent academic research constitutes another world to that of the Enterprise University, and maintenance of the flow of its mysterious benefits depends on respect for its uniqueness, then it is also an 'other' that the managed university is constantly tempted to transform into something more like itself.

Programmed research

Our task was to find out how research matters were dealt with at the level of institutional governance. It seems that regardless of their private commitments, the primary task of research managers is *not* to encourage research and scholarship as ends in themselves. Nor is it particularly to encourage practices based on imagination, criticism, or other scholarly values. The bottom-line is the research prestige of the university and its contribution to the financial balance sheet. In one Sandstone university medical department, a professor noted that he was under pressure to apply for external grants, but the university showed less interest in what the research actually achieved. Others have similar stories. Research managers who strive to maximise the number of major research projects on the university's books are not always so concerned about their content. If this means that academic effort shifts from theoretical, critical or unfashionable subjects to applied, useful and bureaucratically popular topics, such managers may neither notice nor complain.

Despite the specificities of research, with its many voices, its heterogeneous disciplines and networks, research management is caught up in the same imperatives that are shaping the Enterprise University elsewhere. Universities need new control structures and decision-making systems in order to render resources more flexible, and to respond effectively to the external imperatives of government and industry. In these systems and structures the very distinction between 'outside' and 'inside' starts to collapse, unleashing the power of homogenisation. Repeatedly we found that the Commonwealth systems of research financing are among the most compelling of what all universities call the 'external drivers' of institutional standing, performance and resource levels.

As research management sees it, traditions which have long sustained research are not so much a medium for production as a limit to be overcome. Discipline-based research functions on the basis of academic independence, peer review, and merit-based allocations until the budget is gone. Just as collegial traditions are seen as obstacles to the new kind of executive leadership, traditional practices are seen as obstacles to the desired deployment of resources, potential and performance in research. The favoured mediums are supra-disciplinary schools or inter-disciplinary centres, rather than departments with their more robust identities and traditions. The autonomous researcher is not abolished, but is placed in a different setting. This has implications for the kind of work that is done.

Increasingly, university research is programmed, managed from somewhere in the medium distance by sophisticated systems in which control (like the devil) is in the detail. The calibration of research work is changed, so that time is measured in annual university plans, despite the different scholarly calendars. The university is remade towards a singular tradition of a more corporate kind. In this framework the traditional academic disciplines, with their self-organising and republican traditions, define themselves as problematic.

Research as a money economy

The Australian experiment

In the Enterprise University research is the main link between the academic and corporate programs of institutions. Different objectives and forms of esteem have been subtly inter-mixed. Measured research performance combines the intellectual and corporate product. In their survey of universities in the United States, Australia, Britain and Canada, Slaughter and Leslie remark that universities are both prestige maximisers and profit maximisers.[2] Monetary income is one but not the only source of their prestige. High academic standing is an end in itself, while at the same time status breeds income: high academic standing attracts research funding and draws commercial research clients. A rough balance between economic and academic practices is maintained. This picture holds up well for research in the US and perhaps in Canada. We believe that in the decade since Slaughter and Leslie completed their research in Australia, the Australian case has evolved significantly.

System-level changes plus changes in institutional management have re-ordered and re-normed research. This has been made possible by a system of research governance that by international standards is highly centralised. In the Australian 'experiment', research management at every level has been modelled as a competitive economy, with dollar values ascribed to both inputs and the outputs. The Commonwealth research quantum, the corresponding institutional measures of performance, the creation of comprehensive research management in each institution and the sharpening of competition in research: all have entrenched the economic definition of research activity. Crucially, the means to research (funding) has become both the measure of its value, and the end to be sought. As leader-managers see it, academic standing and institutional prestige in research have been 'economised'. Academics do not always see it that way, but they are dependent on funds and their control over the rules of research organisation has diminished.

In relation to Slaughter and Leslie's twin institutional objectives of prestige and profit, in the organisation of research in Australian universities, the balance is moving towards the profit side. This has been achieved by defining research performance (and in a sense research activity) itself in income terms, so that much of the time, prestige and profit meet. Fifteen years ago nearly all financial support for research was implicit, being contained within the general operating grants provided to institutions by the Commonwealth for their use. Almost all core funding for research is now allocated on the basis of measured performance. In world terms, Australia's commitment to performance-based research support, with performance measured in economic terms, is more 'advanced' than most. In 1996 only five other OECD countries (plus a couple of American states) made extensive use of performance-based funding: Germany, Netherlands, Sweden, Denmark and the UK. In the USA, as in Australia, rankings based on research monies (nearly all of which are effectively competitive) have considerable clout. On the other hand, the UK research assessment is ultimately based not on quantity of research grants but on qualitative assessments of performance.[3]

Nevertheless, the creation of a research economy is one logical extension of trends in neo-liberal government which are shaping national programs everywhere. This suggests that Australia's experiment in research governance might have lessons for other countries.

A new renaissance?

The tales that the different Australian universities tell about themselves in annual reports, quality prospectuses and marketing campaigns make it plain how important measured research performance has become. They not only demonstrate that research is central to university image projection; they underline the point that in the Australian system success in research has become openly equated with success in obtaining *money* for research. Prestige is derived from performance. Performance is measured in dollar terms.

Amusingly, despite the objectivity of this measure it seems it is open to conflicting interpretation. Each older university reworks the comparative data on research funding so as to demonstrate its superiority over all of the others. Each new university compels the reader with the picture of its carefully drawn upward trajectory. If a university's work is good it is made out to be better, the nation's best, internationally competitive. If it is not so good, all is not lost. A little research can nevertheless be used to illustrate a lot of brochures. 'Innovation' is expressed as marketing.

A cross-section of university documents from the mid-1990s illustrates the point. UNSW focuses on total Australian Research Council (ARC) large grants and on ARC collaborative grants with industry, where in both cases it leads the nation. It complains because the Commonwealth research quantum does not include commercial income, where again it is number one. On the other hand the University of Melbourne adds to its ARC income its National Health and Medical Research Council (NHMRC) grant income, where *it* is number one, to demonstrate overall national superiority in competitive grants supporting academic research. The smaller universities cannot compete in terms of aggregate grant income, so sensibly they rely on per capita measures. At different times Western Australia and Adelaide have been first in national competitive grant funds per head. Adelaide finds itself number one in ARC large grants per member of the research and teaching staff, provided that performance in medicine is excluded. In 1995 Adelaide published a newspaper advertisement with a battery of selected research data, ranking itself first in South Australia on all criteria. On some measures it placed the University of South Australia, less than a decade old, ahead of rival Flinders. Yet when size is taken into account Flinders could point out that it was second in the land in NHMRC funding. Queensland rests its claim upon its Cooperative Research Centres (CRCs) with industry. James Cook and Tasmania looked best when CRC funding per staff member is calculated. And so on.

Compounding the claims, research is flourishing everywhere. Each university is doing better and better. Mere budget cuts cannot dampen this spirit of inquiry, this remarkable renaiassance. Research is a growth economy without growth in funding. Or so it seems.

The funding system

University leaders have a strong incentive to treat research in economic terms. In 1997 direct Commonwealth research funding was almost $1 billion, with over $600 million from ARC and DEETYA in targeted programs and the research quantum of operating grants, $153 million for the Australian National University (ANU) Institute of Advanced Studies, and about $200 million from other government portfolios, including over $80 million in NHMRC grants (table 6.1). Then there is commercial research. In 1995 'other research grants and contracts' totalled $290 million (almost 4 per cent) of institutional incomes.[4]

When all research dollars are included, in 1995 Australian universities received over $1.3 billion for research purposes. Research sustained almost 20 per cent of total income.

The research quantum

The research quantum of operating grants was negotiated between the Commonwealth government and the Australian Vice-Chancellors' Committee. The quantum was notionally designed to provide infrastructural support for existing research. However, institutions were never required

Table 6.1 Commonwealth university research funding via DEETYA, 1997*

Nature of funding	$ million	Per cent
Research quantum of operating grants	222.0	35.6
Research infrastructure (block grant)	85.2	13.7
Research infrastructure (equipment, facilities)	19.3	3.1
ARC grants	126.0	20.2
Centres, collaborative grants	44.5	7.1
Assistance to research students	83.3	13.4
Research fellowships (ARC fellows etc.)	43.2	6.9
Total	623.5	100.0

*In addition institutions receive research funding under the NHMRC program ($80.2 million in 1996), approximately $120 million more from other Commonwealth portfolios (1997), and $153 million for the ANU Institute of Advanced Studies (1997).
Sources: DEETYA; Williams; Gallagher.[5]

to allocate it to specific projects and from the beginning it functioned as a performance-driven supplement to each university's Commonwealth operating funds. When the quantum began in 1990 the sole measure was each institution's success in obtaining nationally competitive research grants. In 1995 industry and public-sector grants were added and the quantum was further broadened to include publications and higher degree completions, though the dominant element remained that of grant income.[6] In the circular economic logic of the quantum formula, grants begat grants. This was decisive. It created the incentive to focus on money income *rather than* the research activity which the quantum was meant to represent and augment. Exchange value subsumed use value, price became purpose.

Under the quantum arrangement, the Commonwealth makes available a constant proportion of total operating grants – in 1997 4.9 per cent – for distribution between institutions on the basis of their measured research 'activity'. It calculates the quantity of each institution's research activity by using a standard formula, and then distributes each institution's share of the quantum on the basis of proportion of total research activity as so measured. In 1997 the research quantum allocated to individual universities varied from less than 1 per cent to over 10 per cent of their operating funds.[7]

In the all-important formula for the quantum index (table 6.2), the largest single element (82.5 per cent in 1997) is the income from nationally competitive research grants. These include ARC, NHMRC and other recognised national schemes. ARC large grants are scarce

Table 6.2 Components of the Commonwealth research quantum, 1997

Item	Description	Per cent
Research income	Academically competitive grants – ARC, NHMRC and other recognised programs, but not commercial research (calculated by the National Competitive Grants Index (NCGI))	82.5
Publications	Books, book chapters, journal articles, other publications (using a weighted index)	12.5
Higher degree research completions	Number of graduating research students	5.0
Total		100.0

Source: DETYA.

(about 20 per cent of applications succeed), but have strong flow-through effects, affecting three-quarters of other competitive grants, and the allocation of postgraduate awards, as well as directly feeding into the quantum.[8] The other elements in the quantum index are research publications (12.5 per cent) and research higher degree completions (5.0 per cent).

As well as a source of supplementary funds in a resource-poor environment, the quantum soon became seen as the primary measure of the research standing of institutions. Naturally they began to focus on activities which generated the most quantum. Its financial bottom-line provided a simple, convincing distinction between successful and unsuccessful research. In one sense this made research management easier, though in most universities it became harder to do really well. Success in research was now defined as success in the standard competitive schemes that generated quantum, and to a much lesser extent success in producing the relevant publications. Over the years the publications count has been reduced to four standard types (academic books, some book chapters, and refereed journal articles and conference papers), further constraining the definition of high-value research.

Meanwhile other changes instigated by the Commonwealth entrenched the influence of the funding system on research activity. In 1989–91 part of each institution's operating grant for research was redistributed to the ARC, and in the years following, university's remaining operating funds were squeezed more and more tightly. University research activity not tied to a specific allocation of funds diminished. The centralised funding distributed by the government, whether through the quantum, or project and centre programs, now constitutes a majority of all designated research activity.

In turn this has made limited life *projects* into the dominant mode of research activity, rather than open-ended long-term research programs. The project format enables research to become a tradeable commodity: research in a money economy is research that happens in recognisable episodes capable of calculation and sale, like pieces of software. Projects require precise objectives that can be forecast and limited in advance, lending research to utilitarian purposes, including the structured competition for funding support ('Do the things that are most likely to earn us money to do things which earn us ...' etc.).

That the effects of this circular governmental structuring of research are profound was attested by every research manager that we spoke to during the study. Similarly, when Meek and Wood interviewed middle and senior managers in universities they found that 93 per cent mentioned the ARC and 84 per cent the government itself as influential in university research policies. Anderson and Johnson compared university autonomy in 20 countries and found that in Australia the extent of government influence over research and publication was 'notably higher' than average.[9]

The research enterprise

The creation of the performance economy in research has been accompanied by the development of a culture of economic enterprise. This parallels the transformation of research culture in the USA, as Slaughter and Leslie note (see chapter 3). Deliberately fostered by government in the Dawkins years and after, and by the universities themselves, shaped by the programs for industry–university collaboration, and continually reinforced by the economics of research, this culture is one of the keys to the Enterprise University.

In the new lexicon, academic freedom shades into market economic freedom. The Australian research centre heads reported by Slaughter and Leslie talk about 'freedom' from the stifling traditions of the discipline, and the dead hand of university bureaucracy, but the fruits of this liberation are rarely expressed as those of a richer intellectual life. These are freedoms to sign contracts, sell discoveries and retain the income earned, freedom to trade. Likewise, the collegial competition for research prestige is reconfigured as an economic competition between individuals, and between universities as corporations.

'Competition' has one set of meanings when it regulates the sharing of academic status within a collegial system grounded in public funding. It has another set of meanings when researchers are directly struggling with each other for basic support or industry contracts. Yet the language and practices of competition provide apparent continuity with academic tradition as well as a *post hoc* justification for economic reform. Competition is one of the primary techniques of management, whereby universities organise researchers in the same manner that the government controls universities – ranging them against each other, installing scarcity in the form of under-funding and 'soft money', determining outcomes by specifying the object of contest and the rules of the game. Competition is seen as both a given, an inevitable part of the environment, and a desired state to be actively promoted. The Commonwealth's 1995 Hoare Report on university management stated that

Universities ... must balance the traditional benefits of collaboration and collegiality with an environment of increasing competition for domestic and overseas students, staff, research funds, industry support and status.[10]

Consider the many meanings of 'competitive' and 'competition' in this extract from the UNSW *Corporate Plan 1994–99*:

University of NSW operates in a highly competitive local, national and international market for higher education. We have responded positively to changes in government policy on higher education that have opened up the competition for funding, to the broadening array of higher education options and the public's awareness of them, to the growing demand for quality and to an increasingly international environment. Planning is directed towards achieving and maintaining a competitive edge in the intense competition for high performing students, high quality staff, scarce funds and eminent standing.[11]

Competition is the global environment, competition is the method of resource allocation, competition is the signifier of excellence. The meanings shade into each other. Above all, competition is scarcity. 'Concentration and selectivity have been the driving principles of research funding in Australia' stated the official responsible for government higher education programs in 1997.[12] The discourse of selectivity and concentration draws authority from its resonance with older notions of academic excellence to underpin the management of a structured competition for research support and funding. Research rarely turns an economic profit, or even becomes self-sufficient, but 'selectivity', 'concentration' and 'competition' invest research management with an air of allocative efficiency.

The more intensive the struggle for funds, the better the research – or so it seems. In orthodox research management it is taken for granted that a more intensive competition is *automatically* associated with higher academic quality. In the Darwinian logic of the times, more competitive, more scarce and selective, leads to 'fitter' and more worthy of survival, hence 'better'. The Griffith Research Management Plan emphasises that 'the University has a policy of pursuing research excellence through competitive funding mechanisms which emphasise the quality of the project'.[13] Flinders boasts that its internal research grants have been allocated competitively since 1967. We saw plenty of evidence that competition was becoming tougher and spreading to every corner of research. A sense of improved quality – of more and better discoveries, of more original and more penetrating insights – was not so obvious. What was clear was that the privileging of competition as a tool of resource allocation augments research *quantity* and sustains the drive to greater measured performance at every level. It also powers a focus on short-term returns rather than long-term development,[14] a tendency to ever shorter project times, and a disincentive to share project findings or even to collaborate on projects. 'My research' becomes 'my property'.

In the Enterprise University few incentives are provided to encourage collaboration with other researchers (with the single exception of researchers located in industry), while incentives to competition are overwhelmingly present. The collaborative side of research is left to sustain itself. We saw only one clear exception. The University of Technology, Sydney (UTS) has made collaboration with selected partners into a core aspect of its research management strategy.[15]

Economy 'outside-in'

The UTS example underlines the point that while the external pressures in research are plainly inevitable and ubiquitous, institutions (and researchers) can choose to respond to those pressures in more than one way. They can work against the trend to competition by collaborating, though this is less easy, less 'natural': it requires determination and a strong sense of identity. Nevertheless, most institutions that we visited had chosen a more conventional path, focusing on the maximisation of their share of the research quantum at each other's expense (table 6.3). They had translated this imperative into a particular set of utilitarian research behaviours that were surprisingly similar in every university. Much as government had constructed the national research system, so they had built the research system of 'their' institution. Government centralisation called up an equivalent politics of the local centre.

In each university the will to manage research is expressed in a new regulation of previously existing activities, and the spread of performance-oriented research activities and research management to new areas of work and new personnel. Managers use their own versions of funding formulae, competitive bidding and publication counts to shape

Table 6.3 Distribution of Commonwealth research quantum between universities, 1999

Sandstones	$m	Gumtrees	$m	Unitechs	$m
ANU*	n.a.	Newcastle	6.155	Curtin	4.186
Melbourne	26.424	Flinders	5.757	Queensland UT	3.863
Queensland	23.533	Wollongong	5.717	South Australia	3.550
Sydney	20.939	Macquarie	5.651	RMIT	3.231
Western Australia	14.518	La Trobe	5.143	UTS	2.575
Adelaide	13.219	Griffith	4.224		
Tasmania	4.885	New England	3.689	*New Universities*	
		James Cook	3.415	Western Sydney	2.041
Redbricks		Murdoch	3.136	Canberra	1.268
NSW	21.900	Deakin	1.575	Swinburne	1.221
Monash	16.235			Northern Territory	1.169
				VUT	1.163
				Edith Cowan	1.016
				Charles Sturt	0.848
				Southern Cross	0.787
				Central Queensland	0.689
				Southern Queensland	0.570
				Ballarat	0.272
				ACU	0.147

*n.a. means not applicable. The Australian National University (ANU) includes the Institute of Advanced Studies, whose academics were then (1999) ineligible for large grant ARC funding and reckoned as outside nationally competitive grants and the quantum for funding purposes. The faculties at ANU, exclusive of the Institute of Advanced Studies, generated research quantum of $6.447 in 1999.
Source: O'Kane.[16]

research in the faculties, departments, schools and centres. Often, heads of departments or schools do the same further down. The notion is entrenched that better research performance depends on administered incentives and 'shocks'.

This internal research economy has been structured by two main imperatives or 'historic movements': first, the extension of potential research activity throughout each university by universalising a 'research culture'; second, the installation of quantum-type funding distributions, which reward the successful performers by granting them more opportunities to perform, while securing their compliance in the new standardised systems.

Generalising a 'research culture'

Everywhere we found the same relentless pressure to raise ever more research monies and conduct ever more research. Sometimes it is expressed as creating opportunities, at other times as demanding product: the objective is always to generalise a 'research culture', the behaviours deemed appropriate to research, in order to increase quantum and funding.

Only in regard to gender is research management openly committed to dealing with the question of who participates in research. Policies on women and research are couched in terms of opportunity. Management is benevolent – there is valuable human capital here, waiting to be utilised – but it leaves the causes of gender inequality unexamined.

Per capita measured research output is higher among men than women. Because women are concentrated in junior academic positions, where teaching loads are higher vis-à-vis research, there is less access to study leave and research-related infrastructure, as Sheehan and Welch found.[17] In the face of this larger problem, universities provide small scale programs and/or earmarked resources to encourage women. At Central Queensland and at UNSW there is a network of women researchers with official support. At UNSW, funding from the 1993 Commonwealth Quality Assurance grants was used for a women's research development officer. The Women in Research Committee was established in 1994, holding seminars and forums: its work was noted with approval by several women interviewed. Griffith University awards a women's postgraduate research scholarship.[18]

Research culture takes different meanings in different universities. In institutions where research activity is already widespread, the task is to push it into more productive lines. In some universities the task is to create research from almost nothing. Management in those universities, and management definitions of research, exercise more direct control over research culture because management is the engine of research from the start.

At the time we visited some New Universities the forward march of managed research had far to go. At Southern Cross total 1994 income from ARC large and small grants was $278 600,[19] 2 per cent of the level of UNSW. Universities like Southern Cross aim 'to develop world-class research and postgraduate training in a limited number of niche areas',[20] and emphasise applied research which they hope will have commercial potential. Infrastructure is thin. The university does not have a full library and Commonwealth funding is less than when the Gumtrees were new. Southern Cross hopes that in future on-line resources will fill the gap. Meanwhile it is servicing its research students through what it calls the 'Cuckoo' system.

What we did was approach the University of Queensland library and say, 'can we just stick someone in your library to photocopy journal articles for us?' And they said 'so long as it doesn't affect us in any way'. So we installed our own telephone line and fax lines. The way it works is that if you want an article you just bung it through to the library. They fax it through to the Cuckoo who photocopies your article. It's sent by overnight courier and delivered to your desk next morning. 99.7 per cent of requests are satisfied within three days. We can just sit back. (senior executive, Southern Cross)

Central Queensland's management is focused on the creation of research centres with the potential for collaborative local links and private income. Five per cent of the operating budget is set aside for the research centres. CQU began with 'two or three' centres, rising to seven. It also supports partly performance-based funding to reinforce the infrastructure of the centres. Across-the-board research support has been abolished.[21] At the same time research activity outside the centres is still permitted. In a New University research prioritisation is hard to police. Anything that helps to build research capacity is seen as useful, whether or not there are immediate returns, for there is always the hope that new researchers and/or new strengths might emerge. Often a blind eye is turned to private consultancy activities, so as not to frighten away researchers with track records (though such blind eyes are also found in established universities as well).

Track records can be imported. Also at Central Queensland:

We didn't have a lot of people with research qualifications. So we chose to bring in key people ... to provide research leadership and initiative.

It is a kind of botanical propagation model. Established researchers and research programs are appointed from older universities with the hope that they can be grafted onto the new stock, boosting the research harvest (though sometimes rendering havoc with the reproductive habits of local flora). Often these imported researchers are shocked on arrival by the absence of basic resources they previously took for granted – computers, Internet access, international conference support. Their requests for minimum research infrastructure are seen as a claim for special privileges. Yet it is difficult to sustain a personal research program while mentoring staff and students with an inadequate research training, and simultaneously building teaching and administration. In the worst cases, management loses patience with what appears to be slower than expected results; the extra support promised on arrival starts to dissolve, and friction develops.

Older research institutions also focus on generating and spreading an income-generating research culture. At Griffith and Deakin, and parts of Tasmania, academic staff have been provided with financial incentives to prepare funding submissions, such as $1000 for each bona fide ARC large grant application at Griffith in 1994. Reportedly this doubled both the number of applications and the number successful, and spread the skills of submission preparation. But even while generalising research, these universities, like New Universities, want to concentrate resources in predetermined priority areas.

Strikingly, even at the strong research universities research culture is continually being extended and reinvented for even the best can do better (table 6.4). Not only can the quantity of research activity/funding be increased, every change in funding schemes must be matched by changes in local research management. For its size Flinders was always successful at raising ARC and NHMRC funds, but when the Cooperative Research Centres (CRCs) became a principal source, the university suddenly discovered a new zealousness about collaboration with industry. UNSW is by any measure a successful research university, yet its research management plan also talks about 'fostering a research culture'. While three-quarters of academic staff are actively engaged in research, UNSW would like to push the level closer to 90 per cent, the level in some American universities. School and faculty administrators whose 'benchmarked performance' falls below that of their disciplinary competitors at other Australian universities are expected to improve their performance indicators by 10 per cent per annum.[22] This focus on comparative performance statistics provides the new definition of 'meaning' in research, with the symbolic moving ahead of the substantive: we have the sense that a medical scientist who discovers the cure for cancer might expect a citation from the DVC research which reads: 'Congratulations on beating Melbourne and raising more funds than Queensland!'

At the same time, even UNSW and other universities with across-the-board strengths feel impelled to concentrate on targeted areas. The research leader-manager at one of the smaller Sandstone universities states that:

Comprehensiveness is being balanced by the fact that we're a medium sized university in the Australian context, that we can't do everything and that if we really want to succeed we're going to emphasise areas of research concentration.

Queensland's *research management plan* identifies ten areas of outstanding research strength and 34 areas requiring special support.[23] Here policies of concentration/ selectivity, and generalisation/ quantity, are pushing against each other.

In stronger universities the strategy of targeting is partly a matter of image-making and the creation of a sense of purpose. Grouping projects into 'areas of excellence' may have no immediate impact at all upon the way the work proceeds, but it is a signal to DETYA, to industry and to the academics inside the university that senior management will look

148   The Enterprise University

Table 6.4 Research quantum as a proportion of operating grants (1997) and research earnings per staff member (1995), Australian universities

	Research quantum per operating grant (1997)			Total research earnings per equivalent full-time staff (1995)		
	Research quantum ($m)	Operating grant ($m)	Quantum as share (%)	Research income ($m)	FTE staff	Income per head ($)
Western Australia	14.125	122.420	11.54	44.568	893	49 908
Adelaide	14.139	129.285	10.94	45.587	861	52 946
Melbourne	28.243	271.301	10.41	83.087	2190	37 940
UNSW	21.915	226.641	9.67	61.326	1652	37 122
Queensland	21.460	251.347	8.54	70.104	1731	40 499
Sydney	22.331	191.456	7.66	59.274	2090	28 361
Flinders	6.027	84.377	7.14	17.357	667	26 022
Monash	17.575	265.039	6.63	50.263	2214	22 702
Macquarie	5.686	99.921	5.69	17.403	726	23 971
New England	4.202	79.265	5.30	8.366	517	16 182
Tasmania	5.432	102.929	5.28	13.528	738	18 331
James Cook	3.782	76.782	4.93	9.253	575	16 092
Wollongong	4.052	85.067	4.76	10.335	556	18 587
Newcastle	5.949	132.044	4.51	19.556	793	24 660
Murdoch	2.893	64.446	4.49	7.748	406	19 084
La Trobe	5.438	156.021	3.49	12.731	1171	10 872
Curtin UT	4.331	133.077	3.26	10.421	925	11 266
ANU*	6.476	208.398	3.10	19.519	1261	15 479
Northern Territory	0.865	31.845	2.72	2.801	202	13 865
Griffith	3.843	145.800	2.64	11.314	835	13 549
RMIT	3.982	153.010	2.60	11.497	1069	10 755
Canberra	1.288	51.446	2.50	3.221	335	9 614
South Australia	3.003	144.140	2.08	11.012	1033	10 660
Queensland UT	3.600	191.368	1.88	9.212	944	9 758
Swinburne	1.026	56.597	1.81	2.169	374	5 799
UTS	2.368	134.365	1.76	5.616	732	7 672
VUT	1.270	97.525	1.30	3.707	605	6 127
Central Queensland	0.598	58.303	1.03	9.212	944	9 758
Southern Queensland	0.615	62.469	0.98	1.631	360	4 529
Deakin	1.294	133.610	0.97	2.759	844	3 269
Western Sydney	1.665	178.647	0.93	3.999	874	4 575
Charles Sturt	0.806	92.011	0.88	1.938	514	3 770
Southern Cross	0.384	47.104	0.82	0.766	231	3 317
Edith Cowan	0.797	98.953	0.81	1.936	655	2 956
Ballarat	0.195	30.564	0.64	0.667	218	3 060
ACU	n.a.	n.a.	n.a.	n.a.	n.a.	n.a.

*See note to table 6.3.
Source: O'Kane, 'Financing of research', p. 10.

favourably upon further proposals in the defined areas. Does this image-making alter the patterns of research activity? The testimony of our interviewees suggests that it does, and the more so in the smaller and newer universities.

Local funding systems

Each university has established a formula-based system of distribution from the centre to faculties/schools. Like the Commonwealth quantum, the local funding formula is normally grounded in measures of research income, research training and research output. When building their formula most universities start from the Commonwealth quantum, which provides a defensible technique: a case of 'Do unto others as DETYA has done unto you.' When institution-distributed funding is subject to formula and competition, as with Commonwealth funding, outcomes are difficult to contest. Formula funding also forces each academic unit to report on its measurable research activity, using homogenising descriptors that are controlled by management. Most importantly, it installs in the academic units a direct economic incentive to generate more quantum monies. It completes the recreation of research as a performance-based economy.

While the case studies were being conducted a number of universities were in the throes of changing their internal formula so as to distribute Commonwealth quantum monies (and sometimes additional operating funds) back to the faculties/schools/centres according to the contribution of each unit. At Queensland 15 per cent of operating funds were distributed in this manner; at Flinders 10 per cent. Sometimes the exact quantum formula is used for internal distributions, sometimes a modified local version that changes the balance between different measures of research activity in the Commonwealth index, or introduces new elements in distribution such as targeted support for new researchers. Such variations inevitably have implications for the distribution of funding between faculties, and developing the local formula can be a highly political matter.

Griffith and Newcastle routinely distributed Commonwealth quantum monies back to the faculties. At Queensland the full quantum allocation was phased in over 1995–97, and at NSW over 1996–98. In 1992 Monash introduced a simplified quantum distribution to faculties with 55 per cent for external research grants and 45 per cent for publications, broadly defined, a formula which strengthened the arts, law and business faculties relative to the science-based faculties. Later Monash shifted to a 70 per cent grants-based formula. Central Queensland distributed half the Commonwealth quantum to the faculties on the basis of 40 per cent for publications, 40 per cent for higher degree study and 20 per cent for external grants. The other half was kept for university research grants (50 per cent), research awards (30 per cent) and the PVC (Research)'s fund (10 per cent). The research leader at Deakin pointed to Curtin University of Technology where the quantum funding was being distributed not just to the academic unit but to the individual. This was seen as the ultimate performance driver, the horizon to be reached.[24]

Many research managers are enthusiastic, even evangelical about their own success in completing the circle of economic incentives:

A very clear signal has been sent out to the faculties and I think there has been quite a response in the academic community. They see that funding is determined by performance and high performance is actually rewarded by funding flowing in that direction.

Having established central performance-based research funding, research managers typically move to establish this at the faculty/school level, and perhaps the departmental level. Faculties/schools, departments and research centres are also encouraged to become more proactive in creating projects and developing clients, so as to behave almost like entrepreneurial local firms within a large and diversified conglomerate. In some cases research management in the faculties/schools is reformed by decree, in other cases – mostly in older universities – persuasion must suffice. But tradition can be stubborn. This is the challenge facing one research manager:

My biggest disappointment in this position is that I haven't been able to get the schools to take a bigger role in driving research themselves. As long as we drive it centrally, which we do quite hard, it won't be as effective as if it's coming from a lower level.

In many universities performance-based distributions have not been implemented within all faculties. The mix of Commonwealth quantum, local modifications and different faculty/school arrangements can produce a complex system subject to piecemeal accommodations and traditions, and the ebbs and flows of university politics, scarcely an outcome drawn from the management textbook. But the major change has already occurred. One scientist states that:

What's become important is not the generation of ideas, but the accumulation of research funds ... The University makes much more fuss of Professor [name] getting one million dollars a year from [a pharmaceutical company] than someone else being elected to the Academy of Science.

What ought to be prized are the people who travel vast distances on the smell of an oily rag. The people that are prized are the people who get large amounts of money and blow it away in expensive programs that may well be quite unproductive.

The quantity of research funding, its method of allocation, its terms and conditions, have become dominant over research content. It is very different to the old collegial culture. Yet does it work, and what is the price? It is true that invention is not performed by butterflies with instinctive flutter, but nor is it fully encompassed by the model of research as an economic production. The paradox of organising research in systematic fashion is that its requirements remain diverse, and understood best by the researchers themselves.

Creating compliance

Devolution and integration

All institutional research managers set out to integrate research in the academic units (faculties/schools/centres/departments) into the overall research management strategy, while suppressing and 'cooling-out' potential collegial–managerial conflicts. Between different universities there is considerable variation in the systems and techniques of research management. Local history, personalities and the balance between disciplines can all be influential. Universities differ in the functions of manager-leaders, in the role given to central research committees, in the manner in which academic units are 'hooked in' to the centre, in the funding system, and in the precise formulae used.

The configuration of these elements also varies. The different inter-university variations do not in themselves carry the seeds of success and failure (though they provide some insight into individual institutions). There is almost as much variation between strong research universities as there is among lesser performers. Strong research universities are divided from the weaker not on the basis of the committee structure or funding formula, but other factors, such as history, position and accumulated resources. Only one solid generalisation about research organisation and research success is possible: universities which do *not* have a coherent ordering of research, in terms of the orthodox notions of managed research, are unlikely to perform well against indicators such as the quantum that are grounded in orthodox notions. This evident circularity is both a guarantee of standardisation, and a phenomenon which again suggests how dependent institutions have become on their external drivers, and how pliable in following their dictates.

We found one such case at the University of Newcastle in the first year of our study. A relatively strong research university in the past because of its engineering, science and medicine faculties, Newcastle had been slow to modernise its research organisation in orthodox terms. In 1995 there were only two CRCs and the only new ARC large grants were in

engineering and science. The head of one of the best research departments in the university noted that he and others had tended to under-
estimate the importance of the CRC program.[25] Commercial research
was developing only slowly. Some faculties had low levels of research
activity. One dean stated that his staff had no need to make submissions
for funding because the faculty was in surplus due to retirements. Neither
the faculties nor the centre was consistently propelling research performance. Though research managers at the centre were accountable for
overall performance, they lacked mechanisms to drive up the number
of grant applications and projects: that is, responsibility for research
performance was centralised but its determinants were voluntary and
decentralised. (In successfully reformed systems elsewhere, the axis is
reversed: responsibility for outcomes is decentralised, while performance
is driven remorselessly from the centre.) Newcastle faced a mutually
reinforcing downward slide in staff morale and research performance.

This was not the only institution where research management had yet
to achieve the closure it desired. At Sydney, one dean complained:

> There's an awful gap between the rhetoric and the reality. Look at our research
> management plan. It says that all parts of the University will be engaged in high
> quality research scholarship befitting that discipline. Lovely, fine words but after
> those words have been uttered that's the end of it.

Again, at Deakin one dean referred to 'lack of purpose, lack of focus'.
The university had not made up its mind whether the deans or the
central research committee were to carry the main responsibility for
research performance. It had moved 'backwards and forwards' between
a devolved model and a totally centralised model.

No university manages research by explicit direction from above. This
would constitute a frontal attack on the collegial tradition, directly challenging the integrity of the disciplines. In reconfiguring the academic
units as units of a performance economy, the most delicate aspect is
structuring the relationship between the element of centralisation, and
that of devolution/autonomy. Devolution locates the academic units as
the locus of research performance, and the immediate practical decisions
about research activity, including some decisions about new initiatives.
Unit managers often have more financial autonomy than under the collegial tradition, but within tighter constraints. They are autonomous, but
not independent, being tethered to management by the centrally determined systems of priority setting, output measurement, funding and
infrastructure support, which install a pattern of values and incentives
and delineate the boundaries of legitimate research activity.

All universities have at least one research committee composed of members drawn from the academic units, where centralisation/devolution

tensions are played out. On these committees the drive for management control informed by 'feedback' from below meets the autonomy of local units, with vestiges of collegiality. Research committees exhibit a characteristic role dilemma between representing the academic units and implementing a common research policy across the whole institution. The way out is often to restrict such committees to a limited advisory function. Representative structures rarely shape overall patterns, but often provide managers with a potential sounding-board and early warning system. Senior executives frequently describe participatory arrangements as an important part of the quality control cycle, rather than an expression of diversity and pluralism. Some universities also have looser intermediate arrangements, whereby central managers create 'representative' committees drawn from the academic units but in reality controlled from or colonised from the centre. Such groupings can be used to constrain the independence of decentralised managers. They also help to sustain a polite collegial fiction of universities structured from bottom up, and research governed by the real researchers.

At Griffith the research committee is comprised of associate deans (research) from each faculty who are expected to function as agents of the DVC (research) and the research management strategy. At Newcastle the research committee includes faculty representatives who are mostly not the people chairing faculty research committees. The faculties have a line into the central committee but the expression of faculty interest is diluted. At UTS there is a 'strategically focused' research committee of seven chaired by the PVC (research), and a faculty-based advisory group which operates as sounding-board for the PVC and the smaller research committee.

Overall we identified four models of devolution and integration, though in practice many universities combine elements of more than one model. We characterise these four models as:

• people in meetings;
• bosses in offices;
• dollars in projects;
• goals in plans.

First, there is research organisation led by committee decision-making ('people in meetings'). The authority of such committees is fading, as manager-leaders and funding formulae become more powerful, but all universities have at least one research committee and in older universities their role can be very significant, with at least some discretionary funds. One variant of this model has a strong element of decentralised authority in the faculties. This is the older kind of devolution, still clearly marked by collegiality, with strong disciplinary focus, greater

departmental independence, and weak central 'drivers'. Research organisation at Sydney and Monash exhibits some of these features. In future
this model is likely to come under increasing pressure.

Second, there is research organisation led by line managers ('bosses in
offices'), where the research manager-leader is responsible for research
administration and budget and often commands significant discretionary
funds. At the University of NSW the integration of research activities is
secured through line management by the DVC (research and international) and further down, the faculty deans and their common membership of the Vice-Chancellor's Advisory Council. Within the centrally
controlled budget the deans and faculty research management committees enjoy substantial delegated authority. Within the faculties, 67 schools
and 15 non-school departments have budgetary status. Research grant
applications are processed by research management committees at each
level. Although one UNSW leader-manager notes that there is 'no
indicator in the world we would feel happy with', there is increasing
emphasis on performance measurement and the use of targets to drive
measured improvements. The university's Research Management Committee advises the DVC on policy and funding and distributes some
resources, but it is operating within the terms of a classically corporate
system.

Third, there is research organisation led more by performance
measures, funding formulae and budgets ('dollars in projects'), rather
than people or meetings. This enables management to employ 'steering'
less directly than in the corporate model, and thus concede a greater level
of autonomy. There is less pressure on manager-leaders, less manager
stake in the ongoing research programs, less politicking over resource
distribution, and more scope for local entrepreneurship. By the same
token, it is harder for managers to intervene so as to subsidise new
researchers or provide substantial seed-money for promising projects –
though easier to secure a credible identification of poor performance.
This form of devolution appears closer to collegiality, though appear-
ances can be deceptive: management by formulae and budget is as sure a
way of deconstructing the disciplines as intervention by line managers,
and one often harder to resist. Older universities such as Queensland and
WA use elements of this model, often mixed with elements of the first
and second. If there is an overall trend, it is towards a hybrid of models
two and three.

Fourth, there is research organisation facilitated by cultural change,
through the vehicle of the institution's official research strategy ('goals in
plans'). One strand in the management literature emphasises leadership
as a process of cultural change. This has entered notions of leadership in
many universities. In research management the University of Technology,

Sydney is an example of this approach. While UTS uses funding formulae and committee structures, the main emphasis is on securing the
changes in attitudes and behaviour necessary to achieve strategic
objectives such as more industry funding and involvement, inter-
disciplinary, and collaboration with potential research partners. Griffith is
another university where the research management plan is as a cultural
instrument.

Research office and research company

The main elements in the internal administration of research are the
research office, the research leader-manager, in many universities the
central research committee, and the company that manages at least some
commercial contracts, consultancy and intellectual property matters.
Most universities have also developed specific commercial companies for
handling particular projects. Certain university research centres are constituted as companies, such as the joint industry–CSIRO–university
funded CRCs.

The research office provides information about funding sources, helps
academic staff to prepare submissions for funding, is a clearance point
for contracts and cheques, and sometimes handles commercial matters as well. It is the interface between researchers and the ARC, the
NHMRC and other major research programs. In some universities it also
structures devolution. Queensland is divided into six super-faculty
groups under their own PVC. Each group is serviced by a specific officer
who is responsible for co-ordinating research relations with external
funding bodies and who acts as secretary to each of the group research
committees. Crucially, these officers are employed by the research office
and their desks are located there.

The research office is a vital hub in the performance-driven university.
Everywhere it tends to grow, despite the leanness of the times. Research
office personnel are often very good at what they do. They continuously
educate staff in the skills needed to work the funding systems. In older
universities they broaden options and rescue submissions. In newer
universities they are apostles for the formation and spread of a research
culture.

If the money is around, we should be getting our snout in there with applications.
The research office does a good job there. They're not perfect, obviously, but
they're very professional.

The research office office routinely adds value to submissions for
funding, reworking them with care to fit formal and informal bidding

criteria which change every year. In large part the competition for research funds is a competition between the technical know-how of research offices.

> Except for the top few per cent of proposals 'grantmanship' is the thing that carries the day. We all know it, we're not proud of it and it's not the way you'd like the system to be, but the first rule of grantmanship is that you play it like it is.

In some New Universities resources are too thin to provide services such as massaging and polishing applications for ARC funding. It is an unmistakable sign that the research role is a lower priority than in other universities.

We found varied relationships between the administration of research grants and projects, and the administration of postgraduate studies. Often the two are combined in one office, led by the same senior academic and subject to a committee or a common brace of committees. At Queensland the designated leader is the PVC (research and postgraduate studies). Sometimes research administration is brought into conjunction with other areas such as international education or quality assurance. At UNSW and Griffith University the same leader exercises responsibility for both research and international initiatives. At Newcastle the leadership position is designated as PVC (research and information technology).

All universities distribute specific monies of their own for research purposes. Typically, these include project grants for those just missing out on ARC, NHMRC or other competitive grants; smaller seeding grants, especially for new researchers; and incentive schemes designed to achieve particular strategic objectives, such as enhanced collaboration with industry, or regional programs. Institutions also allocate internal postgraduate scholarships additional to Commonwealth postgraduate awards, and funds for research infrastructure and equipment. Sometimes research offices and/or committees and/or research leaders make detailed allocations themselves, at other times they distribute sums of money to faculties/schools/departments where the allocations are determined.

The role of university research companies varies. The late 1980s/early 1990s trend to central managing of all commercial dealings seems to have halted. Though regulation of commercial activities is becoming more comprehensive, centre-based and faculty-based companies are expanding vis-à-vis the central research company. Some academics avoid the university company because it taxes income and can create delays.

During a number of the case studies we identified day-to-day tensions between the research office and the university research company. At Tasmania the two sides operated without reference to each other. This created ambiguities in the case of the many projects which are commercial in character but fall short of full cost recovery. At UTS, the research PVC was trying to overcome a stand-off between the research office and the company Insearch. At Queensland the relationship between the two was more constructive. The Office of Research and Postgraduate Studies is housed in the same building as UniQuest, the commercial arm, opposite the Michy Laboratories and other commercial research tenants. A 'clearinghouse' committee located between UniQuest and the Office of Research consists of the PVC (research), one person from the University Research Committee, the executive director of UniQuest and the director of research and postgraduate studies. It handles decisions relating to major projects, contracts, intellectual property and areas of potential conflict. Unlike some New Universities, Queensland stresses both commercial and non-commercial research and uses the one to feed into the other. Having explored the potential for commercial research more than most, the university is aware of the limits. Commercial research is 'a lemon with bitter sweet juice'.

There's not a lot of money around in Australia, and there aren't many companies that are prepared to invest in research. I think that universities will end up carving out niche areas for themselves. We have particular strength in relation to the mining and minerals industry and ... computer science.

UNSW also emphasises both commercial and non-commercial research. It was the first Australian university to create a commercial arm (Unisearch, 1960) and sees itself as the leader in commercialisation. It has strong links with Australia's largest mining-manufacturing company, BHP, which spends about $3 million a year at UNSW.

University of NSW traditionally has been an academic university with close ties to industry and commerce. That's probably our greatest strength ... We're much closer to the US than to the UK model.

UNSW is one of the few universities to make significant money from patents: since 1991, 40 inventions have generated funding. Unisearch handles all applications.[26] The number of patents lodged by Unisearch increased from 12 in 1991 to 20 in 1994, and in that time the university obtained $5.32 million from commercialisation. Successes included the membrane technology that led to Memtec Limited (a company valued at $200 million in 1995), and the thin film photovoltaic cell which Pacific Power had agreed to develop with $45 million in invested funds. In addition, in 1994 there were 1159 consulting projects carried out by 583 individuals, leading to $8.5 million in consulting work.[27]

The approach at the University of WA is different. It has no commercial arm of its own, though it makes selective use of Technology Innovation Management (TIM) which is owned by the state's four public universities. The research office handles most contracts and intellectual property matters itself. The university sometimes claims ownership of patentable discoveries, and sometimes allows the academic originators to do so. In contrast to UNSW, the university prefers not to finance the full costs of patents itself but to include the cost of worldwide patenting in licensing agreements with private companies. This brings the originators of commercialisable discoveries into closer contact with their industry partners. UWA encourages private consultancy work but expects academics to place their teaching and research on a higher priority. UWA creates the impression that classical academic values are in command, yet it is very successful in both commercial and non-commercial research. It is intriguing to see that in this less overtly managed institution, the flagship areas of research are the projects in science, medicine and engineering with industry relevance, as at UNSW. A number of areas of research strength are linked to the state's resource industries, including oil and gas engineering for off-shore platforms; mineral processing; earth sciences; agriculture and land conservation; and zoological neuroscience, using native fauna.

Research leaders

There is also considerable variation in the role adopted by key managers and university leaders that cover or intersect with research organisation (table 6.5). Sometimes the DVC or PVC research is the line manager in charge of research administration as at James Cook, Griffith and UNSW. At UNSW the DVC (research and international) manages the Research Office, the Office of Postgraduate Studies, the company Unisearch, the International Office, the Institute of Languages and the Asia–Australia Institute, and the many research centres. He deals with deans who themselves are chosen for both managerial and academic qualities. As another senior leader remarks:

We're not policy people, we're actually managers as well. That's a strength of this university.

Other cases are different. At Newcastle the DVC is the main policy adviser on research and chairs the research committee, but does not control the office. At UWA the PVC (Research) advises on policy and monitors its implementation, but research and postgraduate studies administrators report to the assistant registrar (research administration)

Table 6.5 Research leaders in the sample group of universities

University and date	Position	Held by
Queensland 27 June 1995	Acting PVC (Research and Postgraduate Studies)	David Siddle
Griffith 3 July 1995	DVC (Research)	Roger Holmes
James Cook 29 Aug. 1995	DVC (Research)	Peter Arlett
Central Queensland 1 Sept. 1995*	PVC (Research)	John Coll
Newcastle 23 Oct. 1995	PVC (Research and Information Technology)	Ron MacDonald
Southern Cross 27 Oct. 1995	Dean of Graduate Studies	Peter Bavenstock
Flinders 3 Nov. 1995	PVC (Research)	Michael Skinner
Adelaide 1 Nov. 1995	DVC (Research)	Mary O'Kane
UWA 13. Nov. 1995	PVC (Research)	Michael Barber
Edith Cowan 16 Nov. 1995	Director, Office of Research and Development	Sybe Jongeling
Tasmania 28 Nov. 1995	PVC (Research)	Pip Hamilton
UNSW 7 June 1996	DVC (Research and International)	Chris Fell
Deakin 23 July 1996	PVC (Research)	Kerin O'Dea
UTS 11 Dec. 1996	PVC (Research)	Lesley Johnson

*Not interviewed. The interviews on research matters were carried out with Janelle Coe, research services officer.

who is responsible to the registrar, not the PVC. In relation to intellectual property, the PVC (research) chairs the committee but the executive officer is a legal contracts person reporting to UWA's legal officer. This system depends on 'effective dialogue' between the PVC, the dean of graduate studies (also in policy not management) and the administrators.

At most universities the DVC/PVC directly controls some discretionary resources. At James Cook we found a DVC (research) that enjoyed an extensive power to choose projects to support, as at James Cook, though this was an extreme case and the size of the funding bucket under DVC/PVC control – as distinct from research committee, research office or academic unit control – varies greatly. The picture is further complicated by the many vice-chancellors who deploy innovation funds under their own personal control.

Even where the DVC/PVC research exercises no line management authority and little resource power, the position can still be influential. The DVC or PVC research is usually a member of the executive group meeting regularly with the vice-chancellor, and her/his role on the research committee provides another line of authority. And in the last decade the DVC/PVC research position has often proved to be the stepping stone to a vice-chancellorship, something already achieved by two of the people listed in table 6.3.

In some New Universities, there is no research leader-manager and certain of the functions are exercised by a middle level general staff person under a generalist DVC or PVC. In the present environment this kind of structure looks increasingly unsatisfactory. People in junior research 'leadership' positions report heavy workloads rendered more problematic by weak executive authority. The use of junior positions signifies a lack of commitment to research performance, and renders it more difficult to generate a research culture. In the performance and marketing logic of the times, the more senior the position the greater the symbolic commitment to research. In this context, the pressure for the upward escalation of titles is universal, whatever the institution.

Another method of giving status to the research portfolio is to appoint a leading researcher as DVC or PVC. Such a tactic has diminishing returns (unless research leaders are turned over quickly) because very few research leaders can maintain an active research career while holding the leadership position. It is very difficult to combine a genuine involvement in continuing research with 60–70 hours or more of management work each week, including a heavy schedule of meetings.

At UTS, Lesley Johnson has negotiated an appointment as 75 per cent PVC and 25 per cent researcher in the Faculty of Humanities and Social Sciences. The PVCs at Flinders and CQU maintain some research. The DVC (research) at Adelaide still visits her workbench. Nonetheless, few research leaders take up research and teaching positions when their executive appointments end. An exception is Deakin's Kerin O'Dea, who at the time of interview had just announced her intention to return to her research chair.

Research centres

There are many research centres, many kinds of research centre, and no apparent limit on the functions which can be located in these structures. In terms of size, legal and financial framework, commercial role and academic boundaries (inter-disciplinary or discipline-based) the research centre is so eclectic that it is difficult to generalise. Centres range from big budget Commonwealth-subsidised key centres, special research centres and CRCs with postgraduate teaching, research and development, often creating saleable intellectual property; to small self-declared units consisting of a couple of people and a title on a door. Some centres are corporate entities enjoying part-separation from their universities.

Others have some autonomy in relation to the faculty/school/department structures, creating potential conflicts over resources and power. Others, perhaps the majority, fall within departmental organisation but are distinctively identified.

Nevertheless, most centres have one element in common: they are the product of government intervention or university direction in the organisation of research. Research centres have proven to be a flexible and malleable policy mechanism. Centres are a useful medium for discipline-based groups that might want to do something different, especially across the conventional boundaries. They are also a means of securing greater top-down control over research activities by breaking down normal departmental structures, often by breaking down the conventional character of the academic disciplines themselves. This is especially likely to happen when managed and (temporarily) financed centres *replace* rather than supplement the on-going research activity of discipline-defined teacher-researchers. Centres embody in a concentrated form the processes of restructuring evident in the larger university environment. They tend to be smaller than the traditional organisational structures, they are more likely to involve contract and casual employment, they operate in a new 'soft money' economy, and their more flexible structure is often achieved at the price of more fragile and hierarchical systems of co-ordination.

Governments use the selection and funding of research centres to increase control over universities' research priorities, the more so because centres with core government funding tend also to draw down extra resources from the universities concerned. Universities' own creation of centres serves similar purposes. University managers are rarely able to intervene directly in the normal research activities of faculties and departments (though here the use of the school rather than the department as the unit of organisation offers more potential scope for managers). Certainly, university managers have less authority here than do corporate managers in most other organisations. But by concentrating resources in selected areas termed 'centres' they can directly shape research priorities and sponsor favoured individuals. As with government-instigated centres, university centres tend to draw further resources over time from the soft money economy, in a snowballing effect, not only from commercial sources but from endowments, scholarships or developmental funds available inside the institution.

Centre-building is underpinned by assumptions about the benefits of selectivity, concentration and inter-disciplinarity, notions of a 'knowledge economy' based in industry–higher-education networks, and the belief that centres are inherently more responsive to outside agents and market forces than are traditional structures. These assumptions have become joined together in a 'commonsense' understanding of the need for centres. Like all commonsense, the assumptions are little reflected upon, and never seem to be tested by research-based investigation. Yet these assumptions are questionable. There *are* important examples of university–industry centres and commercially applied inter-disciplinary work. The question is whether a research system can be premised on these examples.

Mostly industry is slow to network with universities except for immediate and limited purposes: industry involvement in centres often stops at conversations at the centre board. Nor is it clear that a multi-discipline approach is always superior. Managers report a 'gut feeling' that traditional discipline-based academic structures are less flexible and responsive, especially in generating applications with commercial potential. It is widely believed that collaboration between people in different fields is *ipso facto* more likely to lead to useful applications. Often the argument is supported by examples from bio-medicine or artificial intelligence. But there is no reason to suppose that what holds for some fields necessarily holds for all fields for all time. Further, the long-term capacity to create inter-disciplinary synergies depends on the continuing identity and health of the disciplines themselves.

Well grounded or not, whole research strategies have been premised on the commonsense understanding of research centres. At Griffith researchers are organised in generic fields. At Deakin cross-disciplinary groups that pool resources to form a centre receive a 10 per cent bonus. Again, the underlying metaphor is 'entrepreneurship', defined as flexibility and a willingness to embrace external agendas.

When a centre is created it is usually expected to attract outside funding. Normally it is specified, by both government and university management, that the core funding of a new centre is temporary and it is expected to become self-sustaining. Time and time again, these hopes are disappointed. On the whole, the research centres with the best prospects of long-term survival are those able to attract a significant level of postgraduate student load. Research on its own does not earn enough money. Even centres producing saleable intellectual property and significant consultancy work are rarely able to finance all their salaries and overheads from these sources. At Central Queensland:

The initial idea with centres was that they would generate more funding. People plucked a figure from the air, they said five years would be a reasonable time in which to expect the centres to achieve self funding. We've got one centre now that's currently up for its five year review and it's obvious that it's not going to achieve self-funding. So we've looked at our policies and agreed that this five year performance review will really be a question of redesignation as a university research centre which receives preferential funding from our university research budget.

No doubt one reason for the great growth of centres is that the centre form more closely approximates the paradigmatic modern corporate organisation, that of the business firm. There is a taken-for-grantedness that research autonomy and creativity is best furthered by quasi-independent units of a business kind, even though the drivers of the two forms of innovation are often different. Not surprisingly, the premise holds better in commercial research – where the ultimate test of value is the market – than other research.

There is much variation in the manner in which centres are organised, underlying the ambiguity of the concept, its role as a quick fix for almost any research objective. Again, there is the paradox that an organisational form established to facilitate concentration and specialisation has proliferated in universal fashion.

At QUT centres are the means of both generating research activity and policing its boundaries. Academics may conduct research projects outside the academic areas covered by these centres, but they will receive no research funding from the university to do this. We were told that postgraduate students wanting to research outside the centres might even be denied enrolment. At Griffith, which has a longer and larger research history, centres take a different role. Built on existing research and teaching units or combinations of them, and receiving a small additional subsidy, they are 'the first point of contact for clients in the community', a primary means of fostering commercial and applied research. They are 'supported by a small allocation from the host faculty, and by major external grants and commission earnings'. Griffith's *research management plan* promised to increase the number of 'centres and units' from 44 to 55 by the year 2000, no doubt on the assumption that more centres signifies more outside research income and fee-for-service activity.[28]

At the opposite extreme are universities where the aims of management are fulfilled by closing down centres rather than opening them up. In some universities hundreds of centres have emerged, mostly of the local departmental kind.

We had a proliferation of research centres and they weren't really getting us very far.

Centres have been springing up all over the place. I call them little mushrooms instead of the trees we actually need. People are fairly domestic in their thinking about their research. They don't think about the national and international context and how competitive they need to be, and the need to concentrate resources ... Given the ever-increasingly small amounts of money we have to dedicate to research we have to very seriously educate our staff to think in a strategic manner ... to think about working with other staff, other universities, to be multi-disciplinary, all those sorts of things.

This spring-cleaning is more than routine, and it needs to be talked about. It signifies focus, efficiency and managerial hard-headedness.

UNSW also makes a virtue out of this necessity. In 1994–95 six centres were disestablished.[29]

The common element in both centre building and centre deconstruction is the deliberate re-engineering and re-allocation of research. Many of the centres that were disestablished were the outcome of past management attempts to pick winners. These choices had demonstrably failed to achieve the promised self-sufficient centres. But because of the utility of centres as tools for intervention (and the redistribution of resources away from normal departments), the characteristic management optimism about the centre form is maintained. Disestablishment becomes a virtue as popular as establishment: it suggests 'survival of the fittest', 'moving with the times', even 'transparency'. Whether it also represents failure of vision or effort, the waste of resources and the distortion of optimal research priorities, is rarely if ever questioned.

Discipline without disciplines

Researcher identities

In reinventing research as a system of money, measures, targets and comparisons, amid a competitive economy and an enterprise culture, research management sets out to change the way that researchers think about research, and how they see themselves as researchers. The research system is both very different and just the same. Certainly research continues as the work of autonomous individuals; and the changes in research organisation can only become effective when those changes are in a certain respect self-managed and self-imposed. In an era of self-regulating systems,[30] deceptively consistent with the old collegial principle of academic freedom, researchers must themselves reconcile the differing imperatives of knowledge creation and wealth creation.

In the Enterprise University academic freedom has survived, but it is also transformed. It is now subjected to standardised management systems and also (with the encouragement of management) to commercial market forces. Sometimes there is a direct clash between academic tradition, and bureaucratic requirements or commercial values: for example, when the publication of PhD theses completed on location in industry is restricted for commercial reasons. But the imperative to improve research performance and raise more funds can hardly be avoided. Such conflicts must be side-stepped rather than solved.

What has made the change to researcher identity possible is its implementation as a 'naturalised' system of economic incentives and indicators, which enables both management control *and* a measure of self-governance. As long as management can represent itself as a provider of material incentives, rather than a political power, it appears as a modernising force that is difficult to question or resist. Performance improvement shades into self-improvement, management shades into self-management. Control and devolution become two sides of the same coin. One vice-chancellor says:

The thing I value most is a sense of continuous improvement, a sense of starting each day and saying 'yesterday was fine, but is there something that we need to start looking at today?' I'd like to see that devolved and internalised ... to have this as part of the culture.

This creates a double-bind for researchers. To defy the new effectiveness of research management is to risk falling outside the research system altogether. Yet to acknowledge the dominance of management is to deny the intellectual independence of research.[31]

A complex process of institutional accommodation and self-accommodation takes place. Targets, financial sanctions and incentives steer researchers in strategic directions and away from long-term personal programs. For many, research in areas of third or fourth choice might still be attractive, especially if winning a grant is linked to internal promotion systems. The obligation to raise funding can hardly be avoided. As one scientist puts it:

People like myself who are working in areas which, by and large, don't need funding are being told that it's our duty to the University to seek ARC large grants. I'm applying for ARC large grants, but I won't be displeased if I don't get them because an ARC grant will hurl me into one line of research rather than others that might be more interesting. It's seen as your collective duty to the university because the National Competitive Grant Funding is not just an indicator of success, it's actually one of the factors that determines how much funding the university gets and how much funding goes to Science. So it's your duty to your science colleagues to get a grant even if you don't particularly want the money.

Other researchers also reported that they were under pressure to apply for grants outside their main areas of interest and expertise. One remarked that policies of forming larger groups of researchers to secure 'critical mass' could force people into 'collaborations that they may not appreciate' at the price of more fruitful lines of inquiry.

Intensification

In the Enterprise University the definition of what it means to be an effective scholar has been made more complex. Different roles appear, shifting and fluctuating even within a single individual's work program: self-employed entrepreneur, corporate research worker, public servant, disinterested scholar, and all the fine shading between. Within this diversity of roles there are powerful currents and a definite line of development. With the spread of commercial projects and intellectual property arrangements challenging free publication and exchange as key priorities, there is a shift in the balance, towards quantitative performance targets, money goals and market economic behaviour.[32]

In an economy of material incentives, the quantitative expansion of research is derived by intensifying the work of the researchers. Researchers also spend more effort in chasing funds and satisfying clients. They generate an increasing proportion of research funds themselves. All of this cuts into the space–time for curiosity-driven inquiry.

The University of Technology, Sydney was the only one in our sample that was working on measures to expand the research capacity of academics that were premised on the need to reduce (rather than increase) environmental pressures. According to the PVC (research), UTS tries to apply 'a humane ethical culture' to research management. Though it is 'driving ahead fairly ruthlessly and trying to adapt to the current situation', it wants to hold onto 'things which are very important in a university'. One of these is the need to ensure adequate time for research, including teaching relief. Internal grants include a 'time-release' scheme to enable researchers to complete major research programs. The research management plan calls on faculties to identify 'time-saving mechanisms', such as 'strengthening administrative support' and 'reducing committee meetings'. It is also suggested that faculties alternate 'heavy' and 'light' teaching semesters, and create research-only days for those staff who are active researchers.[33] The PVC states:

I feel some nervousness about this because I think all staff should do teaching and research. But because of the incredible pressures on people now we're going to have to look at people concentrating on particular things.

Most other research managers are sanguine about the pressures on academic researchers. For them budgets, performance measures, shortened time horizons and systematic insecurity are a fact of life, for themselves as manager-leaders and for others. Their objective is not to modify or reduce the pressure on academics, but to intensify that pressure and to channel it more effectively into research priorities and outcomes.

To the extent that the remaking of university research is successful, research is being transformed from collegial practices that are self-determined and other-financed, to practices that are increasingly self-financed and other-determined. In this context success can be as big a problem as failure. The most successful researchers report an ever-greater dependence on outside agencies, an ever-greater reliance on business skills rather than research knowledge, and the demand to ever-expand their aggregate 'performance' while mentoring and organising the work of less productive colleagues.

Homogenisation

In older universities, especially the Sandstone and Redbrick arts and science departments, residual disciplinary research cultures remain strong, though punctuated by newer practices at different points. Researchers live a double life. They perform for the performance indicators and research plan, and they perform for their peers. Their discipline-based traditions are sanctioned by worldwide scholarly networks rather than government policies or managers. These traditions are characterised by loosely defined work programs, relations of power and status that are conservative and often opaque, and the free exchange of published research findings. The specific cultures of each discipline are distinct.

In 1992 the Monash University Academic Board prepared a report on research dominated by these older, pluralistic disciplinary interests. The report argued that every discipline had different kinds of research outcomes and funding requirements. Common administrative systems would negate these differences. 'Managing' academic research from outside the disciplines was a contradiction in terms:

Research administration should *not* be designed to manage, to control or to direct the research efforts of the staff who are employed, wholly or partly, to do research in the university. On the contrary, the role of research administration should be to provide the environment in which those research efforts can flourish ... We specifically reject any model of research administration that places a research 'manager' in a position of authority over those charged with the responsibility of carrying out research. Such management models are not seen as appropriate to the climate of free intellectual inquiry that characterises a great university.[34]

However, much has changed in a few years. Even in Sandstone and Redbrick universities these perspectives now have little force at the level of executive power and institutional strategy. Research *is* managed according to the singular systems and requirements of institutions, rather than the many and various requirements of disciplines.

Inevitably, the homogenising techniques used to measure and fund research collide with the specificities. In tabulating research income and output in a manner consistent across different fields – for example in the calculation of the quantum and its variants – the formulae use arbitrary weightings (such as the proportion allocated to research income as opposed to publications) that more closely approximate the priorities of some research fields than others. Over time, those academic areas closest to the norms of the measures experience an increase in their share of total research resources. For example there is more potential for commercial research in some fields than others. Formulae that reward commercial income with additional grants from university sources tend to produce a shift of resources in favour of areas with commercial potential.[35] At worst, research systems create perverse incentives that weaken core areas of inquiry and scholarship. This was remarked on by several interviewees – though such issues were rarely acknowledged by research managers, who have vested interests in avoiding any line of argument which might open the way to troublesome claims for an internal redistribution of resources.

The use of grant income as the main measure of research activity fits with medicine, engineering and the applied sciences. It is less appropriate for the humanities, theoretical sciences and some social sciences, education and law. In those disciplines, publications are a more useful summary of activity. The main resource needed is not research assistants or equipment, so much as researcher time. (If ARC grants were used to pay researchers' salaries they would constitute a better measure of research activity in these disciplines.)

In addition, different disciplines vary in their publication practices. In science-based disciplines the major breakthroughs are published in journal articles and refereed conference papers. Books are of lesser importance, mostly taking the form of textbooks summarising the already known. While academics working in the humanities and the social sciences also publish textbooks, in these fields books are also a medium for original and path-breaking work. In some disciplines conference papers are habitually fully refereed, in others not. The research quantum includes only the former. The balance between number and quality of publications also varies. In some disciplines the norm is to publish a relatively large number of papers, in others a smaller number of high quality papers. The former disciplines benefit more from quantitative measures of output.

A striking example of the conflict between research norms and discipline specificity is law. The main manner in which academics in law create legal knowledge is through the preparation of legal case books. These books do not fit the conventional definition of a research project. They require scholarship more than fieldwork, and depend largely on researcher time. Academics in law are under pressure to raise ARC money and thereby boost departmental income, directly and through the quantum formula. It is easier for a law academic to gain an ARC grant for a sociological or historical project about law – that is, a project outside academic legal knowledge itself – than to gain an ARC grant for preparing a major case book.[36] Thus orthodox research management might actually reduce legal knowledge.

Law is a strong discipline within Australian universities, and its academics might find compensations. A group with weightier difficulties is those working in the visual and plastic arts. Here the processes of reflection on the field, teaching–reflective synergy, and work at the cutting edge, take place not in laboratory research or even in scholarship, so much as in the production of works. And if the humanities can be difficult to fit into science-oriented definitions of research, it is near impossible to include works of art.

We interviewed one deputy director in a school of art whose main administrative task was 'to establish some sort of research culture', that both met the conventional requirements for research *and* contributed to disciplinary development. One way around the difficulty was to include in a project certain aspects that 'follow more traditional research modes' and could be used as a basis for applications for research funding, the funding thus obtained 'as a spin-off to actually do the production'. For example two staff had received a small ARC grant in ceramics:

They produce moulds and they can pump out the plates and cups and so forth according to a certain design. Then they have them painted by various artists, so they become unique contributions, but they wouldn't get any funding for that. So what they did was take all the preparatory work that was involved in analysing the most appropriate types of clay, the glazes, fire temperatures, shapes and so forth and they built up a systematic way of actually evaluating those components that then go together to make a finished product. They *were* able to get funding for that. That was declared research.

The problem could not always be solved circuitously. At the above school of art, some 'have difficulty stringing four words together in written form', and were reluctant to undertake scholarship in a very different medium, but nevertheless they were 'absolutely brilliant' as visual artists. The only way to adequately encompass these disciplines would be to treat reflective creative work as equivalent to research and scholarship. As it stands, path-breaking work that works against established norms and operates in a loosely self-referential manner contradicts much that a good research manager needs to do.

Ways out

The skills of criticism, deconstruction and reconstruction are endemic to scholarship and research. Are these skills also folded into the technologies of research management? We found that there *are* reflexivities in research management, but for the most part they operate only within quite narrow limits. The most obvious reflexivity is the continual self-questioning about measured research performance. Within this limited form of reflexivity, the orthodox objectives and techniques of research management are not questioned. However, there is a further kind of reflexivity that is less common, but promises more. It is a reflexivity that takes in the relationship between the technologies of research management, and the larger contextual setting in which research is conducted. This enables us to take into account the effects of these technologies in research as a knowledge system (as well as an economic system), and in the larger reshaping of the universities. In our sample, the one university working along these lines is UTS. The UTS research management plan enables the university to reflect on both the organisation of knowledge and research organisation. UTS argues that fields of knowledge are not given or static but are dynamic, in constant motion. Orthodox management models research as a static 'other', the *object* of management. Research is seen as inherently conservative, while management is seen as the dynamic element and the source of change. The fields of knowledge are taken as given (evading the direct confrontation with collegial tradition, even shaping it and negating it). In contrast, research management at UTS acknowledges that the organisation of research is one of the shaping influences in the construction of knowledge. Both elements are dynamic and each has the potential to affect the other.

UTS aims to facilitate and recognise the diverse and rapidly changing nature of research by acknowledging new research paradigms in its own internal processes of support and reward as well as by seeking to influence the national agenda to be more open to these developments.[37]

On one hand the university wants to bring management closer to research so as to infuse field boundaries and research methodologies with an organisational reflexivity, a capacity for reinvention in terms of corporate institutional goals. On the other it wants to infuse the management of research with a better feel for the nature and needs of the different kinds of research, and possible new research. This creates potential for new management–research synergies, varying by field, provided that potential is not pre-empted by narrowly defined outputs, or forced homogeneity between disciplines. Here UTS recognises that 'a diverse range of research cultures exists between, as well as within, faculties'. 'Performance indicators need to be developed that are sensitive to this diversity of cultures as well as stages of development'. It has created an index of 'faculty-based preferred research performance indicators' and is committed to 'lobby for greater recognition and support by government agencies for research from non-traditional areas and with different modes of publication and dissemination'.[38]

What is significant about the intention of the UTS policy is that it treats independent disciplines/fields of knowledge as a resource to be developed rather than a limit to be overcome, and treats researchers themselves as the heart of these independent disciplines.

The limits of 'excellence'

Research, inquiry, discovery, scholarship: these are too open-ended for the Enterprise University. Risk margins must be reduced. The modelling of research as a money economy reduces the dangerous uncertainty of research. By the same token, it has predictable effects in research practices. We want to summarise some of the problems that result: first, the bias in favour of research quantity rather than research quality; second, the bias in favour of short-term research performance not long-term research capacity; third, the bias in favour of track record and conventional approaches, rather than new researchers and emergent approaches.

Because the quantum formula creates a direct economic relationship between research activity and future institutional income, there is a tendency towards continual expansion in the volume of measured research, which appears as a continual 'improvement' in research. This is exacerbated by the ratchet-effect of inter-university competition, which forces each university to work ever harder for its share of a constant pool of funds. In turn the drive towards quantitative growth creates inevitable tension between quantity and quality. Though the capacity to execute projects is finite, as performance management sees it the more research projects the better. Yet the projects that secure the most competitive grants or earn the most income are not necessarily the projects that generate the major breakthroughs or produce works of lasting importance and beauty, or even the projects that create the most economic value in the longer term. Similarly, a quantum-based research system creates an incentive to maximise the number of publications, but not to maximise the quality of publications. Researcher time is finite and at a certain point each increase in quantity tends to produce a fall in average quality. In the longer term this creates a dilemma within the terms of the research strategy itself, for academic quality is one of the sources of institutional status. For Australian research, the risk is that at best, the nation's measured share of world research will increase, but its role at the cutting-edge will weaken.

Everywhere we met the sanguine assumption that a more intensive competition is the guarantor of research quality. But – and aside from the fact that in the strict meaning of 'quality', the 'qualities' of different disciplines are heterogeneous and cannot be compared – competition for research funding is a competition for *rankings*, not for quality. Whether the projects are better or worse, the same total monies are distributed. In most funding schemes the quality of proposals is not referenced against a standard external to those proposals themselves. In the end, research policy and management are not concerned about this. Because research funding has become an end in itself, the outcomes of research do not matter except for their contribution to the research track record.

A system which measures quantity and leaves quality to the disciplines (or the publishers) is not agnostic. It rewards those closest to current government thinking and industry practices. This may have virtues as a means for economic development,[39] but it certainly changes the idea of the university, and the dynamics of research 'excellence', and imposes new risks on researchers. Researchers in areas *not* favoured by the current settings find that the risks have not really been reduced. Those risks have been transferred from management to themselves.

The second problem is related to the first. Research is an accumulating activity, in that present research programs are built on past programs, and the longer the time spent on a line of inquiry the greater the familiarity with the content and the faster the speed of task. But research as a system of economically defined performance tends to focus on short-term returns at the expense of long term ones. One PVC notes that:

The University is, however, caught in the competing demands of a University mission to undertake research which will support the long-term development of knowledge and government policies which are focused more particularly on the short term benefits to the economy that might be achieved from goal oriented project research. The challenge is to achieve an appropriate balance in these activities.[40]

No one has devised a performance measure for regulating 'balances' between long-term and short-term projects. An associated issue is the incentive to shift research to the applied and commercial end of the spectrum, away from basic research. This might undermine the long-term capacity to conduct even applied research. Though in some fields commercial applications seems to drive basic research, in others the chain of invention is reversed. While a number of academic researchers remarked on these issues, managers were less concerned (though their attitudes varied somewhat according to disciplinary backgrounds). But to us it seems that the short term and the long term are often disconnected.

A third problem is that in a performance-based system, an increasing part of research support goes to already active and successful areas and projects. Track record, always important in peer decisions about research, becomes decisive. This creates a barrier to innovations, especially in new or emerging fields. Again, this tends to undermine both quantity and quality in the longer term. There are special funds to assist innovations and new researchers, but these schemes are working against the whole system dynamic.

This is not to say established researchers are incapable of innovations; but it seems plausible to conclude that all else being equal, a system so strongly focused on existing strengths may retard the emergence of major new approaches. Within established fields, tried and tested ways are prolonged at the expense of new ones, and new researchers are unhealthily dependent on the sponsorship of chief investigators/project leaders who have a vested interest in existing paradigms and whose best work is often behind them. Though ARC post-doctoral fellowships and senior research fellowships are meant to provide full-time opportunities for self-determined work at both junior and senior levels, the number of these fellowships is too small to overcome the difficulties.

Management strategies in which research is modelled as a money economy also contain a more immediate self-limitation. On one hand those strategies rest on ever-intensifying competition for funds, and strategies of induced scarcity via the 'increasing selectivity and concentration' of activities. As the Hoare committee emphasised, against the collegial tradition, in this research economy not all academics should be regarded as researchers and funded as such as of right. On the other hand there is the contrary tendency: 'All institutions, including those which incorporate former colleges of advanced education, seek to expand the breadth, relevance and depth of their research.'[41]

Thus the imperative towards quantity (research activity in every corner of every university) collides with the opposite imperative towards concentration and critical mass. In institutions where researchers are free to pursue projects of their own choice in their preferred disciplines, selectivity cannot be enforced, and this contradiction is maximised. Only when management exercises enough control over research activity to enforce a particular policy of concentration – if necessary by moving researchers out of their preferred disciplines and into the designated disciplines or multi-disciplines – is it possible to concentrate research in selected areas *and* maximise measured research output at the same time (and thus escape the dilemma). The downside is that in this framework, only a limited and predetermined diversity is permitted. Every attempt is made to ensure that the butterflies *do* fly in formation. As one vice-chancellor sees it:

The most pervasive force in universities is a centrifugal force: everything wants to spread out and you've got to actively bring them back in if you don't want the natural state to occur.

In our case studies we found a higher education system in which management's priority setting and resource allocation increasingly pre-structured the boundaries and nature of research, and in some cases even prescribe the detailed inquiry itself. This system has clear biases with predictable consequences, such as the individualistic reading of research output and the conditions for research performance; the tendency to growth in measurable and measured outputs; the quantity–quality trade-offs; the tendency in favour of large project research in the science-based disciplines and projects with potential commercial applications; the growing dependence on management as the engine of research activity – witness the stagnation of research in institutions where research organisation is incomplete or falters; and the privileging of competition.

Orthodox research policy and management works through the disciplines as well as across them, but it is *prima facie* disposed to treat disciplinary and departmental structures as conservative obstacles to institutional goals. It tends to negate discipline specificity by treating all disciplines as the same, and it favours inter-disciplinary centres as against single discipline departments and established cultures. In weakening the disciplines, it improves immediate research performance at the expense of the conditions which enable new research to emerge.

We do not seek a return to collegiality in administration: in some respects the new structures described in chapter 5, while two-sided, are an improvement on what they replaced. However in the area of research management, the drawbacks of the Enterprise University are all too obvious. Research is one of two such areas. The other, described in the next chapter, is that of strategies for institutional development. There the growth of imitating behaviour, convergence and timid conformity is again very obvious. In turn, this has implications for the research mission. While the dynamics of disciplinary innovation and of institutional innovation are by no means identical, each has certain implications for the other.

In universities in which, increasingly, resources are marshalled according to an institutional plan, formula or quasi-market competition rather than heterogeneous disciplinary logics, while at the same time, conformity and low risk-taking are common, the intellectual risks provided by basic research tend to find less favour.

7   Many paths, one purpose: Diversity in the Enterprise University

So far we have focused on common elements in the changes in executive leadership, governance and research management in universities. Differences between individual institutions were noted only in passing. Using 'birds eye' vision, chapters 1–6 brought the whole terrain into view, but flattened out the smaller bumps in the landscape.

It is time to correct this imbalance between the general and the particular: to track the differences and the resemblances between universities, and map the dynamics of diversity itself. How much variety is there, within and between institutions? What kind of variety, whether in social status, corporate mission, educational personality, or size and shape? Are these differences reducing or increasing? Is the more business-like approach leading to a flowering of diversity as the prophets of the market hoped? Or is it creating sameness? Do institutions imitate each other? What might enhance the potential for diversity, for robust individual identities? What are the links between academic diversity, institutional diversity and governance? These are the questions to which we now turn.

Conformity in diversity

At once there is a paradox. As chapters 2 and 3 noted, government has withdrawn from part of the financing of universities and from some overt forms of regulation, while at the same time it is using more subtle and severe methods to shape their inner life. In the official rhetoric the emphasis falls on the tasks of institutions rather than the responsibilities of government. This foregrounds university identity, strategy and corporate objectives, and university management as the agent for achieving those corporate ends. Universities are still shaped by the state (suggesting conformity), yet their individuality is highlighted (suggesting diversity).

Market forces call up the same paradox. In higher education as in other industries, the demands of competition are fierce. It forces hard choices to be made, and it penalises those who refuse to conform to its dictates. On one hand managers now have more freedom to carve out their own paths and to reinvent universities as they see fit, having partly detached themselves from the traditional academic networks 'below' and community interests (other than business) 'outside'. On the other, as Harvey notes, market strategies combine differentiation and change, with similarity and conformity.[1]

This paradox of diversity in conformity – and conformity in diversity – is deeply embedded in contemporary universities. It also runs through the academic literature on higher education. The literature is divided between two main schools of thought, representing two opposing sides of the paradox. One school of thought is gee-whiz optimistic, while the other is pessimistic.[2]

Optimism is often associated with American work in higher education studies. The optimists believe that corporate reform and market competition are calling forth a blooming of difference, as self-managing universities, freed from the dead hand of the state, move to align themselves with the diverse needs of a variety of customers.[3] Likewise, in Australian government policy literature, perhaps not surprisingly, there is much talking-up of the potential of economically modelled reform to create diversity, and about the manifold benefits of diversity itself. Since the 1991 report *Quality and diversity in higher education*, references to a more diverse and responsive set of institutions, leading to greater efficiency, quality and relevance, have been standard fare.[4] Exactly what is meant by diversity, what are its positive effects, exactly how corporate management and market reform will achieve it and generate these supposed effects, has never been made clear.

The more pessimistic view is manifest in some European work in higher education studies. As the pessimists see it, the main tendency is for government and market pressures to *homogenise* the universities. They believe institutions are converging in structure, activities and prestige. One reason is the tendency for institutions to track established models and minimise risk in an uncertain world. It is argued that *isomorphism* – that is, imitating behaviour, mimicking – has become a standard characteristic of universities. Isomorphism is a product not just of individual decisions but of the larger setting in which universities operate.

The focus on isomorphism and convergence questions the facile but all-too-fashionable notion that enterprising leadership can somehow overcome the historical and environmental limits facing an individual university. This is an important corrective. We have some sympathy for these arguments, for they have considerable salience in the Australian case. In chapter 2 we discussed the genesis of Commonwealth shaping of the system as a system of derivatives. Chapter 4 traced the imitation of change at the executive level. Chapters 5 and 6 tracked common pathways to reform in governance structure and research management.

The homogenising effect of government is easy to identify. To recap, in Australia since Dawkins the universities have been expected to pursue their own strategic planning in competition with each other, yet within the framework of strong state regulation, and high government expectations about performance and behaviour. The rules are shaped by Commonwealth data requirements, the relative funding model which encourages standardised resourcing of each academic discipline, and the research quantum. The 1993–95 reports of the Commonwealth Committee for Quality Assurance reinforced the perception that Australian universities were similar to each other, rather than diverse.[5] The committee encouraged universities to pursue 'distinctive missions' linked to their own definition of quality, yet it ranked them against each other on what was presented as a common scale, regardless of individual missions and goals. Naturally the universities adjusted their approach to meet the committee's notion of quality (rather than their own). What diversity there has been in the system has been played out against this backdrop of engineered uniformity, with little scope for idiosyncratic readings and diverse purposes.

Even so, the state as homogeniser is only one side of the coin. It is too easy to see this as the only issue, too easy to blame every instance of imitating behaviour on government. As we shall see, governments can facilitate diversity, as well as enforcing conformity. Even when governments are operating as homogenisers, institutions still have real choices. Imitating behaviour is often self-imposed. And imitation and conformity are not the only forces at work. In the last analysis, the pessimists make too much of homogeneity. The tendencies they talk about are in danger of becoming universal laws, an iron cage that closes around us regardless of what we do. This plays down actual existing institutional diversity, and the scope for experiment and betterment in the current environment, and the scope for changing that environment itself.

The arguments in this debate rarely do justice to the complexity of the problem. In the literature, empirical studies of particular universities or systems are mostly read through the lens of one set of assumptions or the other, so as to support claims of either diversity or convergence. As Meek and Wood note, 'empirical examples can be selected to support either case'.[6] It is rare for any one analysis to embrace both kinds of trend simultaneously – *both* diversification and homogenisation. Yet both trends can happen, at the same time and in the same institution. Reality has the uncomfortable habit of failing to fit our preconceptions as neatly as we would like.

By focusing only on one side of the paradox, the larger dynamics of higher education are obscured. It is better to recognise that both state and market can be a force for *either* diversity or homogeneity, that the environment shapes each institution but does not dictate its genetic code, and that there is significant scope for choices, strategies and varying outcomes.[7] Whether diversity prevails over homogeneity in a sector as complex as higher education is a case by case matter. We agree with Levy:

> The balance between isomorphism and diversity depends largely on where we look. But the conclusion here is not that the isomorphism-diversity dichotomy is pointless, much less that isomorphism reigns. What is required in the face of the coincidence of isomorphism and diversity, of a complex and evolving mix of these broad and consequential tendencies, is that we identify the conditions under which each gains strength and that we try to understand those conditions as much as possible.[8]

Those 'conditions' embrace both institution and environment. The environment includes other institutions. Isomorphism and diversity are played out in the complex relations between outer and inner worlds, between networks and identity. Any increase or decrease in diversity is a function of how institutions respond to external factors (political, economic, social, academic and so on), *and* of their shaping of themselves. Here the operations of the environment are not just 'outside-in'. Individual universities, especially the strongest universities, help to structure the environment in which all institutions operate. As Meek and Wood put it, the environment is both the 'medium and product' of the interaction between institutions.[9] This underlines the point that institutions' values, goals and sense of community *do* matter, as the optimists argue, though not quite for the reason they claim. Not because university managers *sui generis* can conquer the world with the right strategy and good marketing. Rather, because all universities are enmeshed in a vast uneven web of relationships (local, regional, national, global), where *cumulative* effects may be surprisingly potent.

Courageous imitations

Diversity and diversity

Why does diversity matter? *Does* diversity matter? It is not as silly a question as it sounds. 'Diversity' has become a taken-for-granted good, like 'freedom', with which it is often identified. Yet when people speak about diversity in higher education as if it is a common ideal, they often have divergent ends in mind.

One argument for diversity assumes that the supply of higher education is driven by demand. Students are diverse, in social and cultural terms, and perhaps 'ability', and a more diverse higher education system with more choices can better cater for diverse needs. A similar argument states that a more diverse higher education system is more flexible in the face of changing economic and social requirements. Both arguments assume that a *de facto* division of labour operates between institutions. When new requirements appear, the 'appropriate' institution or course fills the gap. These are ecological assumptions for both diversity of kinds of institution, and diversity of courses and teaching styles. However, the model of supply and demand is naive. Isomorphism needs to be factored in. Isomorphic supply limits the range of needs that are given form and *can* be demanded. We only know there is a demand after some organisation has come forward to meet it with a successful new program. In that sense, institutions 'choose' their demand.

A third argument is about diversity between different kinds of institution. It models a more diverse system as one composed of institutions with different levels of status, cost and educational difficulty. Providing the different levels are properly articulated with each other, a vertically tiered system allows a broad set of opportunities to coexist with elite institutions. This argument is often asserted in the USA. There it mirrors the actual higher education system, in which research universities are networked downwards to colleges. The case for a vertical hierarchy of status and quality is less compelling than the earlier case for a horizontal range of kinds of higher education. A hierarchy does not really expand choice. In such a system few people have the money or the academic marks to choose elite institutions, and those able to choose elite education are unlikely to opt for lower status alternatives. The dynamics of vertical diversity are very different to those of horizontal diversity. The real reason why hierarchical systems survive – whether based on formal sectoral divisions such as in the old binary system in Australia, or a hierarchy of competitive institutions within the sector – is not because they facilitate choice. Still less is it because they promote diversity in teaching or knowledge. It is because they facilitate a smoother matching between social power and educational scarcity.[10]

A fourth idea associates diversity with a spirit of self-confidence and innovation.[11] The former head of the Tertiary Education Commission, Peter Karmel, refers to 'the desirability of escaping from the strait-jacket of uniformity so that progress can be achieved through experimentation, change and the adoption of successful practice'.[12] The significant factors here are an institution's mission, values and goals, and its strategies in course provision and services. A distinctive profile has both organisational and educational aspects. These are separable, but they might also affect each other. In our view this kind of diversity, focused on genuine innovation, has more policy potential than the others. This is a diversity separated from isomorphism, and a diversity that is not being mobilised as a social selector.

Nevertheless more than one kind of diversity exists in the real world, and the term cannot be used in universal fashion. In the discussion that follows, the term diversity refers to variety of types. *Differentiation* refers to the creation of a particular kind of diversity, consisting of a number of parts which taken together function as a unified whole. Diversity in higher education takes several forms. 'Systemic diversity' refers to different types of institution within one system: for example the binary system in Australia before 1988. 'Programmatic diversity' refers to variety in programs and services, whether between institutions or within one institution. 'Cultural diversity' refers to variety in values or identities, or in the social environment provided in higher education. Vertical differentiation ('positional diversity') refers to the division of higher education into separate segments based on status or prestige.

'Horizontal diversity' refers to differences with no necessary implications for status ranking, while with 'vertical diversity', differences are distinctions of rank. Vertical rankings may or may not be correlated to forms of horizontal diversity (for example, differences in size or course mix), and are often associated with measurable material differences, such as institutional income or research performance. High prestige institutions tend to attract more students and more industry funds because of their prestige, and also attract staff who are good managers or perform above average in the competition for research dollars. In strong institutions, status and political economy reinforce each other.

The multiple character of diversity – its distinct and sometimes contrary forms – is the key to the paradox. For higher education is becoming both more *and* less diverse, depending on which definition of diversity is being used. Both the optimists and the pessimists are right, in a sense. Universities are becoming both more like each other and less like each other at the same time. On one hand, government and market forces are driving universities to imitate each other. Some development of new niches is going on, and entrepreneurial managers do create new kinds of activity. But the isomorphistic trend seems stronger. On the other hand, the government-constructed market is leading to greater vertical differentiation between the institutions. In a competitive system there are bound to be winners and losers, and the gap between the two increases over time.

It is also important to remember that the present trends are not irreversible. The Australian government now supports a 'one size fits all' model of institutional structure, enforcing sameness. Yet the former binary systems in the UK and Australia, and the present binary system in Germany, are examples of government-regulated systemic diversity. Similarly governments can use funding or legal regulation to create greater diversity between institutions in course mix, or provide requirements and incentives which encourage the same course mix everywhere. Some markets encourage conformity (as in the markets for cars and hamburgers). When universities strive for the middle ground and struggle to be all things to all people, this tends to suppress programmatic diversity and collapse systemic diversity. Yet markets can also be associated with a proliferation of niche approaches and a more flexible handling of emerging needs (as in the markets for software and leisure goods), providing isomorphism is regulated and reduced.

Communicating convergence

In the larger settings in which government and institutions work, common models and tendencies towards convergence are readily identified: globalisation, technological innovation, self-managing institutions linked by data systems, more sophisticated marketing and customer relations, intellectual property frameworks, new business principles in financial management, and so on. Above all, communication systems foster a more intensively and extensively networked environment (chapter 3). Globalisation is both a common system in itself, and a medium in which dominant practices are transmitted throughout the university world. At the click of a mouse the web pages of the Ivy League universities provide a compelling model, though few universities in fewer countries will ever attain it. Everyone working in higher education is plugged in to ever-increasing communications:

> You ask me how things have changed. Firstly, people here work a lot harder and think nothing of coming to meetings at 8 am and going along to government things. People come in at the weekends. The other thing is the multifarious modes of communication. My e-mail is banked up a hell of a lot ... [then there's] ordinary brown envelopes and voicemail. The modes of communication mean that people are communicating more because it's there to do. I think you could spend your whole bloody day answering the mail. (centre director, Sandstone university)

There is little choice about this. To stand outside the communications system and the common culture it carries is to court disaster. Remarking on a poor rating in the first quality round, one departmental head at a regional Gumtree university[13] argues that:

> We've been isolated ... we pay for the fact that we don't routinely interact with academics from other institutions.

One Sandstone university sets aside part of its internal initiatives fund just to promote better networking and collaborative systems:

We don't want mini universities in our faculties and we don't want fortress departments.

The DVC believes that to become more competitive in its external response, the university needs to have a universal communications culture inside, with no 'bolt-holes' where recalcitrant departments and eccentric, hermitic academics can escape from managerial performance pressures and external clamourings for service. At the same time, the Web makes institutions increasingly aware of potential external competitors, whether Harvard or commercial training.

Global higher education contains powerful forces for convergence. Most international students are interested in business studies, computing or engineering, areas with a common global core of knowledge. International agencies prescribe generic policies in the different countries they assist. The salience of these models is not confined to nations subject to development packages:[14] they are worked back into all national policies via common understandings of best practice. The example of American higher education has been influential in shaping these global models. The higher education literature refers to a worldwide tendency towards one kind of national system, based on mixed public/private funding, public and private institutions, and 'supervisory governance'. This is the system model of the World Bank/IMF and OECD.[15] It provides for internal diversity of function, with vertical differentiation of resources and status between institutions. At the same time because it is a common model, it reduces global diversity between national systems. And importing dominant models from abroad helps drive imitating behaviour at home.

Yet in other respects the global dimension can enable diversity. 'Thicker' and more intensive communications and exchange bring universities into contact with a great variety of practices, including European, Latin American and East Asian practices as well as Anglo-American. Even those who like to borrow have a wider range of choices. International education foregrounds questions of cultural diversity in the curriculum and student services, and encourages educational innovations, such as bilingual programs. At present much of the diversity evident in the international programs of Australian universities is diversity in the method of recruitment and induction of students, and some limited diversity in delivery of programs. Less willingness to move away from standard forms of curriculum development is evident, leading to a sense of 'a wider funnel with the same narrow neck'. Nevertheless, the potential for more exciting innovation is there. A more pluralistic form of globalisation might enhance the potential for diversity (though that is another story).

Isomorphism

In their survey of management and governance Meek and Wood asked university managers to specify the main influences on their policies. In order, the factors affecting teaching were professional bodies, the Commonwealth, and other universities. In relation to research the factors were official funding agencies such as the ARC, the Commonwealth, and other universities. In relation to financial policies, the factors were the Commonwealth and research funding agencies. It was felt that government had 'too much influence over micro-management issues within institutions'.[16] These data point to the power of official requirements. They also begin to acknowledge the effects of universities on each other.

Isomorphism (imitating behaviour) takes several forms. One is referred to in the literature as 'coercive' isomorphism, whereby conformity to common patterns of behaviour is enforced by an external agency such as government or professional association. Another is 'mimetic' isomorphism, pursued by the institution voluntarily. A third is 'normative' or 'professional' isomorphism resulting from academic norms and practices to a greater or lesser degree common to all institutions.[17]

It can be difficult to distinguish between these different forms. For example, when a government encourages institutions to develop self-managed systems of quality assurance, all three kinds of isomorphism might be involved. In contemporary higher education the distinction between forced and voluntary behaviour is not clear-cut. Much of what appears as free-swinging market behaviour or strategic reinvention takes place within rules and limits set by policy. Neave refers to 'the law of anticipated results'. A particular institutional decision might seem to be autonomous rather than imposed but 'very often it is little more than a reactive response to pressure exerted from above'.[18]

Formal independence provides no guarantee that institutions will use their strategic freedom to adopt approaches that are distinctive and different. One reason is the logic of self-interest in a competitive system. Karmel argues that:

There is another factor that can work against differentiation in spite of autonomy. It is the tendency for institutions to copy other (especially neighbouring) institutions. There is a number of examples of duplication of specialist programs unrelated to the demand for their products on the principle of 'anything you can do, I can do better'. This tendency is exacerbated when there is keen competition among institutions, particularly for students. It is a force against diversity. The recent spread of law schools, MBA and PhD programs illustrates this, as well as the multiplication of specifically named centres for research activities. In this situation some degree of central regulation may, perhaps surprisingly, be the best means of preserving a degree of diversity.[19]

It is a crucial insight into competitive behaviour. Competition involves 'othering', yet in a process of mutual convergence the 'other' becomes more like the self. Indeed, the game-logic of competition demands this from the start. If institutions were sufficiently different to each other that their diverse missions and profiles could scarcely be compared, a system-managed competition would become impossible. A certain level of sameness must be factored in. Isomorphism has a head start, and over time it goes further ahead.

Van Vught identifies two potential limitations on diversity between institutions. First, governmental structuring of the policy environment: the more uniform and universal the environment, the lower the level of diversity.[20] Second, academic norms and values: the stronger their influence, the lower the level of diversity. Academic norms are transmitted especially in the high-status institutions (one reason why they are conservative), which are models for others. Institutional mimicking converges with academic mimicking. Levy notes that the academic standards of strong institutions become universal standards, and these institutions produce academic and managerial professionals that carry the dominant norms. Mimetic isomorphism is displayed especially in the attempts of new or less prestigious institutions to legitimate themselves by emulating the more successful, while minimising the risks of uncertainty. But competitive pressures render even Ivy League universities risk averse. Levy adds that when goals are ambiguous, as in large comprehensive universities, the fear of risk is enhanced. Other factors that enhance the potential for risk are financial instability, and uncertainty about prevailing technologies.[21] (All of these factors currently apply.) Once risk aversion takes hold, a bold and distinctive institutional strategy – even a new educational program – appears to increase the sum of risk. Aversion to risk becomes an aversion to innovation. Bold new ideas give way to courageous imitations.

Isomorphs want certainty in an uncertain world. If mimicking behaviour cannot eliminate risk altogether, it can minimise it. By adopting the same change strategies as their chief competitors (though not the static profile of their competitors, for that would increase risk), isomorphs ensure that even if those change strategies fail, the mimetic university will not lose any competitive position. In a competition, the objective is relative performance, not absolute performance. Better, if the second mover position allows the mimetic university to improve on its competitor's strategies, it can make small gains.

Yet isomorphism is not something that institutions admit to. Universities are reluctant to openly define themselves as similar to other institutions, still less to admit to a deliberate decision to imitate another institution with higher status. To do so is to forgo their own claims to excellence, to set a benchmark which might be difficult to meet, and to appear lacking in originality. In higher education, like art, originality is mandatory. University officers always talk about being distinctive and innovative. If nothing else, it is a good sales pitch. Several manager-leaders interviewed by Meek and Wood emphasised that an institution must do more than 'identify its particular distinctiveness'. It must also present 'an image of its innovativeness to potential students and the wider community'.[22] These strategic imperatives taken together – the need to maximise total market position and the need to be seen to be different, avant garde, cutting-edge – leads to aggressive marketing combined with educational conformity. Readings notes how that in mission statements, all universities claim they are unique and all describe themselves in the same way.[23] As Meek and Wood note, the 'uniqueness' becomes expressed in corporate promotion. 'Where institutions are becoming increasingly sophisticated in distinguishing themselves it is through their marketing and advertising strategies'.[24] Here 'innovativeness' is often confined to innovations in marketing techniques that add nothing to teaching and research.

Sandstones and all that

No one university is the same as another. Each has its own history and geographic location, its social clusters and particular personalities. Nevertheless institutions also fall into recognisable groups. As a system, Australian higher education has three principal aspects. First, the dominant institutional form is the large comprehensive doctoral university, covering undergraduate and postgraduate education, and conducting research in all fields of study. This is virtually the only model, incorporating more than 98 per cent of higher education students.[25] Second, the relationship between institutions is competitive, and incorporates some features of an economic market. Institutions are differentiated from each other according to the outcomes of competition, strung out in a hierarchy from strong at the top to weak at the bottom. Third, institutions are also segmented into groups of institutions, with differing histories and vertically rankable attributes and potentials.

Thus vertical differentiation between institutions is shaped by both inherited patterns of segmentation and the dynamics of market competition. Here inherited status and competition reinforce each other. The historical primacy of certain universities gives them a head start in competition for students, funds and prestige. Not surprisingly, they tend to win in the marketplace and this feeds back into maintenance of the hierarchical status quo. Vertical differentiation breeds vertical differentiation. It is the main driver of diversity in Australian higher education (albeit diversity of a limited kind), though not all the observable diversity between institutions is correlated to this vertical differentiation.

One size fits all

In Australian tertiary education the structural diversity once provided by advanced education has been inherited by the Technical and Further Education (TAFE) institutions, which offer courses up to diploma level. When private training colleges are included, which vary greatly in size and function, more structural diversity is apparent. However, TAFE and private training fall outside this study, which is confined to the formally designated higher education sector. (In some other countries such as the United States, TAFE-type institutions are defined as part of higher

Table 7.1 Size and number of campuses, institutions in this study, change since 1987

Institution	Number of students[a] 1987	Number of students 1998	Change in students 1987–98 (%)	Number of campuses 1996
Monash	14 003	39 742	+ 183.8	6
Sydney	17 961	33 587	+ 87.0	5
QUT	9 504	31 235	+ 228.7	3
Queensland	17 855	28 431	+ 59.2	2
New South Wales	17 825	28 323	+ 58.9	3
Deakin	6 857	27 586	+ 302.3	6
UTS	9 952	22 976	+ 130.9	3
Griffith	4 689	21 514	+ 358.8	5
Edith Cowan	10 471	19 055	+ 82.0	6
Newcastle	5 766	18 463	+ 220.2	3
Adelaide	8 670	13 605	+ 56.9	4
Western Australia	9 625	12 979	+ 34.8	1
Central Queensland	3 262	12 031	+ 268.8	6
Tasmania	5 242	11 839	+ 125.8	2
Flinders	5 537	11 017	+ 99.0	1
James Cook	4 060	9 147	+ 125.3	2
Southern Cross	2 006	9 067	+ 352.0	2

a Includes only the 'core' component of what was to become the 1998 institution and excludes those 1987 institutions that were later to merge with that 'core'. For example, it includes the Queensland Institute of Technology which became the core of Queensland University of Technology, but not the Brisbane College of Advanced Education which was to become a merger partner.
Sources: Commonwealth Tertiary Education Commission (CTEC), *Selected higher education statistics 1987*, CTEC, Canberra, 1987, pp. 41–44; DEETYA, *Selected higher education statistics 1997*.

education.) Within higher education in Australia there is no longer any government-ordained structural diversity. The remaining structural diversity is informal, deriving from variations in the size of institutions and their number of campuses.

Diversity by size is quite limited. As table 7.1 shows, institutions in this study fall within the same broad size category of medium to large university. None of them are small colleges, or mega-institutions like the American state universities with more than 50 000 students. The largest is four times the size of the smallest. All but two enrol more than 10 000 students, ranging up to almost 40 000 students at Monash. The two smallest universities are regional institutions whose size is limited by location and age rather than a conscious desire to remain small. Both want to grow.

There are only a handful of small institutions outside this sample: the Australian Defence Forces Academy in Canberra, the Australian Maritime College in Launceston, Batchelor College educating indigenous students in Darwin, and private institutions such as Avondale College, the Marcus Oldham Farm Management College, Notre Dame Australia and the unfunded Bond University and Christian Heritage College. Notre Dame and Bond would be large comprehensive institutions if they could. There also used to be separate institutions in the arts, music, film and television but since Dawkins these have been annexed to large comprehensive universities, while retaining a measure of autonomy. Undergraduate-only institutions of the American kind have failed to take root. Specialised private business schools have been tried in Australia – for example the Simon School in Sydney and Tasman in Melbourne – but these ventures have failed because of competition from business schools in the prestigious comprehensives.[26]

Though other national systems contain successful small institutions, the norm in Australia is medium to large. This norm is reinforced by government regulation. In the Dawkins reforms it was specified that full funding for research activities would be available only to institutions with more than 8000 students. The norm is also reinforced by market competition, in that a large university with a broad range of fields of study has a wider range of potential 'products' and stronger market share. The national bias in favour of size and comprehensiveness is deep-seated, predating Dawkins. In the development of higher education in Australia, the determining goal was the geographic dispersal of access over a large land area. New institutions tended to replicate the course provision of existing ones. The 1964–88 binary system was an exception to the larger historical pattern, a pattern which helps to explain 'academic drift', the isomorphistic manner in which the CAEs became more like universities over time. Like all forms of upward mobility, academic drift contains strong tendencies towards uniformity.[27]

Because of this pattern of large comprehensive universities, virtually all potential students have access to a wide range of courses, subject to academic entry requirements, within a standard template. At the same time, with less diversity between types of universities, the cultural diversity of student experience is narrower. The focused intimacy of small specialist institutions is missing.

More than two-thirds of all universities in Australia are multi-campus institutions. Institutions in this study vary between one campus and six (table 7.1). The presence of more than one site, especially more than one large site, creates the need for an additional layer of co-ordination. There may be tensions between site loyalties and institutional loyalties. As one would-be break-away academic put it:

I think we'd do much better if this place was called the Gold Coast University ... and we were able to run our own international campaigns and advertising. (senior academic, Gold Coast campus of Griffith University)

Centripetal integration can be attempted via academic organisation, or by central control over site management and administration, or both. To maintain a campus-centred identity risks the long-term fragmentation of the university; yet where two strong sites are involved, academic integration alone is rarely enough. All else being equal, a multi-campus structure tends to weaken the role of academic identities in university organisation. Nevertheless, some multi-campus institutions have strong academic cultures. We found that overall, multiplicity of site has less implications for diversity than we had expected. Diversity in courses mix, institutional role and status, institutional culture or management system do not appear to correlate consistently with diversity in number of sites.

One major consequence of the formation of multi-site institutions has been the effects on institutional competitive position. Growth allowed some universities to augment market share. On the other hand, mergers involving more than one large site absorb resources, energies and strategic capital. Among the leading universities, Sydney and Monash took on major mergers. Per capita research performance suffered, and both were rated on the second level in the 1993 quality round. In contrast Queensland, NSW, Adelaide and Western Australia left large-scale mergers to the other institutions in their respective states.

The segmented system

The market in higher education is no level playing field. Institutions do not compete on the same terms. All else being equal, strong institutions with the greatest capacity to compete tend to become stronger over time relative to other institutions – unless government intervenes to even up the competition, for example by distributing funding on the basis of inter-institutional equity, or a planned division of labour.

In the Australian system there are four clearly identifiable segments of universities and a fifth group more heterogeneous and less stable than the others. Though there is some diversity within the segments, and a couple of institutions are difficult to categorise, the segments are well defined. For a full listing of institutions, including those outside the study, see table 7.2. We have chosen buildings and landscaping descriptors for three of the five segments. For cyber-universities the metaphor would be different. But so far universities remain largely place-bound. Their identities are centred on the main sites where people meet and work together. We suspect that in at least the leading institutions this will continue to be the case. The five segments are set out below:

- The *Sandstone* universities, the oldest foundations in each state, including the universities of Sydney, Queensland, Adelaide and Western Australia in this study. All have some sandstone buildings. (The University of Tasmania is weaker in resources and academic status than the others, but shares their history and architecture.)
- The *Redbricks*, the strongest of the post-second world war universities, including the University of NSW and Monash University. Their political economy – size, academic role, incomes – is near interchangeable with that of the Sandstones. They have had less time to accumulate status benefits. Redbrick is more than evident in their architecture.
- The *Gumtrees*, universities founded later in the post-war period, between 1960 and 1975, the main period of publicly financed expansion. They include the Universities of Newcastle and Griffith, and James Cook, Deakin and Flinders Universities. Many of the sites were planted with natives (hence 'Gumtrees', though 'Acacias' or 'Banksias' are other possibilities) in contrast with the English gardens of the colonial period.
- The *Unitechs*, largest of the old CAEs in five states, with a strong vocational and industry-orientation, including Queensland University of Technology and the University of Technology, Sydney. The architecture in this group is characteristically ugly, ranging from a grimy early Fordism/Taylorism, to utilitarian modern.
- The *New Universities*, a heterogeneous group of post-1986 foundations including Central Queensland, Southern Cross and Edith Cowan universities. In their buildings, utilitarian recency combines with secondary school leftovers from the CAE period.

Table 7.2 Australian universities by segment within the national market

Sandstones	Redbricks	Gumtrees	Unitechs	New Universities
Sydney	**Monash**	**Griffith**	**UTS**	**Edith Cowan**
Queensland	**UNSW**	**Newcastle**	**QUT**	**Central Qld**
West Australia	ANU	**Flinders**	RMIT	**Southern Cross**
Adelaide		**James Cook**	Curtin	Western Sydney
Tasmania		*Deakin*	South Australia	Charles Sturt
Melbourne		La Trobe		VUT
		Macquarie		Southern Qld
		Wollongong		Canberra
		Murdoch		ACU
		New England[a]		Northern Territory
				Swinburne
				Ballarat
				Sunshine Coast

Bold indicates universities included in this study. *Italics* indicates universities that do not share all of the characteristics of others in the group.

a The University of New England was founded in 1954, pre-dating Monash, but was not given a medical faculty and has always been confined by its regional role. It shares some characteristics with the older Gumtrees, some with regional New Universities, and some with other distance education specialists.

Sandstones

The Sandstones and Redbricks are more resourceful and powerful than other universities largely because of their inherited advantages, their accumulated political economy and social status, which are self-reproducing. In any market success breeds success, but in education the element of path dependence is unusually great. This is not the kind of business in which producers freely change product lines overnight (which would liquidate all that slowly accumulated academic and vocational capital). All institutions appropriate selected parts of the past for use in the present. Where they have no past, they invent it, imagining themselves as inheritors of a larger tradition. It is scarcely any wonder that vice-chancellors of New Universities break out in rhetoric about the University of Bologna (said to be the first), or Newman's 'Idea of a University', however unconnected to their daily life. They are clutching for the past they do not have, like a missing limb. What distinguishes the Sandstones is both that they have more of a past to draw on, *and* that their particular model of higher education has a greater capacity to use the past.

Sandstone history is self-sustaining, in more than one sense. Once an institution becomes part of the top group it is difficult to shift. It readily attracts enough academic, social and economic capital to maintain its established position. By doing so, *de facto* it closes off the group to potential competitors. The position of leading universities, like that of elite independent private schools, is practically unchallengeable. Stepping up the intensity of competition does not open the role of market leader to all comers, it only reinforces the hold of the existing leaders. Neither a formal cartel nor a social conspiracy are needed to achieve this effect: it is the result of the normal workings of the market in elite education.

How is this so? Education markets operate in such a manner because of the peculiar nature of the 'positional goods' produced in education. Positional goods are theorised by Fred Hirsch in his *Social limits to growth* (1976). Hirsch notes that educational institutions provide successful students with positions of *social advantage*: access to the professions and other high-paying jobs, and networking with the social elite. These positional goods have a special quality which makes education markets unusual markets. At any time there is an *absolute limit* to the number of positions of social advantage produced. For example, if the number of doctors tripled, the status and remuneration attached to medicine would diminish. There are always many more would-be investors in the leading professional faculties than there are places available. In the car industry an aggressive new producer can win market share by flooding the market with better and cheaper cars. In the education industry, there is no point in trying to flood the market with elite education places. Someone else has got there first. The market in higher education simply is not 'contestable' in the normal economic sense. Leading producers can readily sustain a joint monopoly.

Status goods are grounded in reputation: Sandstone reputations are protected by canny managers, and by academic isomorphism – the academics who lead disciplinary definition of excellence are mostly working at Sandstones or their international equivalents. Customers are slow to accept the claims of new modern producers against venerable old Sandstone producers, especially while fellow customers are tied to the old institutions. Consumers can be risk averse and isomorphistic, too. Maling and Keepes remark that:

> While careers advisers and others might welcome the greater diversity of the university system now as compared with when they were completing undergraduate degrees, when it comes to advising students where to go and considering the possible pathways for their own children, then the status of the older, well established universities has a strong hold.[28]

At lower levels, the competitive position of each institution is open to challenge. New universities can readily enter this part of the market. It is very difficult to do so at the middle level, and impossible at the top. It is also difficult for an established university to move from a lower to a higher grouping, at least under current system settings. The upper level of the hierarchy is stable, except perhaps in the very long term (though globalisation creates a new driver of elite status that might shorten this). In the United States higher education, long subject to competition, membership of the Ivy League group has been near constant since the 1920s.

In elite institutions, positional goods are *always* produced in a sellers' market. The power of the producer is strong relative to that of the consumer, who is in a very weak bargaining position. If a student walks out of a Sandstone or Redbrick course there are more than enough others to take her or his place. Sandstones do not have to market as vigorously as other institutions. Until a decade ago several Sandstones scarcely marketed at all. In one case, the transition to a marketing culture is even more recent, and is still incomplete:

> The University never cared about the external relations stuff because they thought 'We're the University of Sydney, we don't need it'. (non-academic manager)

Nor do they have to operate as efficiently or provide high quality teaching. Sandstones do not necessarily teach undergraduates better than other universities. Dill notes that American studies controlling for ability at the point of entry 'have found little correlation between student learning and the traditional institutional rankings based on research reputation'. However, this does not weaken those traditional rankings. In the value placed on positional goods it is not value added in teaching that matters. It is the scores of the students who enter, the reputation of the academics who teach them, the success of the university in research, and the labour-market status of graduates. These factors create a mutually reinforcing definition of value. Bright students and research performance operate as the universal indicators of excellence that sustain Sandstone and Redbrick reputations.[29]

Whichever way you look at it, the University tends to end up in the top handful of Australian universities. (research leader/manager, Sandstone university)

Leading universities often recruit top scholars and researchers. They want to maintain academic status. For their part, top academics are attracted to the money and status which Sandstones provide, together with their advantageous locations and scholarly ambience.

Harvard, MIT, University of California Berkeley don't pay substantially more to keep people there: people want to be there. Cambridge doesn't pay people very well at all, they want to be there. I don't know if we can aspire to that. (research leader/manager, Redbrick university)

Because the Sandstones have superior economic resources, because they attract leading academics, because they foster a scholarly image, because they are more than the product of corporate management (being sustained also by alumni, professions and international academic networks), their academic cultures are more robust than elsewhere. These academic cultures reproduce themselves despite reductions in public funding and despite managerialism in the Enterprise University, though they are not unaffected. Sandstones do not need to be fully entrepreneurial. They can dip in and out of money-making ventures to secure incomes and maintain hegemony in emerging areas. In a post-collegial era, in the Sandstones and to some extent the Redbricks, disciplinary identity retains much of its salience:

Really the whole university is a bunch of different departments stuck together. (superdean, Sandstone university)

In some Sandstones the old collegial resentment of management survives also, and institutional loyalties are ambiguous. Academics sometimes get sentimental about ivy-clad sandstone, but they also imagine that the university needs them as much as they need it. They're there because of their own academic status and they willingly resist managerialism.

Dealing with this place is like shepherding cats. If you take the whips to them, they'll all just disappear over the fences into the night and most of them you'll never see again. (faculty dean, Sandstone university)

A more robust academic culture provides some protection from the consequences of mouthing off about 'them', though it places faculty deans – poised between corporatised management and academic culture – in a difficult position. Still, critics rarely target the institution itself. Academics in the Sandstones are aware of the benefits of their location and do not want to reduce the flow of those benefits.

Disciplinary cultures both robust *and* pragmatic have a number of consequences. In such settings academics are more open to reforming themselves, or more tolerant of centrally generated reforms, when they can see that reform will maintain their academic reputation and institutional primacy. If an institution is so designed that the only way to change one component is to change all components, the costs of reform are high, and all parts of the institution are forced to adjust at the same rate, whether they need to or not.[30] Partly decoupled institutions are more economical and more flexible. Self-sustaining Sandstone cultures can be changed separately from each other. Reform is more readily made consistent with the long-term evolution of academic capacity. Strong disciplinary cultures explain the manner in which Sandstones are more coherent than they often appear. Canny Sandstone central managements, able to focus interventions selectively while maintaining faculty self-regulation, can tolerate the ritualistic moans about 'them' in the administration, as long as the overall outcomes remain strong.

As these adjustment strategies suggest, Sandstone commitment to Newmanesque notions of higher-education-for-its-own-sake is selective. The rhetoric is in one moment sincerely felt, in another moment it constitutes a form of marketing in itself, albeit one based on non-utilitarian and anti-commercial values. Anti-marketing, marketed with care. Here the Newmanesque rhetoric underpins a claim for academic excellence and freedom from external pressures, whether those of government or consumer. The smart Sandstones also run a counter-line of student friendly communication. They are now in competition across Australia for the top school-leavers, and more than before, they need to be user sensitive and organisationally smart, setting the standard here as in other respects. Other worldly rhetoric survives, but the Sandstones are as utilitarian as other institutions. They work very hard to sustain research reputation and the flow of high-scoring school-leavers.

A formula that succeeds does not have to justify itself further. Yet as the Australian Sandstones lurch into the global era, and some talk about being a great world university, it is not clear that they are ready to straddle the larger stage with quite the same confidence they have at home. Unlike Princeton or Yale they do not have a prior positional value in the global setting. The professional faculties which sustain so much of their domestic influence and their institutional psyche cut less of the mustard in Frankfurt or New York. They are coming from outside, much the more difficult way to do it; and like New Universities in the domestic setting, if they are to carve out a substantial new role it will be not so much through strategies of 'more of the same' as through brilliant innovations.

Here an old colonial isomorphism and a new utilitarian market isomorphism might hold them back. At bottom, the Sandstones always worked off models from elsewhere. In the nineteenth century it was the English redbricks, Edinburgh and a dash of Oxford at Sydney and Melbourne. In the post-war period they drew what they wanted from the pioneering courses and research programs at local Redbricks and Gumtrees, after waiting to see if the ideas worked. If other domestic institutions are becoming more isomorphistic, the Sandstones will have less to borrow. To become serious global players they will have to become not transplants so much as genuine pioneers. This has not been their strength.

All of this is not to argue that the Sandstones do not produce good education. It is to argue that in these institutions there is no *necessary* link between producer competition, consumer pressure and the quality of the education provided. Nor is there a *necessary* link between a reputation for excellence and a capacity for larger innovations. Ultimately it is prior market segmentation, not ability or quality, that maintains Sandstone supremacy. In turn, the historical concentration of resources and prestige substantiates Sandstone claims to be the home of quality. Tellingly, if a Sandstone is less well organised than other universities, or has areas of weakness unaddressed, the price is small. It loses ground relative to other Sandstones, but not its position in the elite group. Sydney exemplifies this. Though it has many brilliant researchers, and has accumulated more total wealth than any other university in Australia, the fruits of its highly developed academic cultures are partly squandered by lack of organisational coherence. The cost of this incoherence has been slippage from leading university to top five status, and some decline relative to the University of NSW. Between 1995 and 1999 Sydney's share of the total research quantum in Australia dropped from 12.0 to 9.7 per cent and the university moved from second to fourth on this measure. Yet it still recruits half the leading school-leavers in the state.[31]

All else being equal, the strongest universities are those which combine positional advantage with two other elements: institutional coherence in its contemporary form (the Enterprise University), and broad-based and vibrant scholarly cultures. Sandstones with all three elements, such as Queensland, are prospering and have improved their relative position in recent years.

Q. Are there any institutions in the country where in terms of management and governance, they're getting it right?

A. I start by thinking about universities which have greatly changed their position in a relatively short time. They can't do that unless the processes are right and some of those processes undoubtedly would be management processes. I'd have to say somewhere like UQ, because they've changed out of sight and from what I can judge it seems to be a reasonably cohesive place ... UQ has done well in research and the whole regard in which the University is held has jumped enormously. (vice-chancellor, Gumtree university)

In 1983 the University of Queensland ranked eighth in allocations from the Australian Research Grants Scheme, forerunner to the ARC. After implementing new research management plans and quality assurance strategies Queensland rose to fourth in the ARC rankings by the end of the decade. Between 1983 and 1992 it moved from tenth to third in NHMRC funding.[32] Between 1995 and 1999 Queensland moved again, rising from 9.9 to 11.0 per cent of the national research quantum, from fourth to second. It is now regarded as one of the top four Australian universities, perhaps number two in the land.

Redbricks

Though the Redbrick universities like University of New South Wales and Monash have similar objectives to the Sandstones, they are less traditionally academic, more openly corporate, modernist and pliable. Their strategies have varied. While Monash moved entrepreneurially into mergers, distance education and off-shore campuses, NSW chose to consolidate at its core site.

Trying to operate a university across distance and with in-built rivalries and in-built sector or background differences is a big challenge. We feel that bigger isn't necessarily more beautiful ... We put funding into infrastructure while other institutions were struggling with video conferencing just to have a faculty meeting. (senior executive, UNSW)

Nevertheless UNSW and Monash have much in common. Both used research to build a merit-based role in the 1960s and 1970s, and both became particularly strong in applied research, despite some pure research strengths such as Monash in chemistry. Both have always valued international education and Asian-focused curricula more highly than do the Sandstones.[33] In law and medicine, both focused on the modern profession more closely than did the Sandstones, and developed a student-centred and skill-centred pedagogy with outstanding undergraduate teaching (though later overshadowed by Sandstone rivals in postgraduate law). Both focus on relations with industry more explicitly than do the Sandstones, except perhaps Queensland. Both emphasise graduate employability. As one senior UNSW executive puts it: 'Recognition was not accorded to UNSW from academic quarters so I guess we turned to other quarters, to commerce and industry.'

At UNSW and Monash the lodestone has been the contest with an older Sandstone in the same city. At Monash, the foundation act specified that standards should be no lower than those of the University of Melbourne. It was not until 1990 that this clause was removed, and the university chose its own developmental strategy, out of Melbourne's shadow.[34] At UNSW the goal was simply to outdo Sydney in school-leaver demand and research performance.

We're not the establishment university, we're elite only on the strength of performance rather than the silver spoon ... [In the 1950s and 1960s] there was a very patrician put-down. It went on through the school system: 'your children would never go to UNSW unless they couldn't get in to Sydney'. The public announcement of quality outcomes [1993] was really defining. We knew we'd overtaken Sydney in so many areas.
... I feel the answers to these questions over the last twenty minutes have been very focused on competitiveness with Sydney and I'm sorry about that. I don't think it's a total preoccupation of the UNSW but it has been a defining feature. (senior executive, UNSW)

In contrast, the Redbrick Australian National University, outside this study, is in many respects like the Sandstones. It has no local Sandstone rival. The ANU's tone was set not by professional education and applied research, but by the collegial research culture in the Institute for Advanced Studies, the founding component of the university.

Unitechs

The third segment that is coping relatively well in the new environment is the Unitechs. Building on their past practices as technical institutes they have created a viable alternative model to that of the Sandstones, if not with the same range, complexity or flexibility. Discipline-based cultures are weaker than in the pre-1986 universities, but graduate professional cultures are strong. Collegial stuffiness is absent. The Unitechs pride themselves on teaching occupational skills, on the reputation of their graduates among employers, on their links to industry and their capacity to move quickly into new markets.[35] They innovate in newer vocational fields such as communications, multimedia, and business computing. They are modern mass-based institutions committed to broad access by students, whatever their age or background.

> Certainly QUT is a competitive institution. I think it has always seen itself as being the university for the real world and different from that mob up the river ... We go out to the market very regularly and get research to find out what we're doing and where we're going. We find out what we can about our competitors.
>
> You find out what you're good at then you market yourself along those lines, and it sort of becomes self-fulfilling. That's certainly true for QUT. (executive administrator, QUT)

The marketing strategy is supervised by the vice-chancellor. Most Unitechs are large, centralised and marketing-heavy, the most singularly corporate of all the universities.[36] This derives from their more hier- archical traditions, wherein line-of-command relations played a stronger part than faculty and collegial authority.

Apart from Curtin all of the Unitechs have a large downtown campus which strengthens their engagement with industry and government, and their role in postgraduate vocational education. The downside of these city locations is the often crowded, ugly sites. Exciting building such as Storey Hall at the Royal Melbourne Institute of Technology (RMIT) in Melbourne highlights the grimy drabness elsewhere. The Broadway building at UTS must be the most intimidating interior in any Australian educational institution, a towering high modern disaster that cruels this relatively postmodern and engaging Unitech. A major building program could completely transform RMIT and UTS. More recent constructions such as those at Curtin and the University of SA have done better.

Gumtrees

The Gumtrees are in a very different position. When they were founded in the 1960s and 1970s there was no reason to believe that universities would not always be 90 per cent publicly funded. Strong academic communities developed, though Deakin, founded at the end of fiscally driven growth in 1975, was never well resourced and remained the runt of the litter. The Gumtrees were aggressively modern, nationalistic (a characteristic that, like the native plantings, they shared with the ANU and with Monash, the last Redbrick which opened in 1961) and some were educationally radical. Flinders, Deakin and La Trobe had distinctive disciplinary mappings. Griffith and Murdoch were more inter-disciplinary than disciplinary, and developed highly democratic

governance and an air of informality. Long-term public funding eliminated the risk factor, greatly facilitating reinvention. Gumtree radicalism
was tempered over time – at Murdoch the original scheme was completely discarded – but on the whole the Gumtrees did well. They
provided opportunities for young staff unable to make headway in
conservative institutions. In many academic fields Gumtrees were more
innovative than Sandstones, and much more exciting places to be.

In those days the number of law, engineering, dentistry, medicine and
other schools was limited by the Commonwealth. Most of the Gumtrees
lacked a medical faculty and some lacked engineering, limiting their
research role and re-confirming Sandstone and Redbrick primacy in
professional education. It was in the sciences, arts, social sciences,
humanities and the newer professions that the Gumtrees became strong.
For a time individual Gumtrees could imagine that they might eventually
equal the Sandstones and Redbricks in resources and standing, especially
if they could break into elite professional education.

After the formation of the unified national system in 1988 it was easier
to start new professional schools (except in medicine where graduate
numbers were tightly controlled by the Australian Medical Association
and the Commonwealth). Yet in other respects the new system was
unfavourable to the Gumtrees. The Gumtree model was built on public
funding not private funding or market position. The decline in the
proportion of costs covered by the government hit them hard, and the
Sandstones, Redbricks and Unitechs mostly outperformed them in fee-
based education. Though several Gumtrees continued to perform well
according to academic research indicators, in commercial research they
lagged behind the Sandstones and Redbricks. The Gumtrees also had less
capacity to raise donations from alumni and others. Academic structures
became more unstable. Some were forced to cannibalise strong areas to
secure short-term returns. In the new zero-sum game, positional advantage was more decisive than before. The Gumtrees lacked positional
advantage. Demand-wise they were mostly the school-leaver's second,
third or fourth choice. Geographically, they were marooned in suburbia.

Publicly funded upward mobility gave way to pressures for downward mobility, eroding Gumtree projects grounded in modernism and
innovation. With their own identity faltering, the Gumtrees demanded to
be grouped with the Sandstones rather than each other. (Meanwhile
wiser Sandstones such as Queensland and Melbourne were beginning to
appropriate modernism, layering it onto their academic traditions.)
Casting around for winning strategies, they often found it difficult to
mobilise their staff. As one Gumtree vice-chancellor stated in interview,
'there's no real corporate spirit'. Fortunes within the group varied.
Flinders had a good medical faculty, which helped. Newcastle had

medicine and engineering, a new hope that its regional role would
generate income, and the old hope that somehow it could outdo the
metropolis.

The next few years will tell if we're going to ... just become a regional university,
one of the better regional universities. There is a strong research base here, this is
a big teaching university, but the pressure's going to be very heavy from Sydney.
Sydney and NSW are going to be very difficult to beat. (dean, Newcastle)

Macquarie had started early and was stronger than most of the others,
almost a Redbrick, though it was now squeezed between Sydney and
UNSW above it, and the downtown location and vocational reputation
of UTS rising from below. Macquarie hung on grimly, moved resources
internally, and worked at promoting its research performance. At the
University of New England, the oldest of the group, high collegial
aspirations were tethered to low student demand and a regional role.
Caught out by the declining role of public funding, it found adjustment
difficult, though its options were broadened by distance education.
Griffith repositioned itself with mergers, and flexible delivery at Logan,
but all Gumtrees with substantial mergers were stretched. James Cook
fell back on its regional specialisation and a selective research role.
Wollongong, whose starting position was weaker than some, played the
entrepreneurial and specialist research cards with success, and became
known as a well-managed institution. Murdoch and La Trobe struggled.
La Trobe seemed to lack strategy, and some of its research began to slip.
This was an effect rather than a cause. The problems faced by the Gumtrees were not a function of weaknesses in quality. They were the direct
and predictable result of the redesign of the national system as a
competitive market with mixed public and private funding.

Deakin, with less academic resources and social cachet than the other
Gumtrees remade itself. It grabbed a large new territory out of the CAE
sector in metropolitan Melbourne. Fancy managerial footwork and
promotional vigour covered for academic weakness and an awkward
cross-regional spread.

It's a funny environment. I've come to the conclusion that two things are critical.
You can achieve a lot of change by setting impossible targets because even if
people only get five out of ten impossible targets, they're still doing a lot better
than ten out of ten mediocre targets. The other thing is to have a good public
relations system, both internally and externally, so if anything goes wrong you can
always manage it.

I think Deakin is a classic postmodernist institution ... there's a lot more
investment in image making and public relations because Deakin had to go from
nowhere to somewhere. It was probably quite a good decision to say 'Let's buy

the [Geelong] Woolstore', which we don't need, and let's go for the University of
the Year award which earnt us a fortune in image and public relations.

If you're somewhere at the bottom of the hierarchy of universities, you have to
do something fairly extraordinary to pull yourself up above those limits ... if we
were UNSW or UWA this would be quite an inappropriate strategy. Take UWA,
50 per cent of their income is from the State and private income. They don't
really need to bother with public relations, it's already there in the history of the
institution. (faculty dean, Deakin)

The university built a separate commercial arm, Deakin Australia,
which secured a major role in occupational training. Employment
packages tied middle managers to the entrepreneurial centre. The School
of Education (which had led the nation) was outside the new money
culture and withered. At Deakin it often seemed that entrepreneurial
development and academic vigour were zero-sum. Reinvention of the
university created broader strategic options than those before the other
Gumtrees but at the price of short-termism, heightened dependence on
marketing, and stalling of research performance. Reliance on the past was
jettisoned. Unable to sustain itself as a struggling Gumtree, Deakin
turned itself into a New University.

New Universities

Like the Unitechs, the other post-1986 universities developed out of
merger or expansion among CAEs. This is a heterogeneous sub-sector
and it may eventually fragment into separate groupings of regional rural
institutions, regional metropolitan institutions, and various specialists. Of
the institutions in this study two are regional rurals – Central Queensland
and Southern Cross – and the other is a multi-site metropolitan institution, Edith Cowan. Outside the study, two New Universities service the
small capitals of Darwin and Canberra; and three are rural regionals
(Southern Queensland at Toowoomba, Ballarat in Victoria and the multi-
campus Charles Sturt University in NSW), two others are located in the
western suburbs of Sydney and Melbourne (the University of Western
Sydney, and Victoria University of Technology). Swinburne University
of Technology is unusual. It chose to remain relatively small, evading
mergers but picking up a small second metropolitan site and a new outer-
suburban campus. It focused on niche disciplinary strengths in business,
computing and applied science, working the fee-based markets for international and postgraduate students, and opportunities for commercial
research.

At the New Universities academic cultures have been less well rooted
and less indigenous than elsewhere, being only recently created by
government and management. At the same time the New Universities are

often outward looking. In 1997 University of Canberra Vice-Chancellor Don Aitkin compared staff at his institution, a New University, to those at three pre-1986 universities where he had worked. Canberra's staff had a quicker 'response time', and a stronger orientation to vocational education, applied research and consultancy. These academics were primarily loyal to the institution rather than to their discipline.[37] In the pre-1986 universities this institution/discipline priority is often reversed.

Though all New Universities are seeking to build postgraduate research and occupational training, research strengths are mostly confined to a handful of areas, and they lack the vocational cachet of the Sandstones, Redbricks and Unitechs. The public money is no longer there with which to construct basic research as the core of each New University: Commonwealth operating grants are channelled into teaching (often more intensive than in the Sandstones) and functions such as marketing and student services. Though some New Universities can mobilise regional electoral pressure to support growth in funded places, their development paths are corporate and entrepreneurial. They must help themselves, financing their own development. It is a difficult task.

Some universities are placed in backwaters and it will take them a long time to get to the forefront. It's a bit like the plant at the end of the garden that misses out on the water and sun. (vice-chancellor, not a New University)

In the absence of a history they can use, the New Universities are precariously free to reinvent themselves with Deakin-style strategies. The other option is to forge niche markets and play them successfully, for example Central Queensland's initiatives in health sciences, Asia-Pacific communications and rural sociology. The conditions set by demography and the positional market cannot be evaded, however. In addition to regional roles the New Universities focus on student access, pastoral care and good teaching, if only to keep the enrolments stable in a competitive market. They are generally not strong in the school-leaver stakes, and have large numbers of mature-age students and students from first generation higher education families. Several want to build a major role in distance education, including Southern Cross and Central Queensland (see below).

Isomorphs with a difference

When we look at comparative data, we find that there is pronounced diversity between universities in course mix, in the character of catchments and student populations, in research activities and performance, and in the presence or absence of independent financial means. These forms of diversity are closely related to the vertical differentiation into Sandstones, Redbricks, Unitechs, Gumtrees and New Universities.

In a small number of areas of comparison, market differentiation is less salient. First, there seems to be surprisingly little diversity in educational programs, whether based on the established hierarchy or any other factor. Second, in three other areas there is substantial variation but it does *not* follow the conventional hierarchy. As we shall argue, these 'rogue' variations are important precisely because they signify a deliberate attempt to break from path dependence and to change the place of the university within the system. It would be exaggerating to claim these strategies as a complete break from isomorphism. These are organisational innovations following standard forms, with little correlation to educational innovation. There is still isomorphism, but with a difference.

Ethos

'Each university has its own "legend"', according to Don Aitkin. This is both an idea of itself connected to its reality, and 'a constructed story intended to serve a purpose'.[38] Discerning the 'legend' or ethos of universities is a subtle problem. Sometimes divergences in institutional ethos can be read off mission statements; more often the mission statement is all things to all people, underlining a cover-all-bases ambition. All universities are committed to world-class research, all strive for excellence in teaching, all are engaged in the global education market, and so on.

Case study interviews, official documentation and publications, and marketing strategies, provide more useful evidence. Table 7.3 summarises the orientations of each institution in the study. It refers to *primary* orientations. Most aspects of ethos appear, somewhere, in every institution. For example, all managements are committed to corporate performance, though in only some universities does this permeate the whole culture. Many Redbrick academics see themselves as involved in elite formation, yet the Redbricks are more meritocratic and less patrician (and members of social elites mostly prefer Sandstones). In some institutions, vocationalism is a defining ethos, in others it takes second place to other practices.

Most universities carry more than one orientation. *Italics* indicate an orientation only partly established, or established in only part of the institution, but too formative not to mention. Not everyone will agree with these interpretations. They are based on case studies carried out in 1995 and 1996 and there have been some changes since then.

Institutional ethos is correlated to institutional segmentation. All of the Sandstones, and only the Sandstones, understand themselves as

Table 7.3 Typology of primary orientations: institutions in this study only, 1995/1996

Formation of social elite	Research excellence	Vocational preparation	Building student load	Corporate performance
Sydney	Sydney	*Monash*	Edith Cowan	*Monash*
Queensland	Queensland	*Deakin*	Central Qld	UNSW
Adelaide	Adelaide		Southern Cross	
Western Australia	Western Australia	QUT		*Deakin*
Tasmania	Tasmania	UTS		
Monash	Monash			QUT
UNSW	UNSW			UTS
	Griffith			
	Newcastle			Central Qld
	Flinders			
	James Cook			

Italics indicate orientation only partly established, or established in only part of the institution, but too formative not to mention.

primarily involved in elite formation, illustrating the persistence of their traditional social role. All institutions are involved in research, but while the Sandstones, Redbricks and most Gumtrees have a primary commitment to research excellence, the post-1986 universities do not. Every institution is involved in vocational training, but the Unitechs and Deakin have the most marked vocational orientation. All universities are concerned to maintain student load, but only the New Universities see building student load as a crucial defining issue.

The last column, commitment to corporate performance, cuts across the segments. This indicates the degree to which the health of the university as an end in itself (as distinct from the health of scholarship, research or students) permeates the institution. UNSW is more corporate than the Sandstones. Of the Sandstones, Queensland comes closest to the 'corporate' label. At Monash and Deakin institutional objectives are sustained by a culture more entrepreneurial than corporate.[39] In both cases entrepreneurialism is uneven (see chapter 5). In the Unitechs, the corporate ethos and the vocational ethos seem to reinforce each other, forming a unified whole. The same is true at Deakin, whose executive leaders have propelled commercial training. Compared to the Sandstones, Monash and UNSW are vocational in orientation, but not to the same extent as the Unitechs and Deakin. It seems that except at Monash and NSW, universities in which research excellence is a primary orientation are not at the same highly vocational, and also *vice versa*. While institutional manager-leaders might want to pursue both orientations, believing with some justification that graduate employability and research excellence are not mutually exclusive, academics often see it differently.

The association between vocational orientation and educational programs is less clear-cut. The Sandstones continue to sustain generalist courses in the humanities, social science and science that are discipline-centred rather than employment-centred. Newer universities might offer a Bachelor of Arts (Tourism) or Bachelor of Arts (Communication). Nevertheless, as noted utilitarianism is strong across the whole system.[40] Whether the goal is preparation for social leadership, preparation for professional work, or simply better job prospects, the end point is the same: employment and career. Meek and O'Neill remark that universities created out of CAEs claim their courses are 'more geared to the demands of industry and serve a student clientele having more vocational and applied interests' than similar courses in older universities. Yet 'there is little available empirical evidence to demonstrate that courses and students are as different as they are made out to be'.[41]

The Sandstones prepare students for future social position by providing an education often presented as an end in itself. The Unitechs

present education specifically as a bridge to work. This distinction between overt utility and covert utility is important in institutional ethos
and culture, but it should not be overstated.

Supply and demand

Fields of study

Though all universities aim to be comprehensive, they do not all provide
the full range of courses, creating some programmatic diversity between
them. Few have veterinary science and some do not offer agriculture,
architecture and building. Not all offer engineering or law. All have enrolments in the arts, humanities and social sciences, in science, mathematics
and computing, and in business studies. The Sandstones tend to be the
most comprehensive, and not merely because of size. Institutions with a
smaller number of fields are mostly newer and often regional. However,
one regional Gumtree (James Cook) will soon provide nine fields of study
if the planned medical school goes ahead, and the largest metropolitan
university (Redbrick Monash) lacks veterinary science, agriculture and
architecture.

Table 7.4 sets down the number of fields of study in each institution,
and also identifies those with courses in medicine. The distinction between medicine and non-medicine universities is very important in
shaping institutional potentials. It is a distinction closely correlated to
inherited segmentation. All Sandstones and Redbricks have medical
faculties. Only two of the Gumtrees do (James Cook would make three),
and no Unitechs or New Universities. Not only does medicine attract the
highest scoring school-leavers, medicine and related biological sciences
attract high levels of research funding, biomedicine and biotechnology
have great commercial potential, and the public good aspect of medicine
draws prestige.

Despite these variations, there is an overall tendency to convergence in
program mix, at both undergraduate and postgraduate level. Since 1987
the number of law schools has doubled and MBA programs are now
universal. There has also been a great growth of higher degree enrolments
in the New Universities. Meek and Wood (1998) identify 'a steep increase
in internal diversity and a corresponding decrease in external/system
diversity ... a further entrenchment of the Australian comprehensive
university has occurred'.[42]

Once the division of labour was managed by Commonwealth and in
the CAE sector by the states. In large part institutions now define their
own course mix. A greater diversity in course offerings would require the
kind of managed or negotiated division of labour that conflicts with the

Table 7.4 Broad fields of study and catchment areas, institutions in this study, 1996

Institution	Broad FOS	Medicine	Engineering	Agriculture	Principal catchment
Sydney	10	Yes	Yes	Yes	State
Queensland	10	Yes	Yes	Yes	State
Adelaide	10	Yes	Yes	Yes	State
New South Wales	9	Yes	Yes	Yes	State
Western Australia	9	Yes	Yes	Yes	State
Tasmania	9	Yes	Yes	Yes	State
UTS	8	No	Yes	Yes	State
QUT	8	No	Yes	No	State
Deakin	8	No	Yes	No	State/Region
Newcastle	8	Yes	Yes	No	Region
James Cook	8*	No*	Yes	Yes	Region
Monash	7	Yes	Yes	No	State
Flinders	7	Yes	Yes	No	State
Griffith	7	No	Yes	No	State
Central Queensland	7	No	Yes	No	Region
Edith Cowan	6	No	Yes	No	State
Southern Cross	6	No	No	No	Region

FOS indicates Field of Study provided at postgraduate level.
*Medical school planned.
Sources: DEETYA, *Selected higher education statistics*, 1997; Meek and Wood, *Higher education governance and management*, Appendix 1.

logic of a competitive system based on self-regulation. There has so far been no indication that institutions themselves are willing to collaborate to the degree required, except in certain areas with low or declining enrolments, such as languages.

Catchments and student populations

Another form of inter-institutional diversity is that between student catchments, that is, the social/geographical region from which the institution draws students. In relation to domestic students there are three kinds of institutional catchment: national, state and regional. Within institutions, catchment varies between fields of study. Some courses in generalist fields such as business, humanities and social sciences, and science, might be pitched at local employers. Others such as teaching and nursing are directed at state-wide employers. Some encourage national and international mobility, for example engineering or graduate business. Some draw on a partly national catchment, for example medicine.

The distinction between student catchments is informal and a bit fuzzy at the edges. Determined by student preference and industry support, it is also shaped by institutional missions and strategies. The national catchment, is underdeveloped in Australia. The Sandstones and Redbricks see themselves as attracting not only school-leavers and research students from one state, but also high achieving students from other states/ territories. Melbourne is now recruiting aggressively among interstate students, offering scholarships to students with high school-leaver scores. Scholarship schemes are mushrooming elsewhere. Yet these produce only marginal changes to the state and city-bound recruitment patterns, which persist. Some Sandstones would like to recruit a worldwide academic elite, in the manner of the American Ivy League. Some Unitechs also imagine themselves with a broad catchment. However, non-local entry is everywhere a small portion of total intake. The ANU comes closest to a national role but even it draws predominantly students from Canberra and from the state of NSW. With less on-campus student residence, mobility is lower in Australia than in the United States, especially in undergraduate education.

Within each state, the Sandstones and Redbricks dominate the metropolitan school-leaver markets, with the Unitechs and some Gumtrees dividing most of the others between them. Among the universities in this study, in 1997 Deakin (76 per cent) and Western Australia (75 per cent) were highly school-leaver dependent, while only 20 per cent of Bachelor-level entrants at Southern Cross used school-level qualifications. The New Universities are comparatively weak attractors of school-leavers, except at the low scoring end. Along with the Unitechs and some Gumtrees, they depend on their capacity to attract students other than school-leavers. Non-school-leavers comprise almost half of all entrants into Bachelor degrees. They include students entering from TAFE, older students, students in full-time work, and those in professional upgrading. In 1997, the proportion of Bachelor-level entrants from TAFE varied between 1 per cent at Adelaide and Western Australia, to 14 per cent at UTS and 18 per cent at Edith Cowan (table 7.5). These latter universities are also more likely to admit students on bases other than previous academic record. In 1995 the vice-chancellor of Southern Cross, Barry Coynygham said that he saw Southern Cross as making its mark not by attracting high-scoring school-leavers, but by 'adding value' to students' education during their university years.[43] The point was pedagogically sound, but smelled of an argument deployed to fit the facts, rather than one designed to put the world to rights. In the absence of positional status, the next best strategy is to focus on educational principles!

Regional institutions, whether Gumtrees or New Universities, service non-metropolitan constituencies centred on the provincial cities. By no

Table 7.5 Student entry, mode of study and access to underrepresented groups, institutions in this study, 1997

Institution and segment	Proportion of Bachelor-level entrants from school (%)	Proportion of Bachelor-level entrants from TAFE (%)	Proportion of students internal part-time (%)	Proportion of students in distance education (%)	Proportion of students from bottom quartile s.e.s. (%)
Western Australia	75	1	18	0	12.5
Sydney	66	2	24	3	6.8
Queensland	66	3	25	4	18.6
Adelaide	64	1	23	4	15.6
Tasmania	45	7	25	3	28.9
Monash	69	8	25	16	7.6
New South Wales	64	2	25	8	5.8
Newcastle	64	5	32	3	25.7
James Cook	60	4	25	6	21.3
Flinders	55	3	30	7	14.7
Griffith	46	6	27	4	22.7
Deakin	76	5	15	38	10.1
UTS	47	14	46	0	6.4
QUT	44	8	31	7	20.0
Central Queensland	44	9	10	51	36.2
Edith Cowan	39	18	27	18	18.8
Southern Cross	20	10	11	46	18.5

s.e.s. means socio-economic status as measured using classifications of postcode of student residence (see n. 44).
Sources: DEETYA, *Selected higher education statistics*, 1997, pp. 25–26; DETYA, *The characteristics and performance of higher education indicators*, 1998, pp. 19, 92, 101 and 107.

means all regional students attend their regional university. There is some leakage to the capital cities, and a trickle of movement in the reverse direction. Certain institutions such as Monash and Deakin combine a state-wide orientation with a regional base – Deakin at Warrnambool and Geelong in western Victoria, and Monash at Gippsland in the east. At Deakin, the state and the regional roles are equally important, creating organisational ambiguities. Several regional institutions try to modify the limitations of their base catchment with spatial reinventions. Central Queensland provides distance education, plays up its international role, and has opened offices in Melbourne and Sydney. Southern Cross also emphasises distance education. Nevertheless, both Central Queensland and Southern Cross factor the regional role into all development strategy.

We weren't embarrassed about the notion of being regional ... I asked 'are we ready to run with this' and everybody said 'yes', and so we've run very hard. In fact, I'm quite pleased to see other universities starting to say they are regional, they didn't say that before. (vice-chancellor, regional university)

Diversity of catchments is not tied to programmatic diversity, except in the localised targeting of some vocational courses. The commitment of Southern Cross to the North and Central Coast region of NSW is specified in its act of parliament. It provides locally focused programs in tourism, sports science, paralegal studies, multimedia technology and coastal management. James Cook focuses on tropical themes in research. There, unlike Central Queensland, regional specialisation is a substitute for a global focus.

There are other sources of diversity in the proportion of students enrolled on a part-time rather than full-time basis, and the weight of distance education (external studies), of which more below. Institutions with a high proportion of part-time students tend to have many students who are older and work full-time. UTS, with 46 per cent part-time study and a downtown Sydney location plays a strong work/study role. QUT has positioned itself in similar fashion. Given the growth of postgraduate education and occupational upgrading, a large number of non-school-leaver students is not necessarily a sign of weakness or low status. In the longer term it is likely that this form of participation will grow particularly rapidly. Some institutions will strengthen their position by catering for 'lifelong learning'. It is less certain whether this will link to a role in research.

There are also variations in the social backgrounds of students, though here there are problems with the measures of social background used. In 1997, 14.5 per cent of all students in higher education were from the bottom socio-economic quartile (25 per cent) of the population as determined by DETYA, a slight decline from 15.0 per cent in 1992. At Central Queensland, Tasmania and Newcastle the proportion was greater than 25 per cent, while it was below 10 per cent at Sydney, NSW, University of Technology, Sydney and Monash (table 7.5). This suggests universities with substantially different social roles and is consistent with other data showing that Sandstones and Redbricks draw disproportionately on upper socio-economic groups.[44] More light could be thrown on this if a better measure of social advantage/ disadvantage was available. DETYA uses the individual student's residential postcode as a proxy measure of socio-economic status. The socio-economic status of the postcode mix on a single national scale determines where the institution falls.[45]

Among universities in the study, the proportion of students who were indigenous varied from a high of 5.0 per cent at James Cook to a low of 0.5 per cent at Flinders.

Research activities

The research functions and activities of institutions exhibit similar trajectories but with segmented performance. Research and research training are one of the modes of institutional isomorphism. The imperatives to generalise the research role within institutions, and to maximise success in the standardised competition for grants and research quantum, together create a tendency for institutions to strive to imitate each other's research profiles. This can undercut strategies of regional or field of study specialisation.

At the same time research is a major element in the vertical differentiation of higher education. Academic success in research, and levels of income from research, distinguish Sandstones and Redbricks from others. Academic success demarcates most Gumtrees from the newer universities. Research income distinguishes Unitechs from New Universities. The presence or absence of medicine is decisive. Formal research roles have converged, but in terms of status and income, the gap between pre- and post-1986 institutions remains. Only in the number of students enrolled in higher degree studies has it closed significantly. Between 1990 and 1996 the proportion of commencing research degree enrolments held by 12 universities created after 1986 rose from 7 to 13 per cent. Their student numbers rose from 381 to 1301.[46] This growth brought with it the need for additional research infrastructure in the form of laboratories, libraries, computers and other equipment, and academic staff with research training and experience, able to act as supervisors.

Crucially, in relation to research quantum, the gap is closing only very slightly. In 1999, the total share of the quantum held by the six

Sandstones was 48.2 per cent, not much less than the level of 50.4 per cent in 1995. After a decade of research building by the post-1986 universities the Sandstones were still overwhelmingly strongest in research. The share of total quantum held by the 12 New Universities remained very low, though it rose from 2.8 to 5.2 per cent. The five Unitechs moved from 6.8 to 8.1 per cent. The share of quantum held by the ten Gumtrees at 20.7 per cent was virtually unchanged from the 1995 figure of 20.6 per cent. The UNSW and Monash share fell from 19.4 to 17.8 per cent.

Table 7.6 summarises the research higher degree activities of institutions in this study, including the number of students in research higher degrees and their proportion of total enrolment, and the proportion of academic staff with doctoral qualifications.

In 11 universities more than 4 per cent of students are enrolled in research higher degrees. All were founded before 1987. Of the other universities, all but Deakin were founded after 1987. Deakin took on major mergers with former CAEs (even so, Deakin's research profile is weak for a Gumtree). At Central Queensland and Southern Cross research higher degree courses are little developed. The pattern of higher degree enrolment correlates roughly with that of staff qualifications. The norm in the pre-1986 universities is for 50–75 per cent staff to have doctorates. In the post-1986 universities it is around 30–40 per cent, though higher in Unitechs than New Universities.

Table 7.6 also draws out the vital connection between having medicine, the strength of the research role, and the income from research. All universities with a medical faculty earn at least $30 000 per effective full-time staff member in 1996, except Tasmania ($29 128), while all others earned less than $20 000. Sandstone strength is sustained not just by self-reproducing claims about excellence: it is firmly grounded in political economy.

Though the measure is biased in favour of research incomes rather than outcomes (chapter 6), the proportion of a university's government operating funds derived from the research quantum has become a key indicator of academic standing in research. Research income as a proportion of total income signifies the economic weight of research. Both measures suggest the degree to which each university is research intensive, in terms of conventional data. The diversity is great. At Adelaide and Queensland, research is 24 per cent of total income. This denotes a very different kind of university to Deakin or Edith Cowan where research income is 2 per cent or less.

The struggle to develop research across-the-board has positive educational spin-offs. All else being equal it has probably improved the standard of teaching, and increased the attractiveness of some universities to international students, facilitating cultural diversity and

Table 7.6 Research activity and income, institutions in this study, 1996, 1997, 1998

Institution and type	Medical faculty	Higher degree research share of all students 1998 (%)	Doctorally qualified as share of academic staff 1996 (%)	Research income per full-time equivalent staff 1996 ($)	Research income as share of all university income 1996 (%)	Research quantum as share of operating funding 1996 (%)
Western Australia	SS	Yes	11.4	74	56 163	23	11
Adelaide	SS	Yes	9.2	66	56 465	24	9
Queensland	SS	Yes	10.2	73	47 969	24	9
Flinders	GT	Yes	5.9	55	41 112	22	8
New South Wales	RB	Yes	7.9	61	57 204	20	7
Sydney	SS	Yes	9.8	58	33 589	15	7
Monash	RB	Yes	6.3	53	33 008	14	7
Newcastle	GT	Yes	4.6	48	31 541	14	5
Tasmania	SS	Yes	6.7	51	29 128	14	5
James Cook	GT	No*	7.2	59	19 598	10	4
Griffith	GT	No	4.2	50	18 115	8	3
UTS	UT	No	2.6	39	12 984	5	2
QUT	UT	No	2.8	37	12 916	5	2
Central Qld	NU	No	1.7	33	10 231	3	1
Southern Cross	NU	No	1.8	29	7 028	3	1
Edith Cowan	NU	No	3.1	30	5 981	2	1
Deakin	GT	No	2.4	38	5 323	2	1

Higher degree research refers to Masters or doctoral level. Research income per FTE staff refers to full-time equivalent academic research or research and teaching staff. 'Operating funding' refers to annual Commonwealth operating grants.

*Medical school planned.

Sources: DEETYA, *Selected higher education statistics, 1997*, p. 23; DETYA, *The characteristics and performance of higher education indicators*, 1998, pp. 95, 128 and 139.

international exchange. At the same time the fuller potential of a universal research orientation has not been realised. The number of strong
research universities is no greater than in 1987 (it might be less, if
Deakin's research role has declined substantially). To build all universities
as research-strong would require pre-1985 public funding. The great bulk
of research activities requires some public subsidy, even those directly
relevant to industry. Commercial research income is not enough, and
anyway, success in commercial research is normally underpinned by
strong basic research (chapter 6).

Financial independence

Institutions vary in the proportion of income deriving from Commonwealth grants; the proportion from market-based sources, including
student fees and the sale of services; and the proportion from other
private sources such as investments and donations. All else being equal,
reduced dependence on the Commonwealth signifies a university that is
economically stronger and has greater discretion to pursue its own projects. It is less vulnerable to the specific requirements of government, to
the effects of fiscal reductions, and to future changes in policy.

There is more than one kind of non-government income, and its
potentials vary. Higher income from fees and charges indicates greater
vulnerability to changes in market fortune and to the isomorphistic pressures of market competition. Private income from non-market sources,
such as investments and properties, and donations and bequests, confers
a greater potential for financial flexibility and educational independence. Institutions with a relatively high income from these sources have
a greater discretion to shape their own path, to develop diverse and
distinctive teaching programs, scholarship and research. It is true that
some income from non-market private sources is tied to particular
purposes, such as endowed professorial chairs, and this can reduce
flexibility. Here market-based incomes can confer greater discretion on
managers. Nevertheless, market-based flexibility is exercised within
narrower educational limits: not only are market activities subject to
powerful isomorphistic pressures, they are also discipline-specific. It is
straightforward to use market revenues to build academic infrastructure
in the disciplines earning those revenues. It is more difficult to use those
revenues to subsidise other disciplines or finance pure research.

The Sandstones, and to a lesser extent the Redbricks, benefit from
relatively high levels of independent assets and non-market private incomes. At nineteenth-century foundations such as Sydney, there are now
several generations of social leaders that have exchanged economic
capital for cultural capital. The University of Western Australia is smaller

than average in size, but has almost a billion dollars in assets, a high proportion in income-generating funds. Almost one-third of its income consists of non-market private revenues, an extraordinary position for an Australian university, one almost akin to an American Ivy League institution. Adelaide is another with an asset base large relative to the number of students, and a substantial flow of non-market private revenues. Other institutions not in the study that enjoy high financial independence are the University of Melbourne and the Australian National University. Melbourne has non-current assets of $1508 million. The ANU has a non-current asset base of $1154 million, and more than one dollar in five (20.2 per cent) is from non-market private sources.

Table 7.7 provides data on financial independence. Of course, whether financial independence is actually translated into educational innovation and diversity cannot be read from the financial base alone. Other factors come into play, including academic cultures, professional associations, management systems, and organisational innovation.

Table 7.7 also includes data on income from market-based private sources. Here, in contrast with income from non-market private sources, the customary hierarchy does *not* determine the position of institutions. None of the institutions where the proportion of market-based incomes exceeds the 1996 national average (13.4 per cent) are Sandstones, though the other types of university are all represented. The two Red-bricks are the highest income earners in this area. Griffith, Deakin, Central Queensland and QUT are also above average. At UNSW almost one dollar in five (18.6 per cent) is derived from fees and charges. (At the Gumtree Macquarie University, outside the study, the figure is even higher at 20.8 per cent.)

Among the Sandstones, Western Australia has the lowest proportion of income from this source (9.0 per cent). Market-based incomes at Flinders and Newcastle are even lower.

Diversity in education and research

Is this vertical differentiation of higher education associated with greater diversity in educational content and method, and in research, enhancing the overall capacity for disciplinary innovation? The Commonwealth has not collected comparative data at discipline level since the discipline reviews of the 1980s. In a study focused on governance and management it was not possible to collect conclusive data on trends towards diversity or isomorphism in education and research programs.[47] However, the study enabled us to develop a sense of overall trends.

In the recent period institutional innovation has been focused on the mission, on the expansion of student catchment (market share), and on

Table 7.7   Financial independence, institutions in this study, 1996

Institution and segment		Total non-current assets[a] ($ million)	Proportion of all income from non-market private sources[b] (%)	Proportion of all income from fees and charges (%)
Sydney	SS	2459	22.4	10.4
New South Wales	RB	1309	12.7	18.6
Western Australia	SS	995	29.0	9.0
Queensland	SS	945	10.0	13.1
Monash	RB	661	14.6	16.9
QUT	UT	453	7.2	14.6
Adelaide	SS	450	14.8	11.4
Newcastle	GT	434	16.0	6.1
UTS	UT	390	14.2	10.9
Deakin	*GT*	390	9.7	16.6
Tasmania	*SS*	342	5.5	10.0
Griffith	GT	326	5.8	16.8
James Cook	GT	265	4.8	11.4
Edith Cowan	NU	256	11.8	10.7
Flinders	GT	213	10.8	6.9
Central Queensland	NU	125	11.8	14.6
Southern Cross	NU	88	4.3	9.8
National mean[b]		*499*	*12.9*	*13.4*

a Mean of non-current assets of full-size universities, excluding the small specialist higher education institutions and all institutions outside the funded national system.
b The proportion of total institutional income that is defined by DETYA as 'investment and other income', which includes rents, interest payments and dividends from institutional investments, donations and endowments to the university, etc.
Source: DETYA *The characteristics and performance of higher education indicators,* pp. 132, 137 and 148.

management systems and financing. There has not been the same pressure to innovate in and across the disciplines. This does not mean that there is no diversity in teaching style, in course contents or in research. But we found no evidence to suggest that such diversity was increasing. A number of interviewees stated that the opposite was the case:

The Unified National System was supposed to create a diversified system and it didn't, everyone became the same. (senior manager, Unitech)

If so, it is not surprising, given that the Enterprise University tends to foster such convergence. Take research. New Universities copy the practices of institutions with more resources and status. There is no real prospect that isomorphistic strategies can overcome their historic disadvantages, and the constraints of the policy setting, and enable these universities to become fully fledged research institutions capable of reworking the disciplines themselves. Why then do these new universities use imitating strategies? In a market, emulation, rather than originality, is the quicker route to legitimacy and to a limited kind of success. When allocating scarce resources to investment in new research programs, the Unitechs and the New Universities are constrained by the quantum formula, and peer assessment of proposals for ARC grants. Where they attempt to develop niches, the need to minimise the width of the band of risk encourages conformism elsewhere: they 'copy in all ways other than the particularly distinguishing one' as Levy puts it.[48] It is not that competition inhibits all forms of innovation. Rather, innovation safe within the terms of market competition is encouraged, while more far-reaching innovations in education and research are not. New competitors find it hard to change the rules of the game.

The fate of Gumtree experimentalism is instructive. Griffith began in 1975 with an inter-disciplinary course structure, a focus on applications and social problems rather than isolated scholarship, and strongly student-centred pedagogies. These approaches were associated with an unusually 'flat' management structure. Educational innovation and organisational innovation were joined by a common participatory culture (it was assumed, mistakenly, that educational and organisational innovation were each necessary to the other). By the mid-1990s, with the university grown to 20 000 students on four sites, most of the original distinctiveness was gone. The original inter-disciplinary ethos had survived only in pockets such as environmental science and Asian studies. There was still a higher than average participation in governance but the management structure was now an orthodox one. The style was modern rather than informal, though it remained less formal than the Sandstones. Ironically, while Griffith was reverting back to the mainstream, courses and research based on inter-disciplinarity, and applications to social problems, had become more widely used elsewhere, without the old Griffith nexus to organisational democracy. Griffith and the other institutions had converged. The outcome was less inter-institutional diversity, in organisational culture and in disciplinary maps.

This is not altogether a bad thing – after all, good innovations *should* be imitated. The question is whether such 'good innovations' are still possible. It is now more difficult for newer institutions to build the kind of institutional and programmatic diversity embodied in Griffith, Murdoch and others in their early days. The need for short-term returns renders problematic those institutional experiments that require a longer time to come to fruition. Much of the competition in higher education is at the level of programs. It is here that institutions attract and retain students. In a student-load and student-fee financed system it is essential to maintain numbers. Institutions have a diminished capacity to endure low enrolments, yet when courses in new areas are being developed, such risks are rarely absent. Innovation in pure research is subject to even greater hazard.

Institutions are dealing with a more heterogeneous clientele, are probably more responsive to that clientele, and are drawing on a more diverse range of funding sources. Institutions are more self-managed and have greater discretion in relation to course mix and delivery. Proponents of conventional institutional reform often argue that a greater diversity in clientele and funding sources generates a corresponding educational diversity more or less automatically, in linear fashion. But innovation is not a generic quality. Organisational innovation does *not* necessarily produce educational innovation, and the two kinds of innovation have somewhat different dynamics. There is no evidence that the linear effects imagined by proponents of reform have actually taken place.

The Sandstones have the greatest capacity to bear the risks of innovation. But they also have the producer power to shape what the student-consumer will demand, they experience strong isomorphistic pressures from professional groups and academic cultures, and their strategic instinct is to stay close to established practices that are associated with their positional advantage. Redbricks and Gumtrees are striving to become like Sandstones. New Universities that want to increase market share have more strategic need to take risks, yet the penalties of failure are far more severe. All of this suggests that when engaging in programmatic innovation in a competitive system, the best strategy is to disguise diversity by marketing it as more of the same.

Of course fields of knowledge evolve not only under conditions of systemic and institutional organisation, but according to their own inner pressures. Academic disciplines are subject to continual diversification, combination and change. There are striking variations between disciplinary cultures, and this is a continuing source of diversity. Research on higher education suggests that among academics, attitudinal variation is greater on the basis of fields of study than on gender, age, promotional level, duties, and the status or resources of institutions.[49] Is the spontaneous variation of the disciplines sufficient to counter the herd tendencies in institutional management and strategy?

Perhaps not. First, the diversifying effects of disciplinary innovation are not infinite. Most disciplines are globally networked and subject to *de facto* international benchmarking, for example the natural sciences, mathematics, engineering and business studies. Peer review of research proposals, for example through the ARC and the NHMRC, is another standardising device. Second, as we have seen, in this period the disciplines are subject to managerial reconstruction (and deconstruction). Research centres often constitute a shift away from discipline-specific identity. Standardised common formulae for measuring research performance tend to push activity towards a common mould. Cross-disciplinary schools are substituted for discipline-based departments. Another sign of the times is the extinction of fields with small student numbers and poor prospects of non-government income, regardless of their intrinsic intellectual importance. One suspects that Clark is right to assert the ever dividing plurality of the disciplines as a source of diversity, but this argument misses the point that in the Australian system, at least, the organisational weight of the disciplines is declining. That seems to us the decisive trend. Because of this, the capacity of these same disciplines to drive diversity throughout the higher education system is also reducing.[50] Under these conditions it would be unrealistic to expect a flowering of diversity in education and research.

Thus while in terms of resources and status the vertical distance between the Sandstones and other institutions has been maintained, diversity in teaching and research has probably diminished. Why hasn't vertical segmentation provided the basis for a division of labour, facilitating a more pronounced educational diversity, as in the USA? The answers to the question are government, competition, and their interactions. The diversifying potential of segmentation is modified by the 'one size fits all' comprehensive university, and the determination of both government and institutions to provide doctoral courses and research in most disciplines. This has headed off American-style institutional diversity between full research universities and undergraduate universities and colleges. And funding is more insecure than in the USA. This promotes low-risk isomorphism in strategies.

Simulacra exposed

In a system premised on a single model, the full force of isomorphism is felt. This isomorphism becomes the primary vehicle for vertical differentiation. Fulton describes a similar outcome in the United Kingdom, which like Australia is a post-binary environment:

What is emerging from student selection, from teaching assessment and ... is confirmed by the composite league table of 'good universities' which several national newspapers now regularly publish – is a single status hierarchy in which all of the main indicators point in the same direction. This is bad news for diversity: it gives great authority to the leading universities to impose their values and practices on the rest of the system, whether deliberately or not; and it renders alternative values and practices distinctly suspect ... Far from encouraging diversification, the new unitary structure is serving to underpin the robustness of the pre-existing hierarchy.[51]

As Clark puts it, in place of formally separated sectors, 'we now find institutions increasingly strung out along extended continua, with finer degrees of difference between neighbours and enormous difference between the extremes'. In the lesser universities, institutional strategy is caught in the logic of the 'simulacrum' much discussed in postmodern theory. A 'simulacrum' is a state of replication in which the difference between the copy and the original disappears. Lesser universities want to become 'simulacra' of the market leaders. The problem is that universities are position-bound, and success is a product not just of clever strategies, but of history and geography. The positional power of the leader stays intact. The 'simulacra' are exposed as inferior copies. What Clark calls 'weak emulating' by new universities, universities that can travel only a quarter or a half of the way to the desired model, sustains vertical differentiation. Institutions, 'become variously sorted out on a continuum of degrees of difference'.[52] Unlike the old binary divisions, the new informal differentiation is never acknowledged by policy-makers.

The result is an ambiguous hierarchy, sustained by differences of price, students, activities, money and social group use. The strong institutions set the content boundaries around potential innovations in education and research (aside from innovations with lower status). The main form of diversity is vertical rather than horizontal. In this manner, market liberal reform is transformed into the social projects of conservatives. Via mixed public/private funding and system competition, the advantages long held by the Sandstones are modernised. Instead of the result of a patrician conspiracy, or of state distribution of largesse, Sandstone catchet, and the social and educational projects associated with that catchet, now appear to be proved in open competition. Inherited privilege has been turned into merit.

Higher education in Australia has been completely transformed. Only the major players and the outcomes remain the same. This presents no problem for the Sandstones. The non-Sandstones, finding the game arranged in someone else's favour, are left with only one way of lifting their place. By reinventing themselves, they can change their agendas and broaden their choices. Reinvention strategies are designed to create strategic room to move, enabling a university to at least partly evade the constraints of its historic role.

Reinvention strategies

Institutional reinvention is no small matter. It means concurrent change in several spheres: ethos, management systems, financing, organisational culture, course structures and teaching programs, research activities, marketing and community relations. It is expensive and requires time. It means jettisoning key elements of the past and this can be difficult and painful. It is a strategy for institutions for whom the past is more a handicap than a help. In the early 1990s the New Universities in Australia all reinvented themselves as comprehensive doctoral institutions, for to cling to CAE identity was to guarantee marginalisation. The Unitechs found that part of their past was still useful, and developed a hybrid model combining university and technical institute. It was a partial reinvention. The Sandstones remained path dependent. They had nothing to gain from riskier reinventions. For the Gumtrees, the options were more ambiguous.

Reinvention continues to be a live option. Some universities are still working through the implications of an earlier episode, while others have engaged in more than one transformation. Here it is necessary to distinguish genuine strategic reinvention from continuous responsiveness and from the marketing campaigns now part of every institution. Often, what appears as a new orientation is just slick promotion: marketing in the absence of changes in academic priorities or internal systems. That is not to imply that marketing is always superficial, an ephemeral superstructure on top of something more fundamental. Marketing itself can be a powerful instrument of reinvention, entrenching a new ethos, changing 'customer' expectations and reshaping the internal climate. Marketing budgets under central control can be used to outflank academic units that resist change.

At one extreme, marketing shapes organisational/educational change as Syme suggests, rather than vice versa.[53] It is always tempting to use marketing to 'solve' short-term problems. At worst, this results in destabilisation. The university finds itself in a grey zone between public relations and real transformation. The colours of one superficial makeover after another start to blur. Marketing and student recruitment become decoupled from teaching and research programs, customer expectations are neither consistent nor met, longer term evolution becomes the random aggregation of short-term market reactions. Institutional identity is undermined. Marketing can be a good servant, but it is a bad master.

Strategic reinvention should also be distinguished from the on-going modernisation and corporate reform affecting all institutions. Most of the Sandstones engage in modernisation, whether reforming recalcitrant faculties, installing performance drivers and creating private funding and a more entrepreneurial culture, installing new technologies in teaching and administration, or changing the university crest to attract alumni and sell more merchandise to young students. Sandstones can afford a good deal of modernisation without challenging their identity. However, it may be significant that the two Sandstones now closest to the label 'corporate', Melbourne and Queensland have improved their relative position the most. Ironically, it is in the once 'naturally modern' Gumtrees, where identity and strategy are more fragile, that modernisation provokes more difficult debate.

The Redbricks have no need to resist modernisation. The difficult question for them is whether to engage in reinvention. For a Redbrick secure in public standing there are less risks in reinvention than for a Gumtree. A new trajectory offers the potential to circumvent a Sandstone rival. On the other hand, reinvention means forgoing the hope that a long slow isomorphism, doing the Sandstone better than the Sandstones, might eventually take the Redbrick past its older rival. UNSW and Monash have reinvented themselves, the ANU has not. The reinvention of Monash has been more profound than that of UNSW.

Making a difference

In the era of the Enterprise University, Australian universities have developed three kinds of reinvention strategies. As noted, these forms of strategy constitute a form of diversity not correlated to the conventional vertical differentiation of universities:

- a very strong commitment to entrepreneurial activity and private income-raising (for example fee-based education for international students, postgraduates and those in short courses, commercial research and consultancy, and the like);
- an advanced investment in globalisation and international education;
- specialisation in distance education and flexible learning.

All three strategies rely on impetus generated from the executive centre of the institutions, and sufficient university-wide support. All three involve organisational innovation, expenditure and risk. These are Enterprise University strategies *par excellence*, resting on the professionalisation of management and broadening of its scope, and changes in student recruitment and financing, communication systems and modes of delivery. It is a sign of the times that all three strategies are 'global', in the sense of working with off-site networks and relationships. All have the potential to generate income. All constitute a limited break from the old path. They are forms of innovation that fit the times. Income-raising, entrepreneurship and internationalisation are qualities favoured by government policy, and are also friendly to market interests. None of the three strategies demands fundamental innovation in course content or research (though a deeper engagement in international education points the way towards longer term curriculum change).

These three reinvention strategies can be discerned statistically. While all institutions are increasing their earnings from entrepreneurship, in a small number the commitment to private income is exceptional (table 7.8). Redbricks UNSW and Monash are notable for their fee-based programs, especially international marketing. In 1997 almost one UNSW student in four (22.3 per cent) was a fee-paying student, compared to Sydney with 10 per cent, and Newcastle and Southern Cross with less than 7 per cent. UNSW and the University of Technology in Sydney are leaders in fee-based postgraduate education. Other major commercial players are Edith Cowan, Central Queensland, QUT and UTS, Deakin (note that enrolments in the commercial entity Deakin Australia do not appear in these statistics), and Griffith, which has quickly built a sizeable international program. Southern Cross is focusing on fee-based post-graduate courses. The University of WA has a high international student enrolment by national standards, but not state standards: international student numbers at Curtin University in Western Australia, outside the study, are much higher. Like Griffith's, UWA's internal culture is less entrepreneurial than these data suggest. Statistically, Tasmania and Flinders are the least entrepreneurial universities in the study. James Cook seems almost indifferent to fee-based earnings, but stronger in commercial research and services.

All universities provide international education. It is a significant source of revenue: in 1997, 92.3 per cent of international students paid fees. However, the mere presence of such students does not mean that the institution has reinvented itself as an internationalised university. It is possible to enrol international students without making changes to programs, services or ethos.[54]

Indicators of a university more internationalised than most include a very high proportion of enrolments from this source (UNSW, Monash, Central Queensland), and an off-shore presence via distance education or franchising arrangements (Monash, Central Queensland). More than half of Southern Cross' small number of international students are off-shore, reflecting its commitment to distance education. Other signs of global engagement include international campuses (Monash has one at Kuala Lumpur in Malaysia and others are planned), 'twinning' arrange-ments whereby local institutions provide the first part of an Australian degree, staff and student exchange, research collaboration, and most

Table 7.8 Market-based activities and internationalisation: institutions in this study, 1997 and 1998

Institution and segment		Fees and charges as share of income 1997[a] (%)	Fee-paying student load as share of total student load 1997[b]			Off-shore students as share of international students 1997 (%)	Total international students 1998
			Postgraduate (%)	International (%)	Total (%)		
New South Wales	RB	21.1	4.8	17.5	22.3	0.4	5011
Edith Cowan	NU	19.1	0.5	9.6	10.1	1.7	1538
Monash	RB	18.3	2.0	15.7	17.7	3.9	6293
Deakin	*GT*	18.0	2.4	7.8	10.2	2.0	2196
Central Queensland	NU	17.5	0.9	12.8	13.7	3.2	1777
Griffith	GT	16.0	0.9	9.7	10.6	0.1	2367
UTS	UT	15.1	4.5	7.7	12.2	0.8	1947
QUT	UT	15.0	1.0	7.5	8.5	0.4	2252
Sydney	SS	13.4	2.4	7.5	9.9	0.9	2700
Queensland	SS	13.3	0.9	7.0	7.9	0.9	1784
Newcastle	GT	12.8	0.7	5.8	6.5	0.5	1096
James Cook	GT	12.5	0	4.7	4.7	0.3	460
Southern Cross	NU	10.9	2.3	3.1	5.4	1.9	406
Western Australia	SS	10.9	1.2	12.7	13.9	0.5	1419
Adelaide	SS	10.5	2.3	9.2	11.5	0.0	1186
Tasmania	*SS*	7.3	0.3	8.7	9.0	2.2	1027
Flinders	GT	6.4	1.0	6.1	7.1	0.7	646
National mean		14.9	2.0	10.3	12.3	2.2	–

a Includes fees from continuing education (short non-award courses e.g. professional upgrading), postgraduate courses, fee-paying international students, and other fees and charges for services such as research and consultancy.

b Fee-paying students are students paying 'up-front' tuition fees directly to the universities rather than incurring liabilities under the Higher Education Contribution Scheme or exempt from fees and charges (for example research students with scholarships are exempt). Includes fee-paying international students and postgraduate students.

Bold indicates a level of activity greater than the national average.

Source: DEETYA 1997, pp. 90–91, 97 and 121–125.

importantly, the internationalisation of curricula to encompass international themes, contents and methods of teaching and learning.

International research collaboration is strongest in the Sandstones and Redbricks,[55] but the Sandstones are less interested in fee-based recruitment than many other universities, and their international research links rarely flow through into course development. In contrast Monash and UNSW have long been strongly engaged in international education, and as providers of Asian languages and courses in Asian studies. This broad involvement in international education, facilitating fee-based recruitment, has strengthened in recent years. One UNSW executive states:

We basically won't get into something if we don't think it's got the right flavour to it ... We're in it for the long-term: 20, 30, 50 years. Reputation. UNSW has been a big international university since day one and we're very anxious to make sure that what we do, we do very well. I know that sounds very trite but it permeates the thinking.

For much of the 1990s Monash styled itself 'Australia's International University'. It is not clear how far UNSW and Monash have taken internationalisation of the curriculum – neither has introduced bilingual programs, or created options in non-western law or medicine – but the groundwork for a more profound internationalisation is partly done.

The other reinvention strategy is learning at a distance. Until recently distance education in mail or broadcast mode never had more than supplementary importance in Australia. A local equivalent of the UK's successful Open University never emerged. Telecommunications and screen-based technologies have now conferred on distance education a greater strategic significance. Institutions attuned to it are best placed to enter web and e-mail based delivery, where a global market is emerging,[56] and develop screen-based delivery into the workplace. They can also augment on-site provision with e-mail communication and print-based materials of distance education kind ('flexible learning').

A small number of universities have made flexible learning a major strategic priority. The original group of distance education specialists was government-determined. In 1988 the Commonwealth named seven institutions – New England, Charles Sturt, Deakin, Monash/Gippsland, Southern Queensland, Central Queensland, the University of South Australia – plus three universities in Western Australia operating as a consortium. This managed division of labour soon began to break down and special funding for the designated institutions was abolished formally in 1994, by which time Southern Cross was emerging as another provider. Table 7.9 shows that Southern Cross, Central Queensland and

Deakin have made a profound commitment to distance education. Those outside the study with a very substantial distance component are Charles Sturt, Southern Queensland and New England.

These six institutions are the flexible learning specialists. It is a distinctive mode of provision. Their students are older than elsewhere (80 per cent of all external students are aged more than 25 years)[57] and often commence on a basis other than school-leaver. Student to academic staff ratios are much higher than average, for example 26 to 1 at Southern Cross, 22 at Central Queensland and 20 at Deakin compared to an average 16 in all universities (1996). In most of these institutions the ratio of non-academic to academic staff is also high.[58] A move away from face-to-face delivery appears to be associated with a lesser role for academics and a greater one for non-academic professionals, technicians and support staff, similar to the trend in the United States.[59]

Edith Cowan and Monash are other institutions where distance education is important, if less dominant. Edith Cowan provides external education to almost one student in five and maintains a changing set of study centres across the state, some oriented to indigenous students in remote communities. As one leader at Edith Cowan sees it, distance education is not just a strategy for reinvention, it might become the whole of higher education:

It would be much more convenient to have one large campus and operate there: much easier, much cheaper and the organisation would be much simpler because of the proximity of the people. However that's not the real world. It's not the way of the future ... It's just unrealistic to expect that in the modern world where the technology allows us to deliver our programs any place any where any time.

Despite this the University of Western Australia, with the same state-wide catchment as Edith Cowan, maintains one metropolitan campus and no external education, commands the support of high-achieving school-leavers, and maintains across-the-board research activities with a very high level of quantum funding per academic staff member. The traditional approach is still successful for some universities, though not for all.

All of the distance education specialists are regional institutions and four of the six are New Universities. Specialisation in distance education enables New Universities to partly escape their history and often, their geography. It is an alternative strategy to building a strong research university and working the school-leaver market. Likewise, it is an alternative strategy for provincial city Gumtrees such as Deakin and New England. At Monash distance education is centred on the regional campus of Gippsland, and most of the courses provided at the 'parent'

Table 7.9 Orientation to distance education: institutions in this study, 1997

Orientation to distance education (DE)	Institution and segment		Proportion of students in distance education (%)	Number of students in distance education	Overall student-staff ratio (all disciplines)
DE a defining feature	Deakin	GT	38	10 256	20
	Central Queensland	NU	51	5 816	22
	Southern Cross	NU	46	4 230	26
DE provision substantial	Monash	RB	16	6 443	17
	Edith Cowan	NU	18	3 452	16
DE a minor component	New South Wales	RB	8	2 153	16
	QUT	UT	7	2 150	19
	Flinders	GT	7	836	15
	James Cook	GT	6	508	14
DE negligible/absent	Queensland	SS	4	1 242	14
	Griffith[a]	GT	4	775	16
	Adelaide	SS	4	541	14
	Sydney	SS	3	1 073	13
	Newcastle	GT	3	632	15
	Tasmania	SS	3	368	16
	UTS	UT	0	0	17
	Western Australia	SS	0	0	15

a Griffith has since launched a major initiative in flexible delivery at its new Logan campus.
Sources: DEETYA, *Selected higher education statistics 1997*, 1997, pp. 25–26; DETYA, *The characteristics and performance of higher education indicators*, 1998, pp. 19, 92 and 132.

campus at Clayton are not in flexible mode. Monash is unique in that its specialisation in distance education is additional to its role as a comprehensive metropolitan university, rather than a substitute for it. Monash has more roles than any other Australian university. It competes with Melbourne for school-leavers. It has some strong research faculties. It is attempting to become a major global player, and it is active in flexible delivery and distance education. The two global aspects, international education and distance education, evolved separately, but off-shore distance education is targeted for future growth. The Monash case suggests there is no reason why a Sandstone or a Redbrick should not make a major commitment to flexible delivery, providing it does not become *the* strategic priority, which would be incompatible with a strong research base.

In the longer term the proportion of students enrolled in distance education will have decreasing value as a measure of flexible learning. In many universities a growing number of internal courses are provided in both face-to-face and flexible modes. In future many students will prefer such dual mode courses. No doubt a university's long-term strength in flexible learning will be partly determined by its strength in other respects. But timing, infrastructure, and expertise also contribute. Institutions that have a head-start in flexible learning will be best placed to meet demand. They have enhanced their strategic flexibility.

Table 7.10 summarises the reinvented universities in this study. UNSW, Monash, Deakin, the Unitechs and Central Queensland are leaders in commercial income. (Griffith and James Cook earn significant private incomes, but have not been *remade* around commercial activities.) In globalisation and international education, the leaders are UNSW, Monash and Central Queensland (UWA has not remade itself). In distance education the major players are Deakin, Central Queensland and Southern Cross, followed by Monash. Notable absentees from these lists are the Gumtrees, underlining their strategic impasse. Also absent are the Sandstones, which do not need to reinvent themselves.

Reinvention and governance

Chapter 5 discussed variations in academic cultures and management cultures. It was noted that in the Sandstone universities academic cultures are collegial, or characterised by the ethos of professional service. Among the Sandstones institutional coherence is relatively strong, except at Sydney, though integration is achieved more by cultural osmosis than enforced consent. UNSW and Monash are characterised by corporatism and entrepreneurialism, and a more overt central management. The Gumtrees sit somewhere between the two cases – some have a stronger

Table 7.10 Universities that have reinvented themselves: forms of reinvention and the organisational attributes associated with them

Universities	Income earning and entrepreneurship	International education and global exchange	Distance education and flexible learning
Universities	New South Wales Monash Deakin QUT Central Queensland	New South Wales Monash Central Queensland	Deakin Southern Cross Central Queensland (Monash)
Orientation	Corporate goals (all) Research excellence (NSW, Monash) Vocational training (Deakin, QUT)	Corporate goals (all) Research excellence (NSW, Monash)	Corporate goals (all) Vocational training (Deakin) Student load (CQU, SCU)
Academic cultures	Largely corporate academic cultures	Largely corporate academic cultures	Corporate academic cultures, with a touch of
Management cultures	Corporate management culture (NSW, QUT) Entrepreneurial management culture (Monash, CQU, Deakin)	Corporate management culture (NSW) Entrepreneurial management culture (NSW, QUT)	Corporate management culture (SCU) Entrepreneurial management culture (Monash, Deakin, CQU)
Engineered consent	Varies from open consent (NSW, Monash, QUT) to tacit consent (ambivalence (Deakin)	Varies from open consent (NSW, Monash) to covert and tacit consent (CQU)	Varies from open consent (Monash) to tacit consent (CQU, SCU) to ambivalence (Deakin)
Managed systems	Centrally integrated (NSW, QUT), flawed integration (Deakin), partly integrated (Monash), or moving towards it (CQU)	Centrally integrated (NSW), partly integrated (Monash), or moving towards integration (CQU)	Flawed integration (Deakin), partly integrated (Monash), or moving towards integration (SCU, CQU)

collegial element than others, while Deakin is notably entrepreneurial – and on the whole are not as organisationally coherent. The Unitechs are top-down and corporate, with elements of the entrepreneurial, though UTS is somewhat different from others in the group. The New Universities, like the Unitechs, have relatively weak academic cultures and depend on management to hold them together. Because systems and programs are still in the early to middle developmental stages, their integration is incomplete. The strong academic cultures inherited by the pre-1986 universities, especially the Sandstones, set some limits on central management. In the Unitechs and the New Universities management has more scope to remake the institution as it sees fit.

Among the universities in this study, the three reinvention strategies outlined above are associated with a more-or-less consistent set of organisational attributes. This 'clustering' of attributes, summed up in table 7.10, is suggestive. The attributes are:

- a widespread (though not necessarily universal) commitment to the interests of the institution as an end in itself;
- internal systems of governance and management more coherent than most;
- academic cultures more corporate than collegial;
- managements more vigorous, interventionist and often entrepreneurial;
- strong engagement in raising market-based incomes;
- often though not always, a vocational ethos.

In contrast with the Sandstones, reinvented universities display systems and processes of integration more overt in character. Less dependent on the consent of independent collegial units, institutional coherence requires a larger commitment of central resources. Where the older collegial element is still in play, as in some aspects of the centre–faculty relationship at Monash, the reinvention strategy seems to be weakened.

These are not the only elements involved in reinvention, but they are elements always present. On the whole, the reinvention strategies used so far have valorised corporate skills rather than academic knowledge, and less often both together. If internationalisation calls up a more profound encounter with cultural diversity, and if new delivery and teaching technologies become associated with new pedagogies and new modes of disciplinary organisation, the scope for innovation – and hence the range of strategies for institutional reinvention – might broaden. This would also create a wider range of opportunities for newer institutions to make their mark. However such potentials have yet to be realised.

In the forms of reinvention pursued thus far, it has apparently been necessary to employ relatively strong central control, if only to achieve the shift away from traditional academic practices embodied in such changes as large-scale fee-charging and flexible delivery. Likewise only a relatively powerful central management can take enough from the common pot to sustain distance education on a large scale. Only strong manager-leaders can push through the creation of income-earning operations separate from mainstream student admissions and course development (international education), or separate from academic units responsible for teaching and research (commercial companies in research and continuing education).

One not-so-necessary corollary of this dependence on centrally driven Enterprise University reform is that reinvention has so far been confined to those strategies where the attributes of managers have been particularly useful, *rather than* those of academics. This may explain why reinvention strategies based on academic innovations are undeveloped. In one respect the narrowing of reinvention strategies lightens the burden on management, for it can mobilise itself more easily than it can mobilise academics. Yet the narrowing of the scope for reinvention means that a whole side of the university is strategically dormant.

Consequently, if academics want to create new strategic options for their institutions, new forms of higher education, too often they must become managers to do it. Bypassing academic units in the reinvention process, while siphoning off strong academics into full-time management positions, probably undermines academic capacity in the longer term. This limits not only the potential reinvention strategies, but academic performance.

Institutions with both strategically competent management and strong research and scholarship have two different sources of strength to draw on. They also have the potential for a wider range of reinvention strategies. Reinvention strategies *not* underpinned by academic strength face severe limits. When we did our case study there in 1996, Deakin had been reinvented, but it remained low in the pecking order (despite being awarded the title of University of the Year for its distance education capacity) and was stretched thin. Too much reliance on good management and entrepreneurial footwork and not enough on talent 'below' is dangerous. In the medium term, management, marketing and reinvention are sometimes enough. In the long term, reliance on management as *the* principal driver tends to choke off academic development. The imbalance becomes permanent.

Highly managed institutions with weak academic cultures are limited not only in their scope for reinvention (especially reinvention dependent on innovations in education and research), but even in the isomorphistic strategies they can employ. In New Universities and some Gumtrees, academic cultures are seriously short of critical mass. The institutions might be shipshape, with competent navigators, but they need more ballast and more sails. Time will tell. The New Universities are far less stable in their current role than any other group, and we need to see further evolution in their strategies. More worrying are the larger institutions in which academic purpose seems to be getting lost. Lack of attention to the nurturing of academic capacity and academic identity is a key weakness in the Australian university. We will say more about this in the final chapter.

8   Conclusion

The Enterprise University

Governance

It is striking not only how far the Australian University has travelled since the Dawkins reforms of more than a decade ago, but also how much potential there is for further change. The future of The University is more contingent and more uncertain, than at any time since world war two. Centrally located at the intersection between knowledge, industry, professions, government and social networking, it will not vanish, despite various alarmist scenarios about the effects of competition from global virtual universities. At the same time, the roles of some individual universities have become unstable and their identities fragile. It is by no means clear where they are heading.

Inevitably, some are managing well under more difficult circumstances and others are doing it hard. The capacity to survive and prosper is of course unevenly distributed, and the distribution owes more to history than to anything else. For the Sandstones, the oldest university in each of the Australian states, the path ahead is well defined. If the going is not always easy, they can be reasonably confident that they are fit for the journey. 'More of the same', laced with modernisation, cybernetics and a dash of international networking, is the prospect here. These are stable institutions with a guaranteed place, though past experience suggests that they are less likely to be brilliant innovators, in either the organisational or the educational sense. A decade of more intensive competition has improved their marketing techniques but has not turned them into aggressive innovators, or produced new and vibrant competitors for the hegemony: the top echelon of the pecking order remains exactly the same. It must be said that the formal creation of a market has done little that is evident to improve either Sandstones or system. Certainly, it has failed to generate any broadening or deepening of the social, cultural and local economic contribution of the Sandstones, though there has been a significant growth in numbers.

Outside the Sandstone universities the outlook is more variable and unstable. Some are travelling strongly. Others are not. All of them are open to reinvention strategies of the type discussed in the preceding chapter. In some non-Sandstones, strategy has become rather more short term than this. The rubric is not 'more of the same', but 'watch this space'. Ethos, systems and culture, student recruitment, course mix and teaching program, research: all are grist to the mill. And both upward and downward mobility are possible. Below the Sandstone group, the inherited hierarchy of Redbricks, Unitechs, Gumtrees, etc. might change dramatically in the next phase.

It is university governance, the subject of this book, that has become the point of origin for these strategic manoeuvres and reinventions. We have already described the main changes to institutional governance in this era: a more emphatic executive leadership (chapter 4); executive strategies that are prone to isomorphism (chapters 4 and 7); the sidelining or co-option of older collegial structures and the rise of vice-chancellors' groups, commercial arms and informal methods of consultation and communication (chapter 5); the declining salience of the academic disciplines in research organisation (chapter 6); the enhanced flexibility and continuous re-engineering (throughout). Proponents of reform urge that there is further to go. All of this might indicate a new form of governance. Certainly, that is how the re-engineering theorists see it. Their story about contemporary universities is that the adoption of more business-like practices has enabled university governance (read 'management and leadership') to become newly effective, just in time to meet the more stringent requirements of an open and competitive economy, and a student-consumer who (*sans* evidence) is said to be suddenly more concerned about 'value for money' than the older educational values of knowledge, ideas and personal development.

But effective in relation to what? We do not question the capacity of Commonwealth (chapters 2 and 3) and university chancelry to reshape the institutions of higher education. The impact of reform was apparent to us again and again during the course of the case studies. What is in question is the capacity of the newly reformed systems to connect organically to the academic side, and to nurture a process of institutional development that is grounded, inner-controlled, distinctive and long term in character. Governance *is* important, but that is not to say that the new systems of governance are achieving all that they might, or that the common template leads to the most productive outcomes.

A close look at university governance shows that it is more fragmented, improvised and temporary than its protagonists might want. When we interviewed grass-roots academics we found that they rarely had much understanding of their university at the organisational level, or of the main considerations motivating managers. Stretched by the day-to-day demands of teaching, research and professional service – all of the academics we spoke to were working hard – they had little time to take in university concerns. Mostly, they responded to what little they knew of that bigger picture with an all-too-easy cynicism. Plainly, the Enterprise University is not yet *their* university. For all its undoubted capacity in new communications, data gathering and informal networking, the more professional university management of this era has yet to succeed in drawing the average academic into its strategic perspectives and its institutional objectives.

Nothing has been reinvented more than governance, yet throw-away techniques of governance lack the kind of gravity that might draw a deeper academic mobilisation. It seems that we may lurch from one extreme to another. Stuffy collegial structures, the old pre-modern Oxbridge pantomime long playing in Australia, are changeless and eternal no longer. What has replaced them is a postmodern alternative. Schools replace departments and are re-arranged again, disciplines change titles, super-faculties rise and fall, informal assemblies appear and disappear, DVC and PVC offices seem to be equipped with a revolving door. The constants are the financial imperatives, the march to the market and the presence of little groups scribbling SWOT analyses on whiteboards.[1] The variables are the plans, the formulae and the people themselves, and the rationale for whatever governance arrangements are currently in place. The optimist might see in this a ceaseless search for effective means, in a university no longer tied to archaic structures and quite rightly kept on its toes. Often it seems more like the trick of creating 'order out of chaos', whereby authority is secured not by establishing stability and a secure working environment for all, but by fostering novelty and instability while staying one jump ahead.

In the worst cases, instead of reformed governance driving a more productive culture in response to the larger set of external demands on the university, governance seems to magnify the dislocations generated by the external environment. The academic units do not have time to accumulate expertise in relation to one set of demands before another is in place. Participation is precarious. Internal constituencies are roaming loose without an on-going connection to key decisions. It is apparent that since the emergence of the Enterprise University, more than one set of governance arrangements is possible. It is also clear that within the terms of that Enterprise University model, most individual universities could do better. Taking the argument about the salience of governance further, if the limitations of the Enterprise University model are to be transcended, all will need to be differently governed.

Enterprise, reinvention, success

All Australian universities are now to a greater or lesser degree Enterprise Universities. The Enterprise University joins a mixed public–private economy to a quasi-business culture and to academic traditions partly reconstituted, partly republican, and partly broken. This is not so much a genuine private business culture, as a public sector variant in which certain of the conditions and techniques of business (such as competition, scarcity, marketing, goals defined in money terms) have been grafted onto existing bureaucracies now opened up to external pressures. In the Enterprise University the capacity to read 'change' and respond to opportunities is crucial. It enjoys a reformed system of governance designed to bring opportunity and capacity into short-term conjunction, and to manage the tensions that are part and parcel of a hybrid institution.

In their political economy, Enterprise Universities sit somewhere between the public academic institutions they were and the private companies that some imagine them to be already. They are responsible for their own output and financial health, and in that sense mirror the business firm. At the same time, they are driven as much by academic and institutional prestige as by the financial bottom-line, and their internal systems are scarcely those of the factory floor, though performance-based personnel administration and resource allocation are partly established, for example in student services and in research. There is mixed public and private funding. The private and commercial side offers greater potential for institutional discretion and independence, and is becoming more central. There is a new emphasis on entrepreneurialism, at both strategic centre and in academic units, though with varying manifestations and to varying degrees. Entrepreneurialism and business modelling brings with it the devolution of responsibility for funding, fund management and performance, so that academic units begin to resemble small specialist divisions or cost centres within a large conglomerate. The Enterprise University is global in the sense of being unbounded (and sometimes ungrounded). It is global in its scope for action, though predominantly national in its character, and it is globalised in its communications systems.

As we have seen, the reformed Enterprise University varies much between its individual cases. In part these variations reflect differences in the extent of reform itself, in part they are the corollary of the long-standing university hierarchy, Sandstones and all that (chapter 7). Arguably, the universities furthermost down the Enterprise University path are those engaged in a thoroughgoing reinvention. The propensity to reinvention is unaffected by place in the hierarchy – individual

Redbricks, Gumtrees, Unitechs and New Universities have all reinvented themselves – except that none of the Sandstones feel the need for it. So far reinvention has taken three forms: the High Entrepreneurial University, the International University, and the Distance Education University. The reinvention universities discussed in chapter 7 are all more organisationally coherent than are most of their fellow universities; and without this coherence, reinvention would not be possible. The Sandstones are also more organisationally coherent than most of the other universities. However, the basis of coherence in the Sandstones is different to that of the reinvention universities. In the Sandstones coherence is derived from grounded academic cultures joined uneasily to street-wise general staff and competent institutional managers, plus a long-standing social role that is continuously reinforced from outside. In the reinvention universities, coherence is highly dependent on ordering from the centre. These are more conventionally corporate – and sometimes more entrepreneurial – institutions than are the Sandstones, and on the whole they are less dependent on autonomous academic cultures.

Correspondingly, the strategies of reinvention used so far have focused on changes in organisation and financing, and have not required the same extent of reinvention in teaching, learning and research. In other words, reinvention strategies have depended largely on techniques taken from the corporate tool-box. Like other Enterprise University moves, reinvention often seems to work around academic cultures. This suggests that if reinvention worked *through* academic cultures, actively engaging them, a larger, more exciting and more educationally enriching range of reinventions might become possible.

Success

When we define institutional success in competitive terms, it is apparent that while re-engineering and reinvention are necessary to success, they are not sufficient in themselves to *guarantee* success. The case studies demonstrated that universities yet to bed down their Enterprise University reforms were under-performing in a competitive sense: for example Sydney and Newcastle. At Sydney, the price of this organisational tardiness was a slippage from leading Australian university to top five status. At Newcastle, the problems common to all Gumtrees were compounded. Yet among those institutions that have reformed or reinvented themselves, not all have improved their relative position, and some are in serious trouble. When reform becomes universal, the competitive edge it can bring begins to disappear.

The findings of the case studies suggest that the most successful of the present Enterprise Universities are those which join three elements together:

- an entrepreneurial capacity to create and exploit income earning opportunities;
- organisational coherence, bringing with it a capacity to focus performance;
- strong academic cultures.

A number of the Sandstones and the Redbrick UNSW incorporate all three elements. This conclusion suggests that non-Sandstones with strong academic cultures and coherent systems should be able to at least hold their ground, for strong academic cultures are by no means universally distributed. The problem for non-Sandstones is *financing* strong academic cultures. Non-Sandstones lack the 'extra rents' deriving from positional advantage that sustain the Sandstones in hard times. Entrepreneurial incomes are not enough to compensate for declining government monies, and too great a reliance on the market tends to skew the research profile in favour of short-term returns rather than long-term basic research programs, and in favour of the disciplines with potential commercial applications. Here the virtues of non-market private incomes, such as those derived from endowments, donations and university investments, become apparent.

'Success' in the immediate competition between Australian universities is one thing, the capacity to meet the larger challenges is another. Are these three elements sufficient in themselves? We suspect not. All the Enterprise Universities reviewed in this book share certain limitations. Whether the institution is successful or not, whether academic cultures are strong or not, the tension between academic and managerial perspectives is endemic. It is a tension that absorbs energy, reduces the scope for organisational coherence, narrows the range of possible reinventions, and does nothing to modify isomorphism. This suggests that universities need more than entrepreneurialism, organisational coherence and academic cultures. They need to bring these three elements into an optimum conjunction.

Entrepreneurial universities

As we were preparing this book in 1998, another study of contemporary universities was released, Burton Clark's *Creating entrepreneurial universities: organisational pathways of transformation*. Like us, Clark focused on organisation and governance at the institutional level. He did not develop a comprehensive study of the institutions in a single national system, but instead looked at five universities, in four European countries, that reinvented themselves comprehensively and successfully in the 1980s and 1990s. Clark's study contained no equivalent of the Australian sandstones. He deliberately left the strong older universities out of the picture, focusing on international equivalents of the Australian universities that have reinvented themselves as discussed at the end of the previous chapter.

The universities in Clark's study all set out to be 'more enterprising, even aggressively entrepreneurial', moving away from 'close governmental regulation and sector standardisation'. They all created unique paths for themselves. In his words, they 'search for special organisational identities; they risk being different'. The five institutions in the study are Warwick University and the University of Strathclyde in the UK, Chalmers University of Technology in Sweden, the University of Twente in the Netherlands, and the University of Joensuu in Finland.[2]

What is it that enabled these universities to transform themselves? Clark isolates five elements common to all of his chosen cases. These are set out below:

- *A strengthened steering core*, taking in both central managerial groups and academic units: 'it must operationally reconcile new managerial values with traditional academic ones', partly by involving academic leaders in management functions. This enables the institution to become quicker, more flexible and above all, more focused in the face of 'expanding and changing demands', with a capacity to remake programs at need;
- *The expanded developmental periphery*: 'outward-reaching research centres', readily created and dissolved at need, and professionalised offices working on knowledge transfer, intellectual property, relations with industry, fundraising, alumni and continuing education. Clark warns that units in the 'developmental periphery' must keep their eyes on the academic ball. 'If not judged by academic values as well as managerial and budgetary interests for their appropriateness in a university, they can move an institution toward the character of a shopping mall'.[3]
- *The diversified funding base* in order to increase the level of discretionary monies in the face of declining government funding, and to increase institutional autonomy, through the augmentation of research grants and contracts, income from foundations, industry, royalties, earned income from campus services, student fees and the like;
- *The stimulated academic heartland*. The academic disciplines, old and new, and some interdisciplinary fields, continue to be the place where most of the work is done. 'Whether they accept or oppose a significant transformation is critical'. It is here innovations are most likely to fail, and the life of the institution proceed largely as before. Each department and faculty needs itself to become an entrepreneurial unit,

connected both to outside agents and to central steering groups within
the institution. Traditional academic values need to become blended
with 'newer managerial points of view', and the required blending for
the most part must take place *within* the heartland. Officers from all
five universities emphasised to Clark that it was crucial to avoid a
schizophrenic split between the managerial and the academic.
* *The integrated entrepreneurial culture.* 'Enterprising universities ... develop
  a work culture that embraces change', and this culture 'becomes particularly important in cultivating institutional identity and distinctive
  reputation'. Here institutional identity is crucial and it is created and
  reinforced through both statements and daily practices.[4]

Clark notes that every university has unique features, deriving from
its geography, history and personalities. There is no single formula for
success. Within the five cases there is considerable variation in governance. For example, Warwick places greater emphasis on the strengthening
of the central steering core than do the other four institutions, where the
focus has been on decentralisation. Warwick has eliminated faculties, so
that the centre interacts directly with the academic departments. All
departments – not just those in the most entrepreneurial disciplines
– have been drawn into the new culture, fostered by institution-wide
measures such as a new graduate school and research fellowship scheme
(40 per cent of Warwick students are graduate students).[5] Still whatever the centralisation/decentralisation mix, change must happen in 'the
trenches', and in their interactions with the centre. Change does not
happen because a university leader or committee asserts a new idea. It
happens because it becomes operational, and it becomes operational
because it is embraced by those that must carry it out.[6]

Clark is more sanguine about declining public funding and commercialisation than we are – for example, he scarcely acknowledges the
problems for long-term basic research programs – and he is considerably
more positive, even romantic, about the entrepreneurial turn. Nevertheless, his empirical findings largely accord with our own. Further, it is
notable that in Clark's five conditions for optimum reinvention he
foregrounds the issue of academic–managerial synergy. It is this element
that we find missing from the Enterprise University model, suggesting
that the Australian Enterprise Universities will find it difficult to replicate
the successful reinvention that Clark talks about.

All Enterprise Universities in Australia display the first three Clark
characteristics, strengthened steering core, expanded developmental
periphery, and somewhat diversified funding base. Universities following
one or more of the three reinvention paths display these characteristics to
an advanced degree. On the other hand, Clark's last two characteristics

are weak or non-existent in Australia. If some Enterprise Universities have created an institutional culture, none seems to be stimulating its academic heartland as Clark describes. Often, centrally driven integration is secured more on the basis of the weakness of academic cultures rather than their strength. In the post-1986 institutions, academic cultures are too weak to play the role assigned by Clark. The Sandstones come closest to integrating academic and management cultures on equal terms, but they still experience the management–academic stand-off typical of all pre-1986 institutions. Everywhere the 'expanded developmental periphery' seems to side-step academic engagement all too quickly.

Limitations of the Enterprise University

In summary, the Enterprise University has several limitations.

First, its leaders are too far detached from that which they lead, while at the same time, too much is asked of them. Our notions of leadership in universities have become conditioned by images of sport stars, movie stars and the free-booting, risk-taking entrepreneur, heroes who seem to make good without group support.[7] The downside of the cult of the muscular leader, the executive class described in Tom Wolfe's *Bonfire of the vanities*, aside from the retrograde gender connotations, is that it creates impossible, inappropriate expectations. Partial detachment from the networks of politicking in the ranks screens university leaders from a range of inputs, but also reduces their potential support base and detaches them from potential instruments of policy. In the early 1990s Monash attempted to overcome this by creating a generalist deputy vice-chancellor responsible for the day-to-day running of the university, like a provost in the American system, leaving the vice-chancellor free for strategic moves and external relations. The more 'organic' leadership position failed, because the rest of the leadership structure continued to operate from a position of detachment, and because a provost was too far from accepted Australian practice.

Second, too often the Enterprise University works around and against academic cultures rather than through them. In his study of the American academic profession, *Managed professionals* (1998), Gary Rhoades notes how academic resistance to new educational technologies has led to the growth of technology-based instruction and delivery separate from mainstream academic work. The number and importance of non-academic professionals and part-time academic labour have grown rapidly. The academic core has often been side-stepped. There has been something of this bypassing in Australia, except that it has extended beyond new technologies to include the new institutional ethos and the new organisational systems. Time and again, the academic disciplines are seen as an obstacle to reform, one to be deconstructed or displaced. Too many initiatives are pursued through temporary detachable units on the developmental periphery rather than through the academic units themselves. Reinvention strategies based on high entrepreneurialism or distance education are particularly prone to clash with academic mores. But by failing to commit the academic units to institutional goals, the Enterprise University perpetuates a productivity barrier within itself. Further, leaving the academic core untouched reinforces collegial conservatism in the long term.

To bypass the academic heartland is to undervalue its potential contribution to strategic development, and to neglect the nurturing of that potential. The academic profession is underfunded and the reproduction of existing quality cannot be taken for granted. This problem is not confined to Australia. Gareth Williams notes that in the UK, marketisation and corporate reform are associated with a decline of academic salaries relative to the salaries paid to other professionals, and a reduction in the security and autonomy of academic work. These trends might turn out to be 'the Achilles heel of marketisation in the long term'. Williams argues that in the reformed universities/enterprises, 'respect for the knowledge and skill of producers' should be seen as 'at least as important as responding to the short-term wishes of consumers and proxy consumers'.[8]

Third – and associated with the second problem – too often the strengthening of 'the steering core' takes place at the expense of the dynamism of academic cultures, rather than in conjunction with it. In a centralised model it is inevitable that surveillance and performance control are never as complete as central managers would like. Where academic resistance is low there is a tendency to suppress grass-roots initiatives, especially paradigm-breaking initiatives. Perhaps the outstanding example of centrally driven improvement is that of the University of NSW. As noted, UNSW has brought together institutional coherence, entrepreneurialism and strong academic units. UNSW also benefits from a strong research role built during the days of near total public funding, and the openings created by the reluctance of its Sandstone rival Sydney to modernise its organisational systems. Nevertheless, our feeling about UNSW was that though its academic cultures were strong, its central management, sustained by a top-down command structure and comprehensive surveillance of the work of the institution, was even stronger. There was always a danger that the steering core would overwhelm the capacity for initiative from below.

Here the orthodox solution is to decentralise in an economic sense, to provide the academic units with market freedom while maintaining central control over the measures used to set objectives, calculate performance and allocate funds: in other words, to use an organisational design that is entrepreneurial rather than corporate. However, this does not really strengthen the position of independent academic cultures, for it *increases* the tendency to focus on short-term returns rather than long-term academic development. At Monash and Deakin the entrepreneurial approach created academic expectations not always fulfilled. Departments and schools found themselves with more freedom to raise funds, but there was less support from the centre. In the end many felt themselves worse off.

Fourth, in the Enterprise University, the internal institutional community has been thinned out. Fewer of the points of institutional decision-making actually matter to overall mission and identity. This is the consequence of a leadership partly detached from internal interests, the partial bypassing of academic networks, the growing salience of external over internal relations (as if one must crowd out the other), the retreat of councils from a community-forming role to the posture of corporate board, and the failure to replace declining collegial governance with more efficient and dynamic forms of participation. Of course non-organic leaders and attenuated community are a recipe for isomorphism. In the absence of a grounding in local vitality that is too powerful to ignore, leaders will naturally tend to fall back on generic management tools and mimic-models of the ideal university.

Fifth, the social ethic of the Enterprise University has also been endangered. In the pure form of the Enterprise University, the goal is not the fulfilment of a range of social, economic and cultural purposes: it is serving its corporate self as an end in itself. It is, to say the least, ironic that an era in which the 'client' and 'customer' have been foregrounded, and universities are more open to the external world than before, their larger purposes have been obscured. There is a corrosive tendency to treat these larger purposes merely as feints or marketing ploys. In the long term this might fatally undermine public support and public investment in the university.

Finally, the Enterprise University is associated with an undermining of identity, a narrow capacity for organisational innovation and a weaker capacity for educational innovation. It faces not just a decline in public funding, it faces a crisis of purpose. *All* Australian universities are touched by this to some degree. Readings argues that the university has been reconceived as a corporation whose functions include the granting of degrees with a cultural content 'but whose overall nature is corporate rather than cultural'.[9] The matter is more complex than he suggests, and more variable. In some universities the corporate and the cultural are in uneasy symbiosis, in others the corporate is dominant. Nevertheless, there *is* a tendency towards the reduction of cultural purposes (including scientific and democratic purposes) to corporate objectives. Far from generating an era of remarkable innovations as the neo-liberal literature suggests, this is associated with an anxious and unstable combination of managerial aggression, academic falter and plastic imitation. By believing that they must imitate business in order to work with business, universities are in danger of forgoing some of the very elements that enable them to make a distinctive contribution: teaching for personal/ cultural development rather than immediate skills, long-term research programs, critical and reconstructive scholarship, an institutional space not owned by one or another powerful social agent but obliged to relate to all.

These are the most serious problems of the Enterprise University model. If untreated, these maladies preclude the self-improvement strategies that enthusiasts seek to define. In our judgement, problems of purpose and isomorphism can most effectively be addressed by re-strengthening the academic heartland, and installing systems in which commitment to institutional objectives is secured on the basis of internal community. But before exploring those solutions, we will return again to the key issue of university identity.

Beyond the Enterprise University

University identity

University identity has three related dimensions: local, provincial/national and global. Without a stable and embracing identity, institutions are deeply vulnerable to the limitations of isomorphism and loss of their way amid a marketing-led strategy. Yet in the post-Dawkins environment in Australia, university identity cannot be assumed, but must be fostered. For all but the Sandstones, that read their identity from their history, the construction of local and state/national identity is now a core issue. In relation to global identity it is an issue for all, including the Sandstones.

Institutional reinvention is about remaking identity. It draws heavily on resources and time, and must be done well and followed through for many years if it is to be done at all. The increasing mobility of VCs and their need to justify their appointments on the basis of successive quick 'reinventions' of each new university is plainly a threat to deeper, enduring change strategies. While uneasy with the limitations of some of the reinvention strategies we encountered, we could only respect the efforts that these universities had made. Reinvention requires courage. It is a major commitment.

In building identity it is important to recognise that the local, state/ national and global dimensions are *not exclusive* of each other. One academic leader at Newcastle saw no necessary conflict between the local/regional orientation and the global orientation:

We've pitched ourselves as being an international university. It depends on how many initiatives we'll take with respect to the other forms of delivery of education. It seems to me that we're a late starter in that whole area and the next few years will tell if we're going to succeed in that or just become a regional university. We have to continue to develop distinctiveness. Medicine, architecture and engineering have given us examples there ... The other thing it's all dependent upon is what happens to Newcastle as a city. If we're going to pull ourselves out of the doldrums and get revitalised, it can become a major growth centre. (faculty dean, Newcastle)

Here local identity is more than a matter of stroking the local feeder population, or raising money from local industry. It is also at the core of the role of universities within the national system – institutions gain much of their rationale from the regions they serve – and it is a necessary part of the pitch of individual universities in a global setting.

When universities were largely government funded, and were implicated in a common project of nation-building, financed from taxation, the identity even of regional institutions could be read from national policy. Now that the old nation-building programs have been placed in doubt by globalisation and by the neo-liberal turn in government, the question of the national/state orientation (the governmental or 'public' dimension of the university) needs to be revisited. Here we are critical of the neo-liberal myth that the public and private sectors have converged, and claims that publicly constituted universities should be treated as equivalent to private companies. It is easy to see why some university leaders would like to privatise their institutions, whether *de facto* or *de jure*. Privatisation would enable them to become more powerful and less accountable, reducing internal and external political pressures. Yet it is hardly the way to strengthen community support for the universities. If the bottom-line of these institutions is their own interest, regardless of the public services they provide, their bedrock constituency has become confined to their own employees.

In one sense there has been a public/private convergence, in that state ownership is no longer as central to the role of government, marketisation is working its way through the public sector, and the funding mechanisms and accountability requirements of contemporary government reach across both public and private institutions, for example in the hospitals and schools. Nevertheless, we still require distinctive outcomes from public institutions. They are expected to be accessible to general use, to serve broad-based communities on an equitable basis, to conduct their own affairs according to principles of accountability, openness and transparency, and in the case of universities, to contribute to national policy objectives. The problem of national/state identity at this time is to rework these meanings of 'public'. Often this is in the absence of clear signals from governments whose own identity is in flux, and which take the easy policy option of focusing on corporate efficiency rather than the policy contribution of higher education. Here one way to address the national ('public') identity of universities is to focus on their contribution to local needs. Another way is to focus on their contribution to national identity and national interests in a global environment. A third way is a longer term project, though one in which universities might be central. It is to rework the notion of the 'public interest' by developing new global forms of 'public' that span national borders – in other words, to construct the global in the form of sustainable organic networks, rather than markets.

In Australian universities much energy has been expended on the building of fee-based international education programs, and there is a growing reliance on techniques such as international benchmarking. It is vital to open teaching and research programs to external referencing. Nevertheless, in the current environment, such developments also seem to readily encourage replication strategies. Australian producers have the choice of competing in the global market for higher education either on the basis of low cost, or on the basis of a distinctive product. The low-cost option is not an attractive one for universities, because of the restrictions it places on the potential quality of educational programs and research. Yet to compete on the basis of distinctive product means to confront the question of what it is that Australian universities might do that is different to (and perhaps better than) universities elsewhere. The answer is likely to be grounded in local and national identity, for the strengths of a university are also the product of the distinctive cultural characteristics of the population it draws on, and the network of relationships in which it is embedded. Foreign students attending German universities do so in order to study in Germany as well as in the university concerned; students studying in America are attracted to the general as well as the specific characteristics of their American university, and so on.

It was of concern to us that during the case studies we found little evidence of thinking about Australian identity and potential Australian educational strengths in the global setting. Australia has been a leader in agricultural and medical research and in future these might form part of a distinctive national contribution on the world scale. It could also be argued that Australia's relatively peaceful, culturally diverse and tolerant social environment provides something distinctive and of larger value to the world.

There is much more at stake here than the marketing strategy used to attract next year's batch of international students. The long-term issue is the place of universities in Australia within a global higher education system – Australia's place in a global division of labour, which in turn will rest on distinctive Australian strengths, in education, research and the socio-cultural context in which they are provided. To build distinctive national strengths is to invest in them over many years, and to foster inter-institutional collaboration in order to augment resources and expertise. On their own, a handful of strong universities cannot create such strengths. The problem of long-term national strategy is simply too large, and the investment required too great, to be addressed effectively by individual universities operating as corporations *sui generis*. It requires a sustained sector-wide program.

There is also another side to the problem. A distinctive identity (local national, global) has more salience when actively supported by all of the university's agents. It becomes less fragile, less leader-dependent, and more self-reproducing. In that sense one answer to the question about identity is to become more successful in mobilising the academic core, and forging university community. Stimulating the academic heartland also brings with it an advanced capacity to innovate in education and research, which enhances potential global offerings.

Stimulating the academic heartland

'Stimulating the academic heartland' is not just a matter of finding more money (though that is an important aspect!). It requires that more respect be given to academic cultures. Techniques of funding and management need to become more sensitive to the variations between disciplines, and, in some universities, systems of organisation will need to foster the independence of disciplines as an end in itself. One feature that the institutions in Clark's study share with most of the Sandstones and Redbricks in Australia is that in those institutions the departments, schools, faculties and centres are actively working on their own development. That is, the fuller resources of the university are mobilised in the tasks of setting strategies, defining objectives, improving performance and shaping identity. Academic cultures both independent-minded and productive are a sign of a confident and self-determining institution, and bode well for the furthering of its identity. It is stating the obvious to note also that respect for academic cultures both independent and diverse is likely to encourage greater inter-institutional diversity, all else being equal.

Here there is more than one form of independence to consider. Berdahl notes the distinction between autonomy of means and autonomy of ends:

Substantive autonomy is the power of university or college in its corporate form
to determine its own goals and programs ... procedural autonomy is the power of
the university or college in its corporate form to determine the means by which
its goals and programs will be pursued.[10]

Berdahl was discussing the relationship between government and
university, but the point also applies to the relationship between the university's manager-leaders and its academic units. The essential autonomy
is not procedural but substantive. The 'means' adopted by each academic
unit are inevitably subject to institution-wide procedures. However, to
dictate the content of programs, to second-guess the academic creator,
is to set the potential of each discipline according to the imaginative
horizon of managers. However able they might be, their training is confined to one specialisation, that of management itself.

Research management is a case in point. The maintenance of independent disciplinary cultures can enable the 'personality' of research
to be sustained in the face of the powerful effects of managing and
financing. Here it is important to move to organisational tools that themselves are sensitive to disciplinary differences in research outcomes and
the manner in which these are produced. The first move is to develop
indicators of activity, and formulae for the distribution of funds, that are
discipline-specific rather than universal. Researchers in all disciplines
have a common interest in moving away from a system in which their
claims become the standard ploys of a zero-sum game. For their part,
enlightened managements can agree, because more sensitive indicators
are also more inclusive and thus enable a more subtle and effective
management. Another move is to create a second set of measures of
research activity that focus not on research grants but on the outcomes
and effects of research. This again would enable a more discipline-specific
approach, and also a focus on a broader set of objectives than the largely
economic ones which dominate the current research indicators, as
chapter 6 discussed. A third move is to respond to the bias in favour of
track record and peer isomorphism inherent in the present system of research funding by allocating more research support to new researchers
and to collaborative innovation.

The deeper problem in the present system of research management is
that too often the mechanisms of funding and project-definition narrow
the boundaries of independent work itself, even pre-setting some of the
outcomes. One solution is to fund not only project costs, but time-relief
for principal researchers. Another is for funding agencies to provide
greater support for those research programs that enable self-controlled
work altogether free of the project format or client control: for example,
postgraduate research, and research fellowships of several years duration

in which the full salaries of researchers are paid. Another mechanism, on a larger scale, would be to structure academic careers so as to enable a mid-career break of two to four years of concentrated full-time or largely full-time research work. The creation of a mid-term research 'window' would provide doctoral-style opportunities for independent work at a time of greater personal and intellectual maturity.

At the same time, academic programs are not sustained in a vacuum, but depend on an institutional setting. This means that academics have a concurrent obligation to sustain that setting. (In the conventions of collegiality this obligation tends to be ignored.) For example, whereas it is wise for managers to give researchers their head in selecting research programs and projects, there can be less licence in determining teaching programs. In a system in which funding is determined by student numbers, student demand and potential demand set fundamental constraints. A university should be able to provide additional subsidies to carry a new teaching program in its early years; nevertheless, such funding is a strategic priority that ought to be negotiated between institutional management and academic units. It should not be seen as a matter of academic right. Likewise, academic units need to share in performance-related objectives: to meet output targets and to contribute to the university's financial bottom-line. This can no longer be passed back to government. If academic units refuse to share these responsibilities, they can scarcely complain when staffing is reduced in order to bring their expenditures into line.

In summary, a post-traditional academic culture in the 'stimulated academic heartland' should embrace five elements. It should be independent-minded. It should be discipline-sensitive. Its programs should be long term in design and character. It should be productive, in terms of both discipline and institution. It should be open and innovative, moving beyond the closed-shop conservatism and professional isomorphism, and the closures against new contributors, that tended to characterise traditional collegial practices.

Generalising the culture

In the Enterprise University the new techniques of governance have been directed towards the exercise of better control of output, and the containment of difference. In networked systems, with high transparency and technology-based data collection and accountability, it has become possible to manage organisations without involving more than a few people in decisions. This has enabled efficiency gains and smoothed institutional reform and reinvention, but there is a price. Shutting most people out is possible, the question is whether this is desirable. In our judgement, the dimension underdeveloped by contemporary university governance is the building of collaboration. The resource under-exploited is that of shared institutional purpose. Markets and career systems do not create such a sense of shared purpose. Often the contrary is the case: a sense of shared purpose needs to be consciously nurtured.

Here building community in governance is not a substitute for stimulating the academic heartland. It is an addition to it. Nevertheless, if the academic core receives stronger institutional support, that will facilitate a more constructive environment, and this has the potential to spill over into governance. In turn this enables governance to serve as a mechanism for generalising institutional culture, strategies and operational plans.

Reformed governance should be able to establish shared ideals concerning the means of sustaining everyone's hopes of work satisfaction and self-development. Community is a source of diversity of purposes, values and methods. This can be untidy, but it broadens an institution's strategic options. Community is also more directly instrumental, a medium for securing consent for, and conscious engagement in, institutional goals and programs. Some of the new informal systems of participation and communication have these objectives in view. Such informal systems can be looked on as the harbingers of a post-collegial, post-managerial form of university community, in which the augmentation of participation is achieved more by transparency and electronic communication, than the endless round of meetings typical of the collegial era. Nevertheless, participation – via consultations and via decisions – needs to be invested with more certainty than ad hoc forums permit.

We are not arguing here simply for rights-based forms of governance in which individuals can construct their interests as selfishly as they wish. Rights are important, but an essential corollary of institutional participation should be a willingness to adopt a performance culture and a shared institutional loyalty – not institutional loyalty as an absolute that transcends other loyalties, but nevertheless institutional loyalty as a practical commitment. In some universities, the capacity to survive and to sustain a viable identity will be dependent on the breadth of this loyalty. Perhaps the Sandstones need this kind of solidarity less than do other Australian institutions, for they are sustained by a kind of collective self-interest in maintaining positional advantage. Other universities are more dependent on loyalty. Arguably, one weakness of the Gumtrees as a group has been their failure to cultivate a genuine institutional solidarity, both within and between them.

Grounded loyalty does not sit easily with the conventional emphasis on individual career, fast mobility and manufactured temporary commitment. Yet it is at least as equally enabling of performance, and it contributes more effectively to the formation of shared agendas. Along with community, loyalty is an underdeveloped asset, waiting to be used. Here general (non-academic) staff are just as capable of sharing commitment to the institution and its work as are academic staff. General staff are still poorly catered for in systems of representation.[11] It has often been pointed out that a principal weakness of collegiality is that it undervalues the craft of management, and tends to exclude general staff from decision-making. It is not surprising that in response, some general staff want to snap the nexus between academic leadership and management. As one put it:

One of the things that institutions need to recognise is that people like me, notwithstanding what everyone says, actually do understand the business of the university. We have genuine concerns about standards and outcomes and whether students are actually going to get a job, whether we've got the best students, whether the program is put together well and all those kinds of things. My personal view, which I would never share with anyone outside this room, is that we should stop mucking about with trying to make PVCs out of academics and have career managers. (senior manager, Sandstone)

Nevertheless, the answer lies not in displacing academic-leader managers *per se* but establishing equality of respect between academic leaders and general staff leaders, and a negotiated division of labour. It also lies in reconstituting governing bodies – keeping them smaller but broadening their functions – so that they take responsibility for the health of the internal community, and effectively encompass general as well as academic staff.

Reflexive networks

An alternative approach to organisational structures that is worthy of future exploration is that of flatter networked structures based on genuine collaboration between management and academic units ('network bureaucracy'). We found that elements of this organisational style were present at UTS, although it would take a larger case study to determine how representative were these elements. This model might be more conducive to nurturing academic cultures and initiatives, and enable institutions to achieve a wider set of objectives than high centralisation permits. Unfortunately not enough universities are using the flatter networked approach to draw firm conclusions about it from this study.

We might have unearthed more evidence of flat structures if the principal unit of analysis had been not the institution, but decentralised forms such as department, school or centre, or the academic disciplines themselves. The continuing salience of disciplinary cultures in an often difficult setting suggests that a closer study of those cultures would be informative. In our view such a study should be a high priority for future research on the governance of higher education in Australia.

A second theme that might guide further research and system development is that of reflexive management. Again, there were hints of this at one or two universities. At UTS leaders talked about the need to be explicit about the effects of organisational systems on academic work, and sought to monitor those effects. They also looked for ways in which organisational systems could better support academic work, rather than – like other leaders – focusing on how to control and channel that work, and curb its wayward independence. The crucial issue here is university management that is capable of being self-critical and acting on itself with the same alacrity as its acts on others. This suggests an approach to management that incorporates the on-going reflexivity of an academic discipline, management that has moved beyond token exercises in self-criticism, and the barren technologies of quality assurance ('we-are-always-alert', 'watch-us-add-value', 'we-can-do-better'), a management that rests in a capacity in genuine critical thinking, and of the kind that facilitates rather than retards action. We suspect that as is the case with the shaping of academic disciplines, such an internal reflexivity needs to be supported by external referencing. How this might best be implemented is another matter for further study.

Identity and diversity

Finally, given these arguments about governance, how might inter-institutional diversity be enhanced? A structured system-wide diversity is an essential condition if universities are to broaden the range of potential institutional identities. The lesson of the recent past is clear-cut. We now know that a national (and global) higher education system modelled as a market game is narrowing rather than broadening the range of identities available. To blunder on blindly with this form of university organisation would be inexcusable.

At a system level, less isomorphism and more collaboration can be achieved by modifying the intensity of competition, reversing the trend of the last decade. Fear does not provide a favourable climate for genuine innovation. Second, government could modify the normalising effects of formulae such as the relative funding model and the research quantum in Australia, for example by introducing a greater level of discipline-specificity and cross-subsidisation to achieve strategic targets. Third, governments need to give specific support to innovative institutional and educational developments, perhaps by the selective deployment of a venture capital fund on a substantial scale.

If the last course is followed, government must be prepared to hand over the judgements about desirable innovations to an arm's length agency, perhaps one including some international members. To limit innovations to a narrow band of policy objectives and safe choices – as with most of the innovation funding of recent years – is to encourage conformism, not creativity. Further, rather than asking institutions to make competing bids against a common brief, it would be better to negotiate publicly supported innovations on a one-to-one basis, on the basis of agreed institutional mission. As a policy, this would have three positive effects. First, it would allow universities to evade the convergences enforced by the pressures of competition. Second, it would allow government to manage a broader division of labour between the institutions, in which diversity could be valued. Third, it would make explicit (and accountable) the key factor: university *identity*.

Within universities, the answer lies in a combination of:

- community building and participation in governance, releasing a diversity of contributions;
- the stimulated academic heartland, creating educational capacity for innovations;
- autonomous academic cultures *in combination* with organisation-savvy managers;
- a vigorous commitment to building self-identity, and sustaining an original strategy that is grounded in both local and global perspectives and attributes.

A return to higher levels of public funding could make a great difference, enabling universities to grasp many more of the immense opportunities that the global environment provides. However, higher funding cannot be made a prior condition for improvements in governance, or any other factor. We suspect that would be to put the cart before the horse. The condition for a change in the politics of funding is a change in the role and standing of universities (and not vice versa). This is unlikely to be achieved by Enterprise University-type reforms which are focused primarily on the interests of the institution as an end in itself.

On the other hand, institutions clearly moving forward in teaching and research, and institutions able to grasp their potential by developing a vigorous strategy of their own are better placed to attract public support. To remake their resource consensus with the nation-state in a global setting, universities will need to become both more effective local players *and* larger global players. The future of universities is affected by many factors, some beyond their own control. Nevertheless, in triggering the transition to something better, universities' own actions will be decisive. And their capacity for sustained and successful action will rest in their governance – especially the success of that governance in creating a healthy and productive synthesis of academic cultures and institutional identity.

Notes

1 INTRODUCTION

1 The formal definition of higher education in Australia excludes vocational education and training institutions, though these offer post-school courses up to diploma (two-year) level and in some cases offer higher education subjects on a 'franchising'basis on behalf of universities. This exclusion contrasts with the definition of 'higher education' in the United States – where community colleges are included within the formal boundaries of the sector – and some other countries. In using this definition of higher education in Australia we are merely following the conventional practice: we do not necessarily endorse it.

2 Burton Clark, 'The entrepreneurial university: demand and response', *Tertiary Education and Management*, 4 (1), 1998, pp. 5–16.

3 See chapter 3, and recent research-based discussion in such journals as *Higher Education* and *Higher Education Policy*. Those publications of the Organization for Economic Co-operation and Development (OECD) and the World Bank that are focused on higher education policy and management are both instruments and illustrations of the global convergence. There is a useful early summary of the trend to markets and private income in the United Kingdom and the OECD region in Gareth Williams, *Changing patterns of finance in higher education*, The Society for Research into Higher Education and the Open University Press, Buckingham, 1992. For a recent comparative study of trends in university–government relations, see Don Anderson and Richard Johnson, *University autonomy in twenty countries*, Evaluations and Investigations Program, Higher Education Division, DEETYA, AGPS, Canberra, 1997.

4 Peter Sheehan and Greg Tegart (eds), *Working for the future: technology and employment in the global knowledge economy*, Victoria University Press, Melbourne, 1998.

5 The term 'drivers' refers, in the language of executive leaders, to structural incentives which can be used to force changes through the organisation.

6 Mark Considine, 'Market bureaucracy? Exploring the contending rationalities of contemporary administrative regimes', *Labour and Industry*, 7 (1), pp. 1–27. And also Mark Considine and Jenny Lewis, 'Governance at Ground Level: The frontline bureaucrat in the Age of Markets and Networks', *Public Administration Review*, 59 (6) 1999.

7 Among the more useful books of the last decade that open up the generality of higher education are Sheila Slaughter and Larry Leslie, *Academic*

capitalism: politics, policies and the entrepreneurial university, Johns Hopkins University Press, Baltimore, 1997 (discussed in chapter 3); Peter Scott, *The meanings of mass higher education,* The Society for Research into Higher Education and the Open University Press, Buckingham 1995; and Ronald Barnett, *Higher education: a critical business,* The Society for Research into Higher Education and the Open University Press, Buckingham 1997. For management and leadership see Paul Ramsden's *Learning to lead in higher education,* Routledge, London, 1998, which is. grounded in the parallel research into teaching and learning; and Robin Middlehurst: *Leading academics,* The Society for Research into Higher Education and the Open University Press, Buckingham 1993. For a comparative perspective, see Ken Kempner, Marcela Mollis and Bill Tierney (eds), *Comparative education,* Simon and Schuster, Needham Heights, 1998.

8 Simon Marginson, *Markets in education,* Allen & Unwin, Sydney, 1997, especially pp. 7–50; Mark Considine, *Public policy: a critical approach,* Macmillan, Melbourne, 1994.

9 Jeffrey Pfeffer and Gerald R. Salancek, *The external control of organisations: a resource dependence perspective,* New York, Harper and Row, 1978; P.J. DiMaggio and W.W. Powell, 'The iron cage revisited: institutional isomorphism and collective rationality in organisational fields', *American Sociological Review,* 48, 1983, pp. 147–160; Fred Hirsch, *Social limits to growth,* Harvard University Press, Cambridge, 1976.

10 Bob Bessant, 'Corporate management and its penetration of university administration and government', *Australian Universities Review,* 38 (1), pp. 59–62; Mark Considine, 'The corporate management framework as administrative science: a critique', *Australian Journal of Public Administration,* 40 (1), 1988, pp. 4–18; Mark Considine, *Public policy: a critical approach,* Macmillan, Melbourne, 1994; Simon Marginson, *Education and public policy in Australia,* Cambridge University Press, Cambridge, 1993.

11 David Harvey, *The condition of postmodernity,* Blackwell, Maldon, 1990, p. 226.

12 Pfeffer and Salancek, *External control;* Jeffrey Pfeffer, *Managing with power: politics and influence in organisations,* Harvard Business School Press, Boston, 1992.

13 Pfeffer, *Managing with power,* p. 65.

14 The two universities which employed the researchers during the life of the study (Melbourne and La Trobe) were ruled out, and Royal Melbourne Institute of Technology was asked to be part of the study but refused.

15 For discussion of these categories see chapter 7, also Simon Marginson, 'Competition and contestability in Australian higher education, 1987 to 1997', *Australian Universities Review,* 40 (1), 1997, pp. 5–14.

2 ROOTS OF THE ENTERPRISE UNIVERSITY (1):
   FROM POLICY TO GOVERNANCE

1 John Button, *As it happened,* Text Publishing, 1998, p. 226.

2 Leslie Martin, chair of committee, *Tertiary education in Australia,* report of the Committee on the Future of Tertiary Education in Australia, Australian Universities Commission, Melbourne, 1964; Roderick West, chair of

committee, *Learning for life, final report*, Review of Higher Education Funding and Policy, Commonwealth of Australia, AGPS, Canberra, 1998.

3 The earlier language of 'industry' speaks to a more plural set of definitions. 'Industry' might include managers, owners, professions, employees and unions. Even non-profit organisations could be embraced within this term. 'Business', on the other hand, is an unambiguous vehicle of the profit-maximising.

4 Keith Murray, chair of committee, *Report of the committee on Australian universities*, Commonwealth Government Printer, 1957. This was the report which established the modern system of Commonwealth-superintended and funded universities in Australia.

5 Martin Report, p. 1.

6 Peter Karmel, chair of committee, *Schools in Australia*, report of the interim committee for the Australian schools commission, AGPS, Canberra, 1973.

7 Simon Marginson, *Educating Australia: government, economy, citizen since 1960*, Cambridge University Press, Cambridge, 1997, pp. 58–59.

8 Mark Considine and Brian Costar (eds), *Trials in power*, ch. 13, Melbourne University Press, Melbourne, 1992.

9 Lois Bryson, 'A new iron cage? A view from within', *Canberra Bulletin of Public Administration*, 13 (4), 1986.

10 See for example the contributions to *Higher Education Policy* 10 (3/4), 1997, on markets in higher education, including Frans van Vught, 'Combining planning and the market: an analysis of the government strategy towards higher education in the Netherlands', pp. 211–224; Larry Leslie and Sheila Slaughter, 'The development and current status of market mechanisms in United States postsecondary education', pp. 239–252; Gareth Williams, 'The market route to mass higher education: the British experience', pp. 275–289.

11 Marginson, *Educating Australia*; Mark Considine and Martin Painter, *Managerialism: the great debate*, University of Melbourne Press, 1986; Ann Capling, Mark Considine and Michael Crozier, *Australian politics in the global era*, Longman, Melbourne, 1998.

12 John Edwards, *Keating: the inside story*, Penguin Books, Ringwood, 1996.

13 Commonwealth Tertiary Education Commission (CTEC), *Review of efficiency and effectiveness in higher education*, AGPS, Canberra, 1986.

14 Clark observes a similar pattern in the UK: 'humanities departments have good reason to be resisting laggards: new money does not flow their way from either government or non-government patrons' – Burton Clark, 'The entrepreneurial university: demand and response', *Tertiary Education and Management*, 4 (1), 1998, p. 11.

15 For a perceptive early discussion of the pros and cons of the mergers see Grant Harman and Lynn Meek, 'Introduction and overview', in Harman and Meek (eds), *Australian higher education reconstructed? Analysis of the proposals and assumptions of the Dawkins Green Paper*, Department of Administrative and Educational Studies, University of New England, Armidale, 1988.

16 Simon Marginson, 'The West report as national policy making', *Australian Economic Review*, 31 (2), 1998, pp. 157–166.

3 ROOTS OF THE ENTERPRISE UNIVERSITY (2):
   FROM ACADEMY TO GLOBAL BUSINESS

1 *Age*, 29 December 1998; Bill Readings, *The university in ruins*, Harvard University Press, Cambridge MA, 1996, p. 10; Simon Marginson, *Monash: the remaking of the university*, Allen & Unwin, Sydney, 2000.
2 Readings, *The university in ruins*, especially pp. 3, 12–14 and 180.
3 Readings, *The university in ruins*, pp. 42–43.
4 Jean-François Lyotard, *The postmodern condition: a report on knowledge*, University of Minnesota Press, Minneapolis, 1984.
5 Readings, *The university in ruins*, pp. 22, 29 and 175–177.
6 Global Alliance Limited, 'Australian higher education in the era of mass customisation', Appendix 11 to Roderick West, chair of committee, *Learning for life, Review of higher education financing and policy: a policy discussion paper*, Commonwealth of Australia, AGPS, Canberra, 1997. The final proposals of the West committee, for a staged creation of a voucher-based market in undergraduate education, the introduction of subsidies for private providers and the opening up of the higher education system to international competition, and parallel steps to create a market in postgraduate training, are contained in Roderick West, chair of committee, *Learning for life, final report*, Review of Higher Education Funding and Policy, Commonwealth of Australia, AGPS, Canberra, 1998. The sway of the Global Alliance report is evident in the recommendations and in references to Global Alliance in the body of the reports, and were indicated to the authors in conversations with members of the committee.
7 Global Alliance, 'Australian higher education', pp. 7–13.
8 Global Alliance, 'Australian higher education', pp. 69 and 93.
9 For example Productivity Commission, *Stocktake of progress on microeconomic reform*, AGPS, Canberra, 1996.
10 David Hoare, chair of committee, *Higher education management review, report of the committee of inquiry*, AGPS, Canberra, 1995.
11 World Bank, *Higher education: the lessons of experience*, World Bank Publications, Washington, 1994.
12 See also Hans-Peter Martin and Harald Schumann, *The global trap: globalisation and the assault on democracy and prosperity*, Pluto Press, Sydney, 1998.
13 Jan Currie, 'Introduction', Jan Currie and Janice Newson (eds), *Universities and globalisation: critical perspectives*, Sage, Thousand Oaks, pp. 1–2
14 As E. Fuat Keyman argues 'the structure and dynamics of the international system'are not 'an onotological given but a historically and intersubjectively constituted practice'. His theoretical take on the problem is summed up as follows: 'Unity in diversity, as the effect of globalisation, is that which has been historically constructed and is always subject to reconstruction, rather than a constituting totality, a unifying force that dissolves diversity into the system'. Analyses that understand globalisation as 'totalising' in fact contribute to the Eurocentric (hence American) totalising practices of the global, based on inclusion/exclusion and the 'Othering'of difference. Eurocentrism can be reconstructed by recognising difference as the basis of human community, and by replacing the demonisation of the Other with the strategy of learning from the Other. See *Globalisation, state, identity/difference: toward*

a critical social theory of international relations, Humanities Press, New Jersey, 1997, pp. 2, 16 and 34.

15 Anna Yeatman, 'Introduction', in Anna Yeatman (ed.), *Activism and the policy process*, Allen & Unwin, Sydney, 1998, pp. 8–9.

16 See Manuel Castells' trilogy *The information age: economy, society, Volume 1: The rise of the network society*, Blackwell, Maldon, 1997.

17 Harvey, *The condition of postmodernity*, Blackwell, Maldon, 1990, p. 147.

18 Ann Capling, Mark Considine and Michael Crozier, *Australian politics in the global era*, Longman, Melbourne, 1998.

19 To this point the best summary and analysis of these developments is that of Stuart Cunningham, Suellen Tapsall, Yoni Ryan, Lawrence Stedman, Kerry Bagdon and Terry Flew, *New media and borderless education: a review of the convergence between global media networks and higher education provision*, Evaluations and Investigations Program, Higher Education Division, DETYA, Canberra, 1998.

20 The growing literature on the universities and globalisation includes Peter Scott (ed.), *The globalisation of higher education*, Open University Press, Buckingham, 1998.

21 Harvey, *The condition of postmodernity*, pp. 286–287.

22 However, an Australian Research Council-financed project on the internationalisation strategies of Australian universities is currently in progress (Fazal Rizvi and Simon Marginson, Monash Centre for Research in International Education).

23 Sheila Slaughter and Larry Leslie, *Academic capitalism: politics, policies and the entrepreneurial university*, Johns Hopkins University Press, Baltimore, 1997.

24 Slaughter and Leslie, *Academic capitalism*, p. 8.

25 DETYA, *Selected higher education finance statistics, 1997*, DETYA, Canberra, December 1998.

26 Simon Marginson, *Markets in education*, Allen & Unwin, Sydney, 1997, especially chapters 2, 5 and 8.

27 We owe this point to Marcela Mollis, School of Philosophy and Literature, University of Buenos Aires, 'The role of the state in the reform of Argentine higher education', Comparative and International Education Society conference, Toronto 1999. For Braudel see for example *The Mediterranean and the Mediterranean world in the age of Philip II*, translated by Sian Reynolds, Harper Collins, London, 1992.

28 Burton Clark, *Creating entrepreneurial universities: organisational pathways of transformation*, Pergamon, Oxford, 1998.

29 Clark, *Creating entrepreneurial universities*, p. xvi.

30 See for example the evidence of Don Anderson before the Senate Standing Committee on Employment, Education and Training, as reported in Parliament of the Commonwealth of Australia, *Priorities for reform in higher education*, AGPS, Canberra, 1990.

31 Harvey, *The condition of postmodernity*, p. 271.

32 Simon Marginson, *Educating Australia: government, economy, citizen*, Cambridge University Press, Cambridge, 1997, pp. 224–231.

33 Simon Marginson, 'Imagining ivy: pitfalls in the privatisation of higher education in Australia', *Comparative Education Review*, 41 (4), 1997, pp. 460–480.

34 Leslie and Slaughter, *Academic capitalism.*
35 Gareth Williams, 'The market route to mass higher education: the British experience', *Higher Education Policy,* 10 (3/4), 1997, p. 284.
36 Ulrich Teichler, 'Diversity in higher education in Germany: the two-type structure', in V. Lynn Meek, Leo Goedegebuure, Osmo Kivinen and Risto Rinne (eds), *The mockers and the mocked: comparative perspectives on differentiation, convergence and diversity in higher education,* Pergamon, Oxford 1996, p. 127.
37 John Dawkins, Higher education: a policy statement, AGPS, Canberra, 1988, pp. 101–102.
38 Roderick West, chair of committee, *Learning for life, final report,* Review of Higher Education Funding and Policy, AGPS, Canberra, 1998, pp. 89–90.
39 Jay B. Barney and William G. Ouchi (eds), *Organisational economics,* Jossey-Bass, San Francisco, 1986.
40 Yeatman, *Activism and the policy process,* p. 3.
41 Marginson, *Markets in education.*
42 Mark Considine and Martin Painter (eds), *Managerialism: The great debate,* Melbourne University Press, Melbourne, 1997.
43 V. Lynn Meek and Fiona Q. Wood, *Higher education governance and management, an Australian study,* Evaluations and Investigations program, Higher Education Division, Department of Employment, Education and Training, Canberra, 1997.
44 For example Barry Sheehan and Tony Welch, *International survey of the academic profession: Australia,* paper prepared for the Carnegie Foundation, University of Melbourne, 1994; Craig McInnis, Margaret Powles and John Anwyl, 'Australian academics' perspectives on quality and accountability', *CSHE Research Working Papers,* 94.2, Centre for the Study of Higher Education, University of Melbourne, 1994.
45 Harvey, *The condition of postmodernity,* p. 261.
46 Meek and Wood, *Higher education governance,* p. 88.
47 Don Aitkin, What is it that vice-chancellors do? Paper to the Australasian Political Studies Association conference, Adelaide, 29 September 1997.
48 Meek and Wood, *Higher education governance,* 1997, p. 79.
49 Meek and Wood, *Higher education governance,* p. 84.
50 Higher Education Division (HED), Department of Employment, Training and Youth Affairs (DETYA), *The characteristics and performance of higher education institutions,* Occasional Paper, November 1998, DETYA, Canberra, pp. 120 and 127.
51 Gary Rhoades, *Managed professionals,* SUNY Press, New York, 1998, especially chapters 4, 5 and 7.

4 TERRITORIES AND STRATEGIES:
   EXECUTIVE POWER IN THE ENTERPRISE UNIVERSITY

1 Pierre Bourdieu, *Distinction: a social critique of the judgement of taste,* RKP, London, 1986, p. 12. Bourdieu's central argument is that these 'games of culture' are protected against objectification by the actions which 'the actors involved in the game perform for each other', raising a serious risk of 'reflexive blindness'.

2 As one American colleague observed in relation to the expanding role of the college president, 'Where does the 600-pound bear sit? Where he wants to!'

3 Close observers of this argument will perhaps see some irony in the use we make of Anthony Giddens' notion of reflexivity. In 1996 Giddens resigned his chair at Cambridge and became director of the London School of Economics.

4 John Hay, 'Managing the pursuit of truth', in *The modern vice-chancellor*, Proceedings of a national conference initiated by the Centre for Continuing Education, Wollongong, NSW, 20–21 April, AGPS, Canberra, 1994, p. 136. At the time, John Hay was vice-chancellor of Deakin University.

5 Don Aitkin, 'What is it that vice-chancellors do?' Paper to the Australasian Political Studies Association conference, Adelaide, 29 September 1997, p. 10.

6 W.R. Ashby, *Design for a brain: the origin of adaptive behaviour*, 2nd edn, Chapman and Hall, London, 1960.

7 Certainly, this was how the VCs in our sample explained it at interview. Nevertheless, we are aware of cases where VCs are more tied to their councils and their chancellors than they might admit, particularly (but not only) at re-appointment time. One or two councils retain a wide-ranging ability to intervene. For VCs, the trick is to maintain a flexible council that stands away from 'management prerogative' (a moveable feast).

5 COLLEGE AND CORPORATION:
INSTITUTIONAL POWER IN THE ENTERPRISE UNIVERSITY

1 David Hoare, who chaired the Commonwealth committee of inquiry into higher education management, was from Bankers Trust, a major player in university-based research and development projects.

2 Hoare, *Higher education management review, report of the committee of inquiry*, AGPS, Canberra, 1995; *Balancing town and gown: Report of South Australian review of university governance*, Department for Employment Training and Further Education, Adelaide, February 1996; *University governance in Victoria: Report of Committee of Advice*, Education Victoria, Melbourne, June 1997.

3 James Cook University, *Review of management structures*, McKinnon Walker, September 1996.

4 *Review of the academic board: Report of the review committee*, July 1995, University of Sydney.

5 'Silo' metaphors are part of a wider management fashion in public and private organisations. They denote exclusive departmental or divisional autonomy and the power to resist a single corporate plan or intent. They may also denote the inability of the organisation to integrate its services in a single 'customer-focused' manner. In our study it was in the first sense that managers used this term.

6 ECONOMIES OF INVENTION:
RESEARCH POWER IN THE ENTERPRISE UNIVERSITY

1 The other metaphor sometimes used by managers is to liken the task of dealing with academics as 'herding cats', words used by more than one of our

interviewees during the course of the study. In both cases one can hardly miss the assumption that gifted intellectuals are by definition incapable of self-organisation.

2 Sheila Slaughter and Larry Leslie, *Academic capitalism: politics, policies and the entrepreneurial university*, Johns Hopkins Press, Baltimore, 1997.

3 Gar Jones, Alison Lee and Kate Poynton, 'Discourse analysis and policy activism: readings and rewritings of Australian university research policy', in Anna Yeatman (ed.), *Activism and the policy process*, Allen & Unwin, Sydney, 1998, pp. 153–154.

4 Ross Williams, Department of Economics, University of Melbourne, 'Funding higher education in Australia', paper prepared for the Commonwealth Review of Higher Education Financing and Policy (the West Committee), August 1997, pp. 28 & 32; Michael Gallagher, First Assistant Secretary, Higher Education Division, DEETYA, 'Current approaches and challenges in higher education', paper to Funding our future conference, Southern Cross University, 28 August 1997, p. 8.

5 Department of Employment, Education, Training and Youth Affairs, DEETYA *Higher education funding report for the 1997–99 triennium*, DEETYA, Canberra, 1996, Table 6.1; Williams, 'Funding higher education', pp. 20 and 32; Gallagher, 'Current approaches and challenges', p. 8.

6 Jones et al., 'Discourse analysis and policy activism', pp. 155–156.

7 Williams, 'Funding higher education', p. 20.

8 Gallagher, 'Current approaches and challenges', p. 9.

9 V. Lynn Meek and Fiona Q. Wood, *Higher education governance and management, an Australian study*, Evaluations and Investigations program, Higher Education Division, DEET, Canberra, 1997, pp. 92–93; Don Anderson and Richard Johnson, *University autonomy in twenty countries*, EIP, HED, DEETYA, 1997, p. ix; Peter Coaldrake, 'Reflections on the repositioning of the government's approach to higher education, or I'm dreaming of a White Paper', keynote address to the Reworking the university conference, Griffith University, December 1998.

10 David Hoare, *Higher education management review, report to the committee of inquiry*, AGPS, Canberra, 1995, p. 6.

11 University of New South Wales, *UNSW Corporate Plan 1994–99*, UNSW, Sydney, 1995.

12 Gallagher, 'Current approaches and challenges', p. 8.

13 Griffith University, *Research management plan 1995*, Griffith University, Nathan, p. 3.

14 The University of Newcastle, *Research report 1994*, The University of Newcastle, Newcastle, p. 3.

15 UTS, *Research management plan, 1997*, UTS, Sydney, p. 3.

16 Mary O'Kane, University of Adelaide, 'Financing of research in higher education', paper to Funding our Future conference, Southern Cross University, 28 August 1997, p. 10.

17 Barry Sheehan and Tony Welch, *International survey of the academic profession: Australia*, paper prepared for the Carnegie Foundation, University of Melbourne, 1994, pp. 50 and 88.

18 UNSW, *Quality portfolio 1995*, p. 5; Griffith University, *Research management plan*, p. 13.

19 Southern Cross University, *Annual report 1994*, SCU, Lismore.

20 Southern Cross University, *Plan 1995: Into the next millennium*, SCU, Lismore, 1994, p. 6.
21 Central Queensland University, *Research development and management plan, 1995–1999*, 1995, CQU, Rockhampton, p. 2; Central Queensland University, Achieving partnership through research and community service at the Central Queensland University, 1995 submission to the Committee for Quality Assurance, 1995, CQU, Rockhampton, p. 9.
22 *Quality portfolio 1995*, p. 3; supplemented by materials from interviews.
23 UNSW, *Corporate plan 1994–99*, 1995, p. 13; University of Queensland, *Research management plan*, 1995, pp. 3–4.
24 University of Queensland, *Research management plan 1995*, p. 3; Monash University Academic Board, *Report of the research review committee*, April 1992, p. 6; Central Queensland University, *Research development and management plan 1995–1999*, 1995, p. 30.
25 University of Newcastle, *1995 quality portfolio: report and appendices*, 1995, p. 9.
26 At the time of the case study that policy was under review.
27 University of NSW, *Quality portfolio 1995*, 1995, Part 1, pp. 6 and 10, and Part 2, p. 5.
28 Griffith University, *Research management plan 1995*, pp. 9 and 15.
29 UNSW, *Quality portfolio 1995*, Part 1, 1995, p. 3.
30 Nikolas Rose, *Governing the soul*, Routledge, London, 1990.
31 This might be called 'Rousseau's paradox', after Rousseau in *Emile*: 'There is no subjugation so complete as that which preserves the forms of freedom; it is thus the will itself is taken captive'.
32 Marginson, *Markets in education*, pp. 257–277.
33 UTS, *Research management plan*, pp. 9–10.
34 Monash University Academic Board, *Report of the Research Review Committee*, April 1992, p. 7.
35 Students of budgetary politics will recognise this as the Matthew Principle: 'to those who have, more shall be given'.
36 Craig McInnis and Simon Marginson, *Australian law schools after the 1987 Pearce Report*, DEET, AGPS, Canberra, 1993.
37 UTS, *Research management plan 1996–7*, p. 4.
38 UTS, *Research management plan 1996–7*, pp. 7–8 and 14–15.
39 These virtues and the policy assumptions about causality are of course open to debate.
40 University of Newcastle PVC (Research and Information Technology) Ron MacDonald, The University of Newcastle, *Research report 1994*, p. 3.
41 David Hoare, *Higher education management review, report of the committee of inquiry*, AGPS, Canberra, 1995, pp. 6–7.

7 MANY PATHS, ONE PURPOSE:
DIVERSITY IN THE ENTERPRISE UNIVERSITY

1 David Harvey, *The condition of postmodernity*, Blackwell, Maldon, 1990, p. 26.
2 V. Lynn Meek and Fiona Wood, *Managing higher education diversity in a climate of public sector reform*, EIP, HED, DEETYA, 98/5, AGPS, Canberra, 1998, pp. xv, 16. Meek and Wood's is the most important Australian study in

recent years, providing an informed overview of the debates and issues. See also Daniel C. Levy, 'Isomorphism in private higher education', paper prepared for the conference on international private higher education, Boston College, May 1998. For examples of both sets of arguments and a useful, if inconclusive discussion of the theoretical problems, see V. Lynn Meek, Leo Goedegeburre, Osmo Kivinen and Risto Rinne (eds), *The mockers and the mocked: comparative perspectives on differentiation, convergence and diversity in higher education*, Pergamon, Oxford, 1996.

3 See for example the argument in Burton R. Clark, *The higher education system: a cross-national perspective*, University of California Press, Berkeley, 1983.

4 For another example see HED, DETYA, *The characteristics and performance of higher education institutions*, Occasional Paper, November 1998, DETYA, Canberra, p. 1.

5 Peter Karmel, 'Funding mechanisms, institutional autonomy and diversity', in V. Lynn Meek and Fiona Q. Wood, *Higher education governance and management, an Australian study*, DEET, EIP, HED, DEET, Canberra, 1997, p. 62. For an account of the history of government-driven quality assurance in Australia see Grant Harman, 'Quality assessment with national institutional rankings and performance funding: the Australian experiment, 1993–1995', *Higher Education Quarterly*, 50 (4), 1996, pp. 295–311.

6 Meek and Wood, *Managing higher education diversity*, p. 16.

7 Daniel C. Levy, 'Where the new institutionalism falls short: implications from higher education's privatisation (Argentina, China, Hungary and beyond)', State University of New York, Albany, April 1998, p. 28.

8 Levy, 'Isomorphism, p. 29.

9 Meek and Wood, 1998, *Managing higher education diversity*, p. 9.

10 Simon Marginson, *Markets in education*, Allen & Unwin, Sydney, 1997, chapter 5.

11 Van Vught, Frans, 'Isomorphism in higher education? Towards a theory of differentiation and diversity of higher education systems', in Meek et al., *The mockers and the mocked*, pp. 44–45.

12 Karmel, 'Funding mechanisms, institutional autonomy and diversity', p. 46.

13 For detailed discussion of the categories Sandstone and Gumtree, see below.

14 Levy, 'Isomorphism', p. 15.

15 For example see World Bank, *Higher education: the lessons of experience*, World Bank Publications, Washington, 1994.

16 Meek and Wood, *Higher education governance and management*, pp. 95–112.

17 Our conceptions of institutional isomorphism in higher education have been influenced by the work of P.J. DiMaggio and W.W. Powell, 'The iron cage revisited: institutional isomorphism and collective rationality in organisational fields', *American Sociological Review*, 48, 1983, pp. 147–160.

18 Guy Neave, 'Homogenisation, integration and convergence', in Meek et al., *The mockers and the mocked*, p. 30.

19 Karmel, 'Funding mechanisms, institutional autonomy and diversity', p. 50.

20 Van Vught, 'Isomorphism in higher education', pp. 42–58.

21 Levy, 'Isomorphism', p. 6. See also Larry Leslie and Sheila Slaughter, 'The development and current status of market mechanisms in United States postsecondary education', *Higher Education Policy*, 10 (3/4), 1997, p. 247.

22 Meek and Wood, *Higher education governance and management*, p. 155.
23 Bill Readings, *The university in ruins*, Harvard University Press, Cambridge, MA, 1996, p. 12.
24 Meek and Wood, *Higher education governance and management*, p. 155. See also the brilliant study of marketing and market differentiation by Colin Symes, 'Selling futures: a new image for Australian universities?', *Studies in Higher Education*, 21 (2), 1996, pp. 133–147.
25 This includes unfunded private institutions. Among the Commonwealth-supported institutions, all but 0.6 per cent are enrolled in comprehensive doctoral universities.
26 Simon Marginson, 'Imagining ivy, pitfalls in the privatisation of higher education in Australia', *Comparative Education Review*, 41(4), 1997, pp. 460–480.
27 Van Vught, 'Isomorphism in higher education?', p. 47.
28 Jillian M. Maling and Bruce D. Keepes, 'The Australian higher education system – diversity: sought or neglected?', in Meek and Wood, *Managing higher education diversity*, p. 41.
29 David Dill, Higher education markets and public policy', *Higher Education Policy*, 10 (3/4), 1997, p. 180.
30 Stefan H. Thomke, 'The role of flexibility in the development of new products: an empirical study', *Research Policy*, 26, 1997, pp. 105–119.
31 There is a longer discussion of the social and economic dynamics of positional goods in Marginson, *Markets in education*, especially chapters 2 and 5.
32 University of Queensland, *Quality portfolio 1993*, pp. 13–14.
33 They were in fact the pre-eminent 'Colombo Plan' universities, which also helps explain their capacity to exploit government funding and policy shifts.
34 Simon Marginson, *Monash: the remaking of the university*, Allen & Unwin, Sydney, 2000.
35 In this case 'industry' means industry, not just business. Many of the Unitechs have long-established relationships with unions and professional organisations.
36 Symes, 'Selling futures'.
37 Don Aitkin, 'What is it that vice-chancellors do?' Paper presented to the Australian Political Studies Association conference, Adelaide, 29 September 1997, p. 3.
38 Aitken, 'What is it that vice-chancellors do?', p. 6.
39 Here the Redbrick ANU has little in common with UNSW and Monash. Its academic cultures are strongly defined, discipline-specific and notably impervious to central intervention. Although it is more modern in tone, the university it most resembles is Sydney.
40 Aitkin, 'What is it that vice-chancellors do?', p. 7. The same point is made by the Commonwealth's Higher Education Division in DETYA, *The characteristics and performance of higher education institutions*, p. 2.
41 V. Lynn Meek and Arthur O'Neill, 'Diversity and differentiation in the Australian Unified National System of higher education', in Meek et al., *The mockers and the mocked*, p. 73.
42 Meek and Wood, *Managing higher education diversity*, p. 194.
43 Cited in Meek and Wood, *Higher education governance and management*, p. 36.

44 The best study is still Don Anderson and Art Vervoorn, *Access to privilege*, Australian National University Press, Canberra, 1983.
45 DETYA, *The characteristics and performance of higher education indicators*, pp. 12 and 107. The data in table 7.5 are affected by the fact that the s.e.s. classification of Sydney and Melbourne suburbs is higher than the national norm, and this is prior to the s.e.s position of individuals living within those suburbs. Differences in the socio-economic background of students as determined by a common national measure are partly determined by variations in incomes in the different states/territories. The better measure would tell us the social composition of each university relative to its own catchment. However, catchments are hard to determine, and regionally based s.e.s. measures are not available. Apart from this, the postcode classification used to determine socio-economic status is flawed in certain respects. For example, DETYA itself notes that the postcodes are allocated a socio-economic status on the basis of the average characteristics of persons in that postcode and 'this is unlikely to be a precise indicator of a student's socio-economic status where there is significant heterogeneity in socio-econoic status within postcode districts'– p. 11. Further, students from wealthy back-grounds might take up temporary residence in poorer suburbs, students from poor backgrounds might take up marginal housing in wealthier suburbs, postcodes are subject to 'gentrification'and other changes in their socio-economic character over short time spans, and so on.
46 Meek and Wood, *Managing higher education diversity*, pp. 124–125.
47 Meek and Wood reach the same limit in their study of diversity, *Managing higher education diversity*, pp. 133 and 194.
48 Levy, 'Isomorphism', p. 23.
49 The best-known study is by Tony Becher, *Academic tribes and territories*, Open University Press, Milton Keynes, 1989. See also Burton Clark, 'Diversi-fication of higher education: viability and change', in Meek et al., *The mockers and the mocked*, pp. 16–25.
50 Clark, 'Diversification of higher education'.
51 Oliver Fulton, 'Differentiation and diversity in a newly unitary system: the case of the UK', in Meek et al., *The mockers and the mocked*, pp. 174–175 and 179.
52 Clark, 'Diversification of higher education', p. 23; Harvey, *The condition of postmodernity*, p. 289.
53 Symes, 'Selling futures'.
54 Marginson, *Markets in education*, pp. 242–244.
55 Paul Bourke and Linda Butler, *International links in higher education research*, NBEET Commissioned Report No. 37, AGPS, Canberra, 1995.
56 Stuart Cunningham, Suellen Tapsall, Yoni Ryan, Lawrence Stedman, Kerry Bagdon and Terry Flew, *New media and borderless education: a review of the convergence between global media networks and higher education provision*, EIP, HED, DETYA, Canberra, 1998.
57 DETYA, *The characteristics and performance of higher education institutions*, p. 6. Note also that two-thirds of internal part-time students are aged over 25.
58 DETYA, *The characteristics and performance*, pp. 19, 117 and 132.
59 Garry Rhoades, *Managed professionals*, SUNY Press, New York, 1998.

8 CONCLUSION

1 Standardised strategic planning in a competitive environment using the four headings of strengths, weaknesses, opportunities and threats (SWOT).
2 Burton Clark, *Creating entrepreneurial universities: organisational pathways of transformation*, Pergamon, Oxford, 1998, p. xiv.
3 Clark, *Creating entrepreneurial universities*, p. 139.
4 Clark, *Creating entrepreneurial universities*, pp. 5–8 and pp. 137–144.
5 Clark, *Creating entrepreneurial universities*, pp. 11–38.
6 Clark, *Creating entrepreneurial universities*, p. 145.
7 Ann Capling, Mark Considine and Michael Crozier, *Australian politics in the global era*, Longman, Melbourne, 1998, p. 70.
8 Gareth Williams, 'The market route to mass higher education: the British experience', *Higher Education Policy*, 10 (3/4), 1997, pp. 288–289.
9 Bill Readings, *The university in ruins*, Harvard University Press, Cambridge, MA, 1996, pp. 10–11.
10 Cited in V. Lynn Meek and Fiona Q. Wood, *Higher education governance and management*, EIP, HED, DEET, Canberra, 1997, p. 55.
11 Don Aitkin, 'What is it that vice-chancellors do?' Paper to the Australasian Political Studies Association conference, Adelaide, 29 September 1997, p. 8.

Index

academic boards 4, 11, 12, 16, 64, 76–7,
 82, 84–7, 89–92, 96–8, 102, 107,
 108–26 *passim*, 128, 130–1
academic capitalism *see* markets
Academic capitalism (Sheila Slaughter
 and Larry Leslie) 4–5, 49–53, 136–7,
 141
academic disciplines and cultures 6, 7–8,
 10, 12, 16–17, 53, 58, 64–7, 75,
 78–81, 91, 94, 98, 108–15, 131,
 135–6, 141–2, 144, 149, 151–2, 154,
 160–5, 167–9, 174, 184, 188,
 191–202 *passim*, 205, 215, 218–19,
 221, 228–32, 234–42, 247–9, 251–2
 see also academic work; collegiality;
 democratic elements in governance;
 research
academic work 17, 48–9, 49–51, 59, 65–7,
 141, 164–74, 180–1, 225–8, 235,
 241–2, 248–9, 252
accountability *see* government–institution
 relations
Aitkin, Don 31, 65, 73, 202, 203
'Americanisation' of Australian higher
 education *see* United States of
 America
Asian countries, including Southeast Asia
 29, 30, 42, 54, 72, 84, 92, 93, 103,
 182, 197, 223–4
Australia, government of *see* government
 and government policy
Australian Catholic University 33, 144,
 148, 190
Australian National University 31, 33,
 144, 148, 190, 197, 198, 208, 215,
 222
Australian Research Council (ARC) ix,
 31, 137–41, 145–7, 151, 155–6, 165,
 168, 169, 173, 183, 196, 217, 219
Australian Vice-Chancellors' Committee
 (AVCC) 94, 138
autonomy of universities *see*
 government–institution relations;
 identities of universities

Bond University 31, 57, 187
business and industry, relationships with
 universities 4–5, 8, 22 n.3, 49–53, 74,
 76–7, 83, 86, 93, 96, 99–100, 103–4,
 106, 110, 126, 129, 130, 141, 147,
 157, 158, 162, 164, 176, 180, 197,
 205–6, 207, 214, 239
butterflies in formation 133

Canada 49, 53, 54, 136
case studies 12, 14–17
categories of Australian university 15, 72,
 75, 185–202 *passim*, 188–90
Central Queensland University 16, 33, 60,
 63, 66, 73, 88, 110, 113, 118, 144–6,
 148, 149, 159, 160, 162, 186, 189,
 190, 201–2, 204, 207, 209–16, 223–9
chancellors 102
 see also governing bodies of universities
Charles Sturt University 33, 72, 144, 148,
 190, 201, 225–6
Clark, Burton 52, 218–19, 220, 238–41
colleges of advanced education (CAEs)
 and the binary system 25, 30, 32–3,
 34, 56, 116–17, 180, 187, 200, 205,
 206, 221
collegiality 4, 11, 14, 30, 51, 64–7, 70–1,
 71, 79, 86–7, 91, 96–8, 108–12
 passim, 151–4, 164, 174, 193–4, 197,
 200, 228–32, 235, 242–3, 249–51
commercial activities in higher education
 see markets
commercial companies in universities 4, 9,
 10, 84, 85, 97, 102–4, 106, 132,
 155–7, 160, 231
Commonwealth Committee for Quality
 Assurance in Higher Education
 (CCQAHE) *see* quality
Commonwealth Tertiary Education
 Commission (CTEC) 31, 179
communications inside institutions 9,
 47–9, 78, 84–5, 96–7, 102, 105, 106,
 121, 123, 123–32 *passim*, 181–2,
 222, 250

267